THE SCIENCE AND
POLITICS OF I.Q.

COMPLEX HUMAN BEHAVIOR

A series of volumes edited by
Leon Festinger and **Stanley Schachter**

WICKLUND · *Freedom and Reactance, 1974*

SCHACHTER AND RODIN · *Obese Humans and Rats, 1974*

KAMIN · *The Science and Politics of I.Q., 1974*

WYER · *Cognitive Organization and Change: An Information Processing Approach, 1974, in preparation.*

THE SCIENCE AND POLITICS OF I.Q.

BY LEON J. KAMIN

PRINCETON UNIVERSITY

LEA **LAWRENCE ERLBAUM ASSOCIATES, PUBLISHERS**
POTOMAC, MARYLAND
1974

Lawrence Erlbaum Associates, Inc., Publishers
12736 Lincolnshire Drive
Potomac, Maryland 20854

Library of Congress Cataloging in Publication Data

Kamin, Leon J.
    The science and politics of I.Q.

    (Complex human behavior)
    1. Intellect. 2. Mental tests. 3. Nature and
nurture. I. Title. [DNLM: 1. Intelligence tests.
BF431 K153s]
BF431.K3646   153.9'3   74-13883

Printed in the United States of America

CONTENTS

INTRODUCTION 1
    Notes to Introduction   4

1   **THE PIONEERS OF I.Q. TESTING IN AMERICA** **5**
    Notes to Chapter One   12

2   **PSYCHOLOGY AND THE IMMIGRANT** **15**
    Notes to Chapter Two   30

3   **SEPARATED IDENTICAL TWINS** **33**
    The Work of Cyril Burt   35
    The Shields Study   47
    The Newman, Freeman, and Holzinger Study   52
    The Juel-Nielsen Study: Age and I.Q. Again   61
    Some Conclusions   65
    Notes to Chapter Three   67

4   **KINSHIP CORRELATIONS** **73**
    The Erlenmeyer-Kimling and Jarvik Figure   74
    Predicted Kinship Correlations and Genetic Models   87
    MZ and DZ Twins   96
    Notes to Chapter Four   105

5 STUDIES OF ADOPTED CHILDREN 111
The Freeman, Holzinger, and Mitchell Study   113
Studies by Burks and by Leahy   115
The Skodak and Skeels Study   124
Notes to Chapter Five   133

6 THE ACCURACY OF SECONDARY SOURCES 135
Burt's Assessments Again   153
Notes to Chapter Six   157

7 I.Q. IN THE UTERUS 161
A Note on Inbreeding Depression   171
Notes to Chapter Seven   173

CONCLUSION 175
Notes to Conclusion   179

AUTHOR INDEX 181

ACKNOWLEDGMENTS

There are many people to whom I am indebted for help. The drafts of all chapters were read by Professor Tom Trabasso, and some were read by Professor Ronald Kinchla. Their criticism has been helpful, and I have tried to incorporate it. They, of course, are not responsible for the way in which I have finally expressed myself, but I fervently hope that they agree with what I have said.

What I owe to the graduate students working with me, I cannot express. They have been understanding beyond words in allowing me to retreat from a conditioning laboratory while thinking about I.Q. They, with Dr. R. F. Westbrook, have maintained a functioning laboratory in my virtual absence. There is a very real sense in which the book could not have been written without the patient assistance of Xenia Coulter, Mary Cross, Steve Gaioni, and Gary Szakmary.

The Department of Psychology which I am supposed to administer has been kept afloat during this period by Ms. Inna Tults, who managed somehow to type portions of the manuscript as well. The bulk of the manuscript was prepared by Ms. Claire Myones, Ms. Teri Crump, and Ms. June Kreuz, to all of whom I express my thanks.

To Marie-Claire
and to
Richard L. Solomon

who taught me different, and wonderful, things

INTRODUCTION

In psychology as in politics, the pendulum of fashion swings to and fro; and the vacillations roughly synchronize. During the nineteenth century, the associationists preached an egalitarian doctrine, and three reform bills were passed.

—Sir Cyril Burt, 1955[1]

This book is concerned with a single major question: are scores on intelligence tests (I.Q.'s) heritable? The answer, in the consensus view of most intelligence testers, is that about eighty percent of individual variation in I.Q. scores is genetically determined. That is not a new conclusion. Pearson, writing in 1906, before the widespread use of the I.Q. test, observed that "the influence of environment is nowhere more than one-fifth that of heredity, and quite possibly not one-tenth of it."[2] Herrnstein, reviewing the history of intelligence testing to 1971, concluded, "We may, therefore, say that 80 to 85 percent of the variation in I.Q. among whites is due to the genes."[3]

The present work arrives at two conclusions. The first stems from a detailed examination of the empirical evidence which has been adduced in support of the idea of heritability, and it can be stated simply. There exist no data which should lead a prudent man to accept the hypothesis that I.Q. test scores are in any degree heritable. That conclusion is so much at odds with prevailing wisdom that it is necessary to ask, how can so many psychologists believe the opposite?

The answer, I believe, is related to the second major conclusion of this work. The I.Q. test in America, and the way in which we think about it, has been fostered

1

by men committed to a particular social view. That view includes the belief that those on the bottom are genetically inferior victims of their own immutable defects. The consequence has been that the I.Q. test has served as an instrument of oppression against the poor — dressed in the trappings of science, rather than politics. The message of science is heard respectfully, particularly when the tidings it carries are soothing to the public conscience. There are few more soothing messages than those historically delivered by the I.Q. testers. The poor, the foreign-born, and racial minorities were shown to be stupid. They were shown to have been born that way. The underprivileged are today demonstrated to be ineducable, a message as soothing to the public purse as to the public conscience.

These are, of course, political considerations. This book is about the politics of intelligence testing, as well as the science of intelligence testing. To pretend that the two are separable is either naive or dissembling. The opening chapters of the book document how, with respect to I.Q. testing, psychology long ago surrendered its political virginity. The interpretation of I.Q. data has always taken place, as it must, in a social and political context, and the validity of the data cannot be fully assessed without reference to that context. That is in general true of social science, and no amount of biology-worship by "behavior geneticists" can transfer I.Q. testing from the social to the biological sciences.

The attempt to blame social disaster on fixed biological causes has an ancient, if not honorable, history. The I.Q. test has been psychology's main contribution to that continuing effort. The first stirrings of the intelligence testers had provided sufficient data for the Director of the New York State Board of Charities' Bureau of Analysis and Investigation, Dr. Chester Carlisle, to write the following in 1918:

> The particular types of symptom-behavior accompanying the individual who is an economic failure . . . are all determined by . . . an individual constitution inadequate to meet the demands made upon him . . . His biological mechanism was imperfectly developed. . . .
>   . . . Those lacking in intelligence capacity drift into the lower levels of our social life and come to be the denizens of city slums. . . . The more active and higher types among them leave their more defective kin. The residue which remains is, therefore, composed of those of least social value. . . . Hence their progeny show . . . gross intelligence defect. . . . "Pauper," dreaded word in every land, has epitomized the dregs of failure. . . . There often remains a residue of families who . . . cannot find work. . . . The old doctrine of predestination now dressed in terms of modern psychology reasserts itself.[4]

Fifty-three years of subsequent scientific advance did little to modify Dr. Carlisle's conclusions or language, which appeared anew in the 1971 pages of *Atlantic Monthly*, now authored by Professor Richard Herrnstein of Harvard:

> as technology advances, the tendency to be unemployed may run in the genes of a family about as certainly as bad teeth do now.

. . . As the wealth and complexity of human society grow, there will be precipitated out of the mass of humanity a low-capacity (intellectual and otherwise) residue that may be unable to master the common occupations, cannot compete for success and achievement, and are most likely to be born to parents who have similarly failed. . . . The troubles . . . have already caught the attention of alert social scientists, like Edward Banfield, whose book *The Unheavenly City* describes the increasingly chronic lower class in America's central cities. . . .[5]

The I.Q. test, it appears, helps to identify a "residue," separate from normal hard-working people, predestined to unemployment because of imperfect "biological mechanisms" and defective "genes." The residue has little redeeming "social value," but it can cause "troubles." The "denizens of city slums" were, in Dr. Carlisle's time, the native-born poor and the immigrants from southeastern Europe. Today, the residue in our "central cities" is largely black. Patriotism, we have been told, is the last refuge of scoundrels. Psychologists and biologists might consider the possibility that heritability is the first.

The plan of this book is first to review briefly the social history of I.Q. testing in America. Then we shall examine in detail the empirical evidence for the heritability of I.Q. That idea has in recent years enjoyed a remarkable resurgence in American academic circles. The work of Professor Arthur Jensen in summarizing past research literature has figured prominently in that resurgence.[6] Professor Jensen has argued vigorously not only that individual differences in I.Q. are largely inherited, but also that average differences between blacks and whites are possibly determined by genetic differences between the races. Professor Richard Herrnstein has popularized Professor Jensen's summary for large nontechnical audiences.[7,8] Professor Herrnstein shares Professor Jensen's view that individual differences in I.Q. are very largely inherited, but he is much more cautious about possible racial differences: "the case is simply not settled, given our present state of knowledge."[9] Professor Herrnstein's social emphasis is not upon race, but upon class. The case is settled for Professor Herrnstein that in our open society those who have risen to the top have better genes than those who are mired at the bottom.

Throughout my own review of the empirical evidence I have commented on the differences between my reading of the data and those of Professors Jensen and Herrnstein. Their views, I believe, are fundamentally incorrect. There is more involved here than a disagreement among scientists about how to interpret a particular set of complex data. The views of Professors Jensen and Herrnstein have been influential in circles extending considerably beyond the academy. Their interpretations of the I.Q. data have been presented to committees of the Congress concerned with the formulation of domestic welfare policies. The hope I have had in writing this book is not only to contribute to scientific knowledge, but also to influence policy makers, and, perhaps, some scientists who do not recognize that their science and their politics are not clearly separable.

NOTES TO INTRODUCTION

1. C. Burt, "The Evidence for the Concept of Intelligence," *British Journal of Educational Psychology*, 25, (1955), 167.
2. K. Pearson, *Nature and Nurture*, (London, Dulau, 1906).
3. R. J. Herrnstein, "I.Q.," *Atlantic Monthly*, September 1971, p. 57.
4. C. L. Carlisle, "The Causes of Dependency Based on a Survey of Oneida County," *State of New York State Board of Charities, Eugenics and Social Welfare Bulletin*, 15, (1918), pp. 459–460.
5. Herrnstein, *I.Q.*, p. 63.
6. A. R. Jensen, "How Much Can We Boost I.Q. and Scholastic Achievement?", *Harvard Educational Review*, 39, (1969), 1–123.
7. Herrnstein, *I.Q.*
8. Herrnstein, *I.Q. in the Meritocracy*, (Boston, Atlantic Monthly Press, 1973).
9. Herrnstein, *I.Q.*, p. 57.

1
THE PIONEERS OF I.Q.
TESTING IN AMERICA

Terman was unapologetic about where he thought I.Q.
comes from. He believed in the inheritance of I.Q., at
least to a considerable degree.

—Professor Richard Herrnstein, 1971[1]

The first usable intelligence test was developed in France by Alfred Binet in 1905. The basic facts are known to everybody who has taken a college course in psychology, and are available in any textbook. The French Minister of Public Instruction had commissioned Binet to develop a testing procedure that could help to identify students whose academic aptitudes were so low as to necessitate their placement in "special schools."

The test developed by Binet was very largely atheoretical. He viewed it as a practical diagnostic instrument and was not concerned to "make a distinction between acquired and congenital feeblemindedness."[2] Binet in fact prescribed therapeutic courses in "mental orthopedics" for those with low test scores. His chapter on "The Training of Intelligence" began with the phrase "After the illness, the remedy," and his judgment on "some recent philosophers" who had given their "moral support" to the idea that "the intelligence of an individual is a fixed quantity, a quantity which one cannot augment" is clear: "We must protest and react against this brutal pessimism."[3]

With this orientation, it is perhaps as well that Binet died in 1911, before witnessing the uses to which his test was speedily put in the United States. The major translators and importers of the Binet test were Lewis Terman at Stanford, Henry Goddard at the Vineland Training School in New Jersey, and Robert

Yerkes at Harvard. These pioneers of the American mental testing movement held in common some basic sociopolitical views. Their "brutal pessimism" took a very specific political form, manifested by their enthusiastic memberships in various eugenic societies and organizations. They arrived at the remarkable conclusion that the questions asked of children by the Binet test provided a fixed measure of "innate intelligence." The test could thus be used to detect the genetically inferior, whose reproduction was a menace to the future of the state. The communality of their views—and their divergence from Binet's—can best be illustrated by quotations from their early writings.

The Americanized "Stanford-Binet" test was published by Terman in a 1916 book.[4] The promise of the test was made explicit in the opening chapter:

> . . . in the near future intelligence tests will bring tens of thousands of these high-grade defectives under the surveillance and protection of society. This will ultimately result in curtailing the reproduction of feeble-mindedness and in the elimination of an enormous amount of crime, pauperism, and industrial inefficiency. It is hardly necessary to emphasize that the high-grade cases, of the type now so frequently overlooked, are precisely the ones whose guardianship it is most important for the State to assume.

Terman asserted that "there is no investigator who denies the fearful role played by mental deficiency in the production of vice, crime, and delinquency." The cause of mental deficiency — and by implication of crime — was transparently clear. "Heredity studies of 'degenerate' families have confirmed, in a striking way, the testimony secured by intelligence tests."

The test, in Terman's view, was particularly useful in the diagnosis of "high-grade" or "border-line" deficiency; that is, I.Q.'s in the 70–80 range. That level of intelligence

> is very, very common among Spanish-Indian and Mexican families of the Southwest and also among negroes. Their dullness seems to be racial, or at least inherent in the family stocks from which they come . . . the whole question of racial differences in mental traits will have to be taken up anew and by experimental methods. The writer predicts that when this is done there will be discovered enormously significant racial differences in general intelligence, differences which cannot be wiped out by any scheme of mental culture.
>
> Children of this group should be segregated in special classes. . . . They cannot master abstractions, but they can often be made efficient workers. . . . There is no possibility at present of convincing society that they should not be allowed to reproduce, although from a eugenic point of view they constitute a grave problem because of their unusually prolific breeding.[5]

The theme will reappear, so it is of interest to note that Terman did not draw a simple distinction between the white and the "colored" races. The "dull normals," with I.Q.'s between 80 and 90, were said to be "below the actual average of intelligence among races of western European descent. . . ." The "New Immigration" from southeastern Europe was already, by the time Terman wrote, a matter of considerable national concern. The distinction between the "races" of western and southeastern Europe was made forcefully by Madison Grant's influential "The Passing of the Great Race,"[6] and Terman's attribution of a high intelligence level to "races of western European descent" was clearly made in the light of concern over immigration policy.

Professor Terman's stern eugenical judgment fell, in any event, even-handedly on the very poor of all colors. Writing in 1917 under the heading "The Menace of Feeble-Mindedness," he observed that

> only recently have we begun to recognize how serious a menace it is to the social, economic and moral welfare of the state. . . . It is responsible . . . for the majority of cases of chronic and semi-chronic pauperism. . . .
>
> . . . the feeble-minded continue to multiply . . . organized charities . . . often contribute to the survival of individuals who would otherwise not be able to live and reproduce. . . .
>
> If we would preserve our state for a class of people worthy to possess it, we must prevent, as far as possible, the propagation of mental degenerates . . . curtailing the increasing spawn of degeneracy.[7]

The violence of Terman's language stands in melancholy affirmation of Binet's earlier reproof to teachers of the "feeble-minded." "The familiar proverb which says: 'When one is stupid, it's for a long time' seems to be taken literally, without criticism, by some school-masters; those who disinterest themselves in students who lack intelligence; they have for them neither sympathy nor even respect, as their intemperance of language makes them say before these children such things as: 'This is a child who will never accomplish anything . . . he is poorly gifted. . . .' Never! What a large word!"[8]

The views of Henry Goddard, who began to use the Binet test in 1908, did not differ in any important particular from those of Terman. The test data, to his mind, could be used to provide statistical support for the already demonstrated proposition that normal intelligence and "weak-mindedness" were the products of Mendelian inheritance. Perhaps the foremost of the "heredity studies of 'degenerate' families" cited by Terman was Goddard's lurid tracing of the family lines descended from one Martin Kallikak. With respect to the social menace of hereditary feeble-mindedness, Goddard had in 1912 predated Terman: ". . . we have discovered that pauperism and crime are increasing at an enormous rate, and we are led to pause and ask, 'Why?' Even a superficial investigation shows us that a large percentage of these troubles come from the feeble-minded."[9] The "troubles" had evidently caught the attention of alert social scientists who labored long before Professors Banfield[10] or Herrnstein.[11]

The sociopolitical views of the early mental testers are perhaps nowhere more clearly revealed than in Goddard's invited lectures at Princeton University in 1919. There Goddard discoursed on the new science of "mental levels." That new science made possible the accurate assessment of the mental levels both of children and of adults, and those levels had been fixed by heredity. The new science had generated data of profound social significance, and in particular, it invalidated the arguments of gentlemen socialists.

> These men in their ultra altruistic and humane attitude, their desire to be fair to the workman, maintain that the great inequalities in social life are wrong and unjust. For example, here is a man who says, "I am wearing $12.00 shoes, there is a laborer who is wearing $3.00 shoes; why should I spend $12.00 while he can only afford $3.00? I live in a home that is artistically decorated, carpets, high-priced furniture, expensive pictures and other luxuries; there is a laborer that lives in a hovel with no carpets, no pictures, and the coarsest kind of furniture. It is not right, it is unjust." . . . As we have said, the argument is fallacious. It assumes that that laborer is on the same mental level with the man who is defending him. . . .
>
> Now the fact is, *that workman* may have a ten year intelligence while you have a twenty. To demand for him such a home as you enjoy is as absurd as it would be to insist that every laborer should receive a graduate fellowship. How can there be such a thing as social equality with this wide range of mental capacity? The different levels of intelligence have different interests and require different treatment to make them happy. . . .
>
> As for an equal distribution of the wealth of the world that is equally absurd. The man of intelligence has spent his money wisely, has saved until he has enough to provide for his needs in case of sickness, while the man of low intelligence, no matter how much money he would have earned, would have spent much of it foolishly and would never have anything ahead. It is said that during the past year, the coal miners in certain parts of the country have earned more money than the operators and yet today when the mines shut down for a time, those people are the first to suffer. They did not save anything, although their whole life has taught them that mining is an irregular thing and that when they were having plenty of work they should save against the days when they do not have work. . . .
>
> These facts are appreciated. But it is not so fully appreciated that the cause is to be found in the fixed character of mental levels. In our ignorance we have said let us give these people one more chance — always one more chance. [12]

The progress from Binet's position is staggering. The feeble-minded, the paupers, and the unemployed coal miners now seem scarcely distinguishable. This is something more than the "brutal pessimism" protested by Binet. Whatever else we call it, this was a perversion of psychological "science." There are few more vivid examples of the subordination of science to political and economic ideology.

The point of view of the third major importer of Binet's test, Robert Yerkes, is sufficiently indicated by his 1917 appointment as chairman of the Committee on Inheritance of Mental Traits of the Eugenics Research Association. The relation of I.Q. to heredity and to economic factors is made clear in Yerkes' prescription for how "To make a true diagnosis of feeble-mindedness . . . never should such a diagnosis be made on the I.Q. alone. . . . We must inquire further into the subject's economic history. What is his occupation; his pay . . . we must learn what we can about his immediate family. What is the economic status or occupation of the parents? . . . When all this information has been collected . . . the psychologist may be of great value in getting the subject into the most suitable place in society. . . ." [13]

To be diagnosed as feeble-minded during this period, and to be assigned to a "suitable place," was not an enviable lot. There were few fine discriminations drawn, as we have seen, among the criminal, the poor, and the dull-witted. The public institutions to provide for such degenerates were in many states administered by a single official, the "Commissioner of Charities and Corrections." We catch some glimpses of the great value of mental testers to such institutions in the annual reports of Commissioner Wight to the Governor of the State of New Jersey. The commissioner's 1909 report, in discussing "the idiotic," indicated that "They are now in the families, or distributed among the almshouses, and county and State institutions. I find a number of families where there are two or more such imbeciles, suggesting increased necessity for a careful inquiry into causes."[14]

That careful inquiry was not long in forthcoming. Commissioner Wight's 1910 report contained for the first time a section headed "Research Work."

> This is the name we give to the inquiry into heredity, habit, environment, etc., of criminals and defectives, to locate more definitely the primary cause of crime and dependency. The initiative of this important movement was taken by Prof. E. R. Johnstone and Dr. H. A. Goddard of the Training School for Feeble Minded Children . . . The recent meeting of the Eugenic Section at Skillman . . . was well attended by experts . . . who seemed greatly interested in the results of our research work . . . the investigations show that the union of drunken fathers, and feeble minded or epileptic mothers is rapidly increasing the number of imbeciles whom the State is expected to support. . . .
>
> I respectfully ask that a small appropriation be made to prosecute this research work, and send the facts out to the public.[15]

By 1911, having received his appropriation, Commissioner Wight was able to report the results of the research:

> . . . enough has already been accomplished to demonstrate the fact of the transmission of criminal tendencies and mental and physical defect. . . . How to remedy this is another matter. It may be done in part by a more rigid enforcement of the marriage laws, by a better control of the sale of liquor, cigarettes, and dopes known as soothing syrups. If the sterilization law of last winter shall be enforced it will also do much to prevent the evil.
>
> . . . Blanks have been prepared to record such information concerning persons in custodial care as is deemed important in tracing the causes of crime and defectiveness, as they appear connected with heredity and environment. Under the indeterminate sentence act, the Court of Pardons is to determine the time of penal service between the minimum and maximum sentence, and it will be an important factor in settling the question of the fitness of the prisoner for parole if the Court should have his personal record and his family history before it.[16]

This was the social climate into which Terman, Goddard, and Yerkes introduced the intelligence test. The judgments of psychologists were to have social consequences even graver than the prohibition of soothing syrups. The measurement of the fixed mental level was to have a role in determining who was set free and who was jailed; and it was to aid in determining who was sufficiently fit to be allowed to reproduce. There is no record to the effect that the pioneers of American mental testing experienced the awe reported by the physicists who first split the atom.

The early history of testing in America fixed upon the Binet test an apparently indelible genetic interpretation. The hereditarian interpretation shared by Terman, Goddard, and Yerkes did not arise as a consequence of the collection of I.Q. data. Their involvement in the eugenics movement predated the collection of such data. There was, at the time they wrote, no quantitative genetics; there was in fact no tenable theory of how mental traits might be inherited. The notion that dependency, defectiveness, weak-mindedness, and other social ills were attributable to the genes was, in America, an idea whose time had come. We can trace the force of that idea — and its utter divorce from any meaningful scientific data — in the successful efforts of the eugenicists to enact sterilization laws. The rise of the mental testing movement coincided precisely in time with the passage of such laws by a large number of states. These sterilization laws, many of which—but not all —were never enforced, had two features in common. First, they were to be applied exclusively to inmates of publicly supported corrective or "charitable" institutions. Second, they asserted as a matter of fact that various forms of "degeneracy" were hereditarily transmitted.

The first reference which I have found to such a law was provided by Dr. Everett Flood in his 1898 article in the *American Journal of Psychology*, "Notes on the Castration of Idiot Children."[17] Dr. Flood indicated that "A castration bill was introduced into the Michigan Legislature providing for the castration of all inmates of the Michigan Home for the Feeble-Minded and Epileptic . . . also for that of all persons convicted for a felony for the third time." The Michigan bill seems not to have been passed, but it was in any event irrelevant to Dr. Flood's report on the therapeutic castration of 26 Massachusetts male children. Of these, "24 were operated on because of persistent epilepsy and masturbation, one for epilepsy with imbecility, and one for masturbation with weakness of mind."

The first bill actually passed by a legislature was in Pennsylvania. The year, ironically, was 1905, the year in which Binet first published his test. The bill was described as an "Act for the Prevention of Idiocy," but it was vetoed by Governor Pennypacker. Binet would have applauded with his whole heart the governor's veto message.

> These feeble-minded and imbecile children have been entrusted to the institutions by their parents or guardians for the purpose of training and instruction. It is proposed to experiment upon them; not for their instruction, but in order to help society in the future . . . without their consent, which they cannot give. . . . Laws have in contemplation the training and the instruction of the children. This bill assumes that they cannot be so instructed and trained. . . . This mental condition is due to causes many of which are entirely beyond our knowledge. . . .[18]

The first fully enacted law was passed by Indiana in 1907. The law's preamble, with slight modification, appeared repeatedly in sterilization laws subsequently passed by other states. The preamble stated very simply, "Whereas, heredity plays a most important part in the transmission of crime, idiocy, and imbecility.''[19] This legislative fiat occurred before Terman and Goddard sketched out in detail the interrelations among crime, feeble-mindedness, and dependency. They were in large measure following the lead provided by the would-be behavior geneticists of the state legislatures.

The advancement of human behavior genetics seemed now to lie in the hands of politicians, and few could resist the temptation to contribute to science. To Indiana's list of traits in which ''heredity plays a most important part'' New Jersey added in 1911 ''feeble-mindedness, epilepsy, criminal tendencies, and other defects.''[20] The Iowa legislature in the same year provided for the ''unsexing of criminals, idiots, etc.'' The ''unsexing'' provision, however, went beyond any valid eugenic need, and a scientifically sounder measure was adopted by Iowa in 1913. The new bill spelled out the ''etc.'' of the 1911 law. The new measure provided for ''The prevention of the procreation of criminals, rapists, idiots, feeble-minded, imbeciles, lunatics, drunkards, drug fiends, epileptics, syphilitics, moral and sexual perverts, and diseased and degenerate persons.''[21]

Presumably the Supreme Court of the State of Washington had in mind the work of the pioneer mental testers when it upheld the Washington sterilization law on September 3, 1912. The court pointed out that ''modern scientific investigation shows that idiocy, insanity, imbecility, and criminality are congenital and hereditary. . . . There appears to be a wonderful unanimity of favoring the prevention of their future propagation.''[22]

The Attorney General of California, in upholding the California statute in 1910, succeeded in relating the views of the testers to a viable physiological theory. He wrote that

> Degeneracy is a term applied when the nervous or mental construction of the individual is in a state of unstable equilibrium. Degeneracy means that certain areas of brain cells or nerve centers of the individual are more highly or imperfectly developed than the other brain cells, and this causes an unstable state of the nerve system, which may manifest itself in insanity, criminality, idiocy, sexual perversion, or inebriety.* Most of the insane, epileptic, imbecile, idiotic, sexual perverts, many of the confirmed inebriates, prostitutes, tramps, and criminals, as well as habitual paupers, found in our county poor-asylums, also many of the children in our orphan homes, belong to the class known as degenerates. . . .[23]

Within seven years, Terman, at Stanford, was to write: ''If we would preserve our state for a class of people worthy to possess it, we must prevent, as far as possible, the propagation of mental degenerates.'' The meek might inherit the kingdom of Heaven, but, if the views of the mental testers predominated, the orphans and tramps and paupers were to inherit no part of California. The California law of 1918 provided that compulsory sterilizations must be approved by a board including ''a clinical psychologist holding the degree of Ph.D.''[24] This was eloquent testimony to Professor Terman's influence in his home state.

*This affliction has now been renamed. The term used by modern school systems is ''minimal brain damage.''

The *Harvard Law Review* in December, 1912, grappled conscientiously with the implications of the findings of modern science. Discussing the constitutionality of sterilization laws, the *Review* observed that "Asexualization can only be justified in the case of born criminals . . . born criminals who cannot be proved to be such must be granted immunity. However, there are probably some criminals whose degenerate character can be ascertained, and if a statute can be so drawn as to limit its operation to such as these it should be constitutional. . . . Larceny is common among born criminals. . . ."[25]

The scientific documentation offered by the mental testers that degeneracy and feeble-mindedness were heritable did not occur in a vacuum. Their views were responsive to social problems of the gravest moment. Their "findings" were politically partisan, and they had consequences. We can see clearly with hindsight how ludicrously beyond the bounds of science those views and "findings" extended. They fixed upon the succeeding generations of psychometricians, equipped with more sophisticated scientific tools, a clear predisposition toward a genetic interpretation of I.Q. data. That predisposition is still with us.

Though sterilization measures were fitfully enforced against the poor — most notably in California — they had no major impact on American society. There are, however, contemporary stirrings by advocates of sterilization. Thus, for example, a South Carolina obstetrician announced in 1973 that he would not take care of welfare mothers with three or more children unless they agreed to be sterilized. The rationale for this policy was not explicitly eugenic; instead, the physician expressed concern for the welfare burden assumed by taxpayers. The advocacy of sterilization as a policy measure does not necessarily imply a belief in the genetic determination of "undesirable" traits. This was made elegantly explicit by Reed and Reed in their massive 1965 study of mental retardation.[26] They concluded: "Few people have emphasized that where the transmission of a trait is frequently from parent to offspring, sterilization will be effective and it is irrelevant whether the basis for the trait is genetic or environmental." The belief in the heritability of I.Q. may thus merely have provided a convenient and "scientific" rationale for policies and laws which would have been enacted on other grounds.

The sterilization laws may have been largely dead letters, but in another sphere the mental testing movement was deeply involved in a major practical accomplishment. The findings of the new science were used to rationalize the passage of an overtly racist immigration law. The mental testers pressed upon the Congress scientific I.Q. data to demonstrate that the "New Immigration" from southeastern Europe was genetically inferior. That contribution permanently transformed American society. This disgraceful episode in the history of American psychology — one not without contemporary relevance — is the subject of the next chapter.

NOTES TO CHAPTER ONE

1. R. J. Herrnstein, *I.Q. in the Meritocracy,* (Boston, Atlantic Monthly Press, 1973), p. 138.

2. A. Binet and T. Simon, "Sur la necessité d'établir un diagnostic scientifique des états inferieurs de l'intelligence," *L'année psychologique*, 11, (1905), 191.

3. A. Binet, *Les Idées modernes sur les enfants*, (Paris, Flammarion, 1913), pp. 140 – 141.

4. L. M. Terman, *The Measurement of Intelligence*, (Boston, Houghton Mifflin, 1916), pp. 6 – 7.

5. Terman, *Measurement*, pp. 91 – 92.

6. M. Grant, *The Passing of the Great Race*, (New York, Scribner's, 1916).

7. L. M. Terman, "Feeble-minded Children in the Public Schools of California," *School and Society*, 5 (1917), 165.

8. Binet, *Idées*, pp. 140 – 141.

9. H. H. Goddard, "How Shall We Educate Mental Defectives?", *The Training School Bulletin*, 9, (1912), 43.

10. E. C. Banfield, *The Unheavenly City: The Nature and Future of our Urban Crisis*, (Boston, Little Brown, 1970).

11. Herrnstein, *I.Q.*

12. H. H. Goddard, *Human Efficiency and Levels of Intelligence*, (Princeton, Princeton University Press, 1920), pp. 99 – 103.

13. R. M. Yerkes and J. C. Foster, *A Point Scale for Measuring Mental Ability*, (Baltimore, Warwick and York, 1923), pp. 22 – 25.

14. *Fifth Annual Report of the Department of Charities and Corrections, State of New Jersey*, (Somerville, N.J., 1910), p. 14.

15. *Sixth Annual Report of the Department of Charities and Corrections, State of New Jersey*, (Burlington, N.J., 1911), p. 23.

16. *Seventh Annual Report of the Department of Charities and Corrections, State of New Jersey*, (Trenton, N.J., 1912), pp. 17 – 18.

17. E. Flood, "Notes on the Castration of Idiot Children," *American Journal of Psychology*, 10 (1898), p. 299.

18. H. H. Laughlin, *Eugenical Sterilization in the United States*, (Chicago, Psychopathic Laboratory of the Municipal Court of Chicago, 1922), pp. 35–36.

19. Ibid, p. 15.

20. Ibid, p. 24.

21. Ibid, pp. 21 – 22.

22. Ibid, pp. 160 – 161.

23. Ibid, pp. 324 – 325.

24. Ibid, p. 60.

25. Ibid, pp. 123 – 124.

26. E. Reed and S. Reed, *Mental Retardation: A Family Study*, (Philadelphia, Saunders, 1965), p. 77.

2
PSYCHOLOGY AND
THE IMMIGRANT

*Were we set out on a sensible program regarding the
immigrant, we should be led ultimately into an analogous
one concerning the inferior stocks already extant in our
population. Linking up these two programs with a sane
educational policy we might look forward to a true national
greatness. For who doubts that the contributors
to a high culture must be of a high-minded race?*

—Professor Kimball Young, 1922[1]

The United States, until 1875, had no federal immigration law. The 1875 law, and all subsequent amendments until 1921, placed no numerical limitation on immigration. The first federal law simply listed a number of excluded classes of individuals. The 1875 list was modest — it barred coolies, convicts, and prostitutes.

The control over immigration developed slowly, and at first by the gradual addition of new excluded classes. There was also a "gentlemen's agreement" with Japan, and circuitous regulations having to do with the longitudes and latitudes from which immigration was debarred served to assure an appropriate racial balance. There were, however, no discriminations drawn among the various European countries which provided the bulk of immigration. Throughout the nineteenth century, the preponderance of immigration flowed from the countries of northern and western Europe.

The advances of psychology can be seen reflected in the changing terminology of the list of excluded classes. The 1882 immigration act debarred lunatics and idiots, and the 1903 law added epileptics and insane persons. By 1907, a differentiation had been made between "imbeciles" and "feeble-minded persons," both of which classes were excluded. The fullest development of modern mental science informed the law of 1917, which excluded "persons of constitutional psychopathic inferiority."

With the turn of the century, the "New Immigration" from southeastern Europe began to assume massive proportions. The English, Scandinavian, and German stock which had earlier predominated was now outnumbered by a wave of Italian, Polish, Russian, and Jewish immigrants. The popular press and the literary magazines of the period were filled with articles questioning the assimilability of the new and exotic ethnic breeds. There arose a public clamor for some form of "quality control" over the inflow of immigrants. This at first took the form of a demand for a literacy test; but it could scarcely be doubted that the new science of mental testing, which proclaimed its ability to measure innate intelligence, would be called into the nation's service.

The first volunteer was Henry Goddard, who in 1912 was invited by the United States Public Health Service to Ellis Island, the immigrant receiving station in New York harbor. The intrepid Goddard administered the Binet test and supplementary performance tests to representatives of what he called the "great mass of average immigrants." The results were sure to produce grave concern in the minds of thoughtful citizens. The test results established that 83% of the Jews, 80% of the Hungarians, 79% of the Italians, and 87% of the Russians were "feeble-minded."[2] By 1917, Goddard was able to report in the *Journal of Delinquency* that "the number of aliens deported because of feeble-mindedness . . . increased approximately 350 percent in 1913 and 570 percent in 1914. . . . This was due to the untiring efforts of the physicians who were inspired by the belief that mental tests could be used for the detection of feeble-minded aliens. . . ."[3]

This accomplishment of the fledgling science won sympathetic attention from the Eugenics Research Association. That society's journal, *Eugenical News,* was edited by the biologist Harry Laughlin. Writing in his journal in 1917, under the heading "The New Immigration Law," Laughlin observed: "Recently the science of psychology has developed to a high state of precision that branch of its general subject devoted to the testing of individuals for natural excellence in mental and temperamental qualities. When the knowledge of the existence of this science becomes generally known in Congress, that body will then be expected to apply the direct and logical test for the qualities which we seek to measure. . . ."[4]

This appears to have been a relatively modest proposal, presumably pointing toward the use of mental tests in detecting would-be immigrants who fell into the debarred classes. There were, however, historical forces at work which were to catapult the science of mental testing to new levels of public acceptance, and which were to provide the scientists of the Eugenics Research Association with opportunities scarcely imaginable in early 1917. The United States was soon to enter the World War, and mental testing was to play a critical role in determining the ethnic and racial composition of the republic.

The president of the American Psychological Association when the country declared war was Robert Yerkes. The "point scale" version of the Binet test had been developed by Yerkes, and his views on the heritability of I.Q. were clearly formulated. They had led to his appointment to the Committee on Eugenics of the National Commission on Prisons, and to his chairmanship in 1917 of the Eugenics Research Association's Committee on Inheritance of Mental Traits. With the country mobilizing to prosecute the war, the APA, under Yerkes' leadership, suggested that the major contribution of psychologists might be the mass intelligence testing of draftees. The proposal was accepted by the military, and psychologists were commissioned in the Army's Sanitary Corps, under Major Yerkes. Their mission was to provide mental assessments, and hopefully to aid in the job classification of draftees.

The psychologists quickly developed a written group intelligence test— "Alpha"—which could easily be administered to large bodies of men. For "illiterates," a supplementary test—"Beta"—was designed. This test was "non-verbal," of the "performance" type. To accommodate non-English speakers, instructions were to be given to groups of men in pantomime. The work on test development was planned by a committee meeting at the Vineland Training School. The committee's membership included Terman, Goddard, and Yerkes.

The tests appear to have had little practical effect on the outcome of the war. They were not in fact much used for the placement of men. The testing program, however, generated enormous amounts of data, since some 2,000,000 men were given standardized I.Q. tests. The mental tests were very widely publicized. Public interest was doubtless excited by the finding that the "mental age" of the average white draftee was only 13.

Following the war, an intensive statistical analysis was performed on the scores of some 125,000 draftees. The results of this analysis, together with a detailed history of the testing program, were published in 1921 by the National Academy of Sciences, under Yerkes' editorship.[5] The publication of the data occurred in the same year in which Congress, as a temporary measure, first placed a numerical limitation on immigration.

The World War I data provided the first massive demonstration that blacks scored lower on I.Q. tests than did whites. That, however, was not a matter of pressing concern in 1921. The chapter in the Yerkes report with immediate impact was that on "Relation of Intelligence Ratings to Nativity." The chapter summarized I.Q. results for a total of 12,407 draftees who had reported that they were born in foreign countries. A letter grade, ranging from A through E, was assigned to each tested draftee, and the distribution of grades was presented separately for each country of origin. The results are reproduced from the Yerkes volume in Figure 1.

The style of the Yerkes volume was to refrain from editorial comment, and the

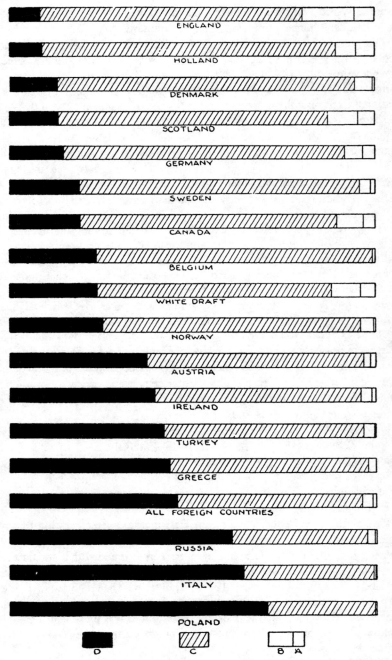

FIG. 1. Percentage distribution of letter grades in intelligence by nativity of foreign-born men in draft (from Yerkes, 1921).

discussion of Figure 1 was value-free. The chapter, edited in fact by Boring, observed: ''The range of difference between the countries is a very wide one. . . . In general, the Scandinavian and English speaking countries stand high in the list, while the Slavic and Latin countries stand low . . . the countries tend to fall into two groups: Canada, Great Britain, the Scandinavian and Teutonic countries [as opposed to] the Latin and Slavic countries. . . .''[6]

These scientific data speedily became ''generally known in Congress,'' with the considerable assistance of the scientists of the Eugenics Research Association, and of (by now) Colonel Yerkes, employed since after the war at the National Research Council in Washington. The flow of events may provide sustenance to those who entertain a conspiracy theory of history. The *Eugenical News* of 1918 had reported that in April of that year ''a group of students of man'' had gathered at the home of Professor Henry Fairchild Osborn to found the Galton Society. The original Charter Fellows were only nine in number, but provision was made for the election of further students up to a total of 25. The founder of the society, and its chairman, was Mr. Madison Grant, author of ''The Passing of the Great Race.'' The purpose of the Society had been made clear in a personal letter from Grant to Osborn, dated March 9, 1918. ''My proposal,'' Grant wrote, ''is the organization of an anthropological society (or somatological society as you call it) here in New York City with a central governing body, self elected and self perpetuating, and very limited in members, and also confined to native Americans, who are anthropologically socially and politically sound, no Bolsheviki need apply.''[7] These students of man met monthly in the Members' Room of the American Museum of Natural History. The minutes of some meetings were published in *Eugenical News*. They make clear that the Society served two major functions. The members read, and invited, scientific papers on subjects of interest. They also provided expert scientific advice to relevant government agencies. Psychology was ably represented among the Charter Fellows by Edward L. Thorndike—a politically sound native psychologist of the first rank, then serving as a consultant to Yerkes' Army testing program.

There occurred in 1920 a massive influx of experimental psychologists, who had worked during the war under Yerkes, into the Eugenics Research Association. The secretary of that association, Harry Laughlin, was appointed ''Expert Eugenics Agent'' of the House Committee on Immigration and Naturalization of the U.S. Congress. The Division of Anthropology and Psychology of the National Research Council established a Committee on Scientific Problems of Human Migration under Yerkes' leadership. The function of that committee was to remove serious national debate over immigration from politics, and to place it instead on a firm scientific basis. This was to be done by the support of relevant scientific research. The psychological and biological scientists of the Eugenics Research Association were equally committed to the goal of relevance. They elected as chairman of their association in 1923 the Honorable Albert Johnson. That honorable gentleman, as fortune would have it, was the congressman who served as chairman of the House Committee on Immigration and Naturalization.

The exchange of ideas with eminent scientists doubtless did not impede Representative Johnson in his task of composing the Immigration Act of 1924.

The first research supported by the National Research Council's committee was that of Carl Brigham, then an assistant professor of psychology at Princeton University. The Princeton University Press had already published in 1923 Brigham's *A Study of American Intelligence*.[8] The book is a landmark of sorts. Though it has disappeared from contemporary reference lists, it can be argued that few works in the history of American psychology have had so significant an impact.

The book's foreword was composed by Yerkes, who "consented to write it because of my intense interest in the practical problems of immigration. . . ." The foreword declared that "Two extraordinarily important tasks confront our nation: the protection of the moral, mental, and physical quality of its people, and the re-shaping of its industrial system so that it shall promote justice and encourage creative and productive workmanship." Professor Brigham was said by Yerkes to have "rendered a notable service to psychology, to sociology, and above all to our law-makers. . . . The author presents not theories or opinions but facts. It behooves us to consider their reliability and their meaning, for no one of us as a citizen can afford to ignore the menace of race deterioration or the evident relations of immigration to national progress and welfare."

The empirical contribution made by Brigham consisted of a reanalysis of the Army data on immigrant intelligence. The performance of Negro draftees was taken as a kind of bedrock baseline; fully 46% of the Poles, 42.3% of the Italians, and 39% of the Russians scored at or below the Negro average. The most original analysis, however, centered about the "very remarkable fact" that the measured intelligence of immigrants was related to the number of years that they had lived in America. This had been demonstrated by pooling the scores of immigrants from all countries, and then subdividing them into groups categorized according to the years of residence in America prior to being tested. This analysis indicated that foreigners who had lived in the country 20 years or more before being tested were every bit as intelligent as native Americans. Those who had lived in the country less than five years were essentially feeble-minded. To some analysts, this finding might have suggested that I.Q. scores were heavily influenced by exposure to American customs and language, but that was not the tack taken by Brigham.

"We must," Brigham declared, "assume that we are measuring native or inborn intelligence. . . ."[9] The psychologists had, after all, deliberately devised the Beta test to measure the genetically determined intelligence of the illiterate and the foreign-speaking. "The hypothesis of growth of intelligence with increasing length of residence may be identified with the hypothesis of an error in the method of measuring intelligence. . . ." That hypothesis was not likely to be congenial to a mental tester, and Brigham quickly disposed of it with a number of statistical and psychometric arguments. With this accomplished, "we are forced to . . . accept the hypothesis that the curve indicates a gradual deterioration in the class of immigrants examined in the army, who came to this country in each succeeding five year period since 1902.''

Forced by the data to this conclusion, Professor Brigham was at no loss to provide a clarifying explanation—"the race hypothesis.'' He proceeded to estimate ''the proportion of Nordic, Alpine and Mediterranean blood in each of the European countries,'' and to calculate the numbers of immigrants arriving from each country during each time period. These combined operations produced a sequential picture of the blood composition of the immigrant stream over time. There was thereby unearthed a remarkable parallelism; as the proportion of Nordic blood had decreased, and the proportions of Alpine and Mediterranean blood increased, the intelligence of the immigrants was deduced to have decreased. This is a nice example of the power of correlational analysis applied to intelligence data. There was no attempt by Brigham to discover whether, *within* each of the ''races,'' measured intelligence had increased with years of residence in America. The conclusion reached by Brigham followed in the footsteps of the testing pioneers who had taught him his trade. He urged the abandonment of ''feeble hypotheses that would make these differences an artifact of the method of examining'' and concluded forthrightly that ''our test results indicate a genuine intellectual superiority of the Nordic group. . . .''

The final two chapters of Brigham's book might fairly be described as reactionary. They pile together quotations from the racist ideologues of America and Europe with Brigham's own opinions. The quoted excerpts in the following sentence are in part Brigham's, and in part his quotations from Grant and others.

> The Nordics are . . . rulers, organizers, and aristocrats . . . individualistic, self-reliant, and jealous of their personal freedom . . . as a result they are usually Protestants. . . . The Alpine race is always and everywhere a race of peasants. . . . The Alpine is the perfect slave, the ideal serf . . . the unstable temperament and the lack of coordinating and reasoning power so often found among the Irish. . . . we have no separate intelligence distributions for the Jews. . . . our army sample of immigrants from Russia is at least one half Jewish. . . . Our figures, then, would rather tend to disprove the popular belief that the Jew is intelligent . . . he has the head form, stature, and color of his Slavic neighbors. He is an Alpine Slav [pp. 182–3, 185, 189, 190].

The final paragraphs of the book raised the eugenic spectre of a long-term decline in the level of American intelligence as the consequence of continued immigration and racial mongrelization. ''We must face a possibility of racial admixture here that is infinitely worse than that faced by any European country today, for we are incorporating the negro into our racial stock, while all of Europe is comparatively free from this taint. . . . The decline of American intelligence will be more rapid than the decline of the intelligence of European national groups, owing to the presence here of the negro.''[10]

With national problems of this magnitude, nothing short of a radical solution seemed likely to be of much avail. From this stern logic, neither Professor

Brigham nor his sponsor, Professor Yerkes, shrank. The final sentences of Brigham's book mean precisely what they say.

> The deterioration of American intelligence is not inevitable, however, if public action can be aroused to prevent it. There is no reason why legal steps should not be taken which would assure a continuously progressive upward evolution.
> The steps that should be taken to preserve or increase our present intellectual capacity must of course be dictated by science and not by political expediency. Immigration should not only be restrictive but highly selective. And the revision of the immigration and naturalization laws will only afford a slight relief from our present difficulty. The really important steps are those looking toward the prevention of the continued propagation of defective strains in the present population. If all immigration were stopped now, the decline of American intelligence would still be inevitable. This is the problem which must be met, and our manner of meeting it will determine the future course of our national life.

With this work behind him, Brigham moved on to the secretaryship of the College Entrance Examination Board. There he made further contributions to psychometric theory, and designed and developed the Scholastic Aptitude Test, the primary screening instrument for admission to American colleges. By 1929 Brigham had been elected secretary of the American Psychological Association and, after his death, the library building of Educational Testing Service was named in his honor.*

There is no record of the psychological community reacting with shock or outrage to Brigham's policy proposals. Perhaps none could be expected from a community in which Terman, Goddard, and Yerkes had helped to set an ideological tone—and which, in the year of publication of Brigham's book, had elected Lewis Terman president of the American Psychological Association. The review of Brigham's book in the 1923 *Journal of Educational Psychology* was probably representative of the psychology establishment's response: "The thesis is carefully worked up to by a logical and careful analysis of the results of the army tests . . . we shall certainly be in hearty agreement with him when he demands a more selective policy for future immigration and a more vigorous method of dealing with the defective strains already in this country."[11]

There now existed an alliance of scientific and political thinkers committed to "vigorous methods" in the solution of the nation's problems. The political usage of Brigham's book and of the Army data was immediate and intense. That branch of the subject of psychology "devoted to the testing of individuals for natural excellence" was to enlighten the Congressional assault on immigration to an extent that Harry Laughlin could not have fully appreciated early in 1917.

---

*Professor Brigham, in 1930, retracted as incorrect his 1923 analysis of the Army I.Q. data. The retraction appears on page 165 of the *Psychological Review* of that year. The Immigration Act of 1924 had by then been in force for six years. Whether Professor Brigham's opinions about the character of Alpines and Mediterraneans changed is not known, and is not relevant.

Francis Kinnicutt, of the Immigration Restriction League, testified to the U.S. Senate Committee on Immigration on February 20, 1923. He desired:

> to further restrict immigration from southern and eastern Europe . . . [since] the evidence is abundant . . . that . . . it is largely of a very low degree of intelligence. . . . A large proportion of this immigration . . . consists . . . of the Hebrew elements . . . engaged in the garment-making industry. . . . some of their labor unions are among the most radical in the whole country. . . . The recent Army tests show . . . the intelligence of the Italian immigration . . . is of a very low grade, as is also that of the immigration from Poland and Russia. All . . . rank far below the average intelligence for the whole country. See A Study of American Intelligence, by Carl C. Brigham, published by the Princeton University Press.
> This is the most important book that has ever been written on this subject . . . Col. Robert M. Yerkes . . . vouches for this book, and speaks in the highest terms of Prof. Carl C. Brigham, now assistant professor of psychology in Princeton University. This comes as near being official United States Army data as could well be had . . . examine the different tables, which are very graphic and bring the facts out in a most clear way . . . they had two kinds of tests, alpha and beta. . . . They took the greatest care to eliminate the advantage which native Americans would otherwise have had. . . .[12]

The chairman of the committee, Senator Colt, thanked Mr. Kinnicutt for having sent him a copy of Brigham's book, and asked him to leave the additional copy which he had brought with him, explaining "I think every member of the committee ought to read that book and then arrive at his own judgment in regard to it."

The views of Dr. Arthur Sweeney, on "Mental Tests for Immigrants," were made part of the appendix to the hearings of the House Committee on Immigration and Naturalization on January 24, 1923. Those hearings were chaired by Representative Albert Johnson, also chairman of the Eugenics Research Association. Dr. Sweeney had written:

> We have been overrun with a horde of the unfit. . . . we have had no yardstick. . . . The psychological tests . . . furnished us with the necessary yardstick. . . . The Army tests . . . revealed the intellectual endowment of the men. . . . The tests are equally applicable to immigrants. . . . All that is required is a staff of two or three trained psychologists at each port. . . .
> . . . See Memoirs of the National Academy of Sciences. . . . We can not be seriously opposed to immigrants from Great Britain, Holland, Canada, Germany, Denmark, and Scandinavia. . . . We can, however, strenuously object to immigration from Italy . . . Russia . . . Poland . . . Greece . . . Turkey. . . . The Slavic and Latin countries show a marked contrast in intelligence with the western and northern European group. . . . One can not recognize the high-grade imbecile at sight. . . .
> They think with the spinal cord rather than with the brain. . . . The necessity of providing for the future does not stimulate them to continuous labor. . . . Being constitutionally inferior they are necessarily socially inadequate. . . . Education can be received only by those who have intelligence to receive it. It does not create intelligence. That is what one is born with. . . . The D minus group can not go beyond the second grade. . . . we shall

degenerate to the level of the Slav and Latin races . . . pauperism, crime, sex offenses, and dependency . . . guided by a mind scarcely superior to the ox. . . .
. . . we must protect ourselves against the degenerate horde. . . . We must view the immigration problem from a new angle. . . . We must apply ourselves to the task with the new weapons of science . . . the perfect weapons formed for us by science. . . . it is now as easy to calculate one's mental equipment as it is to measure his height and weight. The examination of over 2,000,000 recruits has tested and verified this standard. . . . this new method . . . will enable us to select those who are worthy and reject those who are worthless.[13]

Though Dr. Sweeney's remarks contain some infelicities of phrasing, they do not distort the views of the pioneers of mental testing. With disciples of this caliber pressing for vigorous action, there was no need for Professor Terman to abandon his duties as president of the American Psychological Association in order to testify before the Congress. Professor Boring's scholarly observation in the Memoirs of the National Academy of Sciences—"the Slavic and Latin countries stand low"—was done no serious violence by Dr. Sweeney's reference to "the level of the Slav and Latin races." There is nowhere in the records of the Congressional hearings—nowhere—a single remark by a single representative of the psychological profession to the effect that the results of the Army testing program were in any way being abused or misinterpreted. That program had been organized officially by the American Psychological Association under its then president, Robert Yerkes. The data not only came "as near being official United States Army data as could well be had," they came as near being official data of the psychological profession as could well be had. They reflected the almost universal belief, already established among psychologists, in the heritability of I.Q. scores, and in the potency of the testing methods developed by such scientists as Terman, Goddard, and Yerkes.

The psychologists failed to appear before the Congressional committees, but other patriotic thinkers carried their message for them. To be sure, in the case of the House Committee, chaired by the chairman of the Eugenics Research Association, it was carrying coals to Newcastle. There was an Alice-in-Wonderland quality to Representative Johnson's placing into the minutes of his hearing of January 10, 1924, the "Report of the Committee on Selective Immigration of the Eugenics Committee of the United States of America." The Eugenics Committee had been chaired by Brigham's patron, Madison Grant, author of The Passing of the Great Race, and founder, together with Thorndike, of the Galton Society. The Eugenics Committee included in its membership Harry Laughlin, Expert Eugenics Agent of the House Committee itself, and Representative Johnson, the House Committee's chairman.

The eugenic scientists had reported that "The country at large has been greatly impressed by the results of the Army intelligence tests . . . carefully analyzed by Lieut. Col. R. M. Yerkes, Dr. C. C. Brigham, and others. . . . with the shift in the tide of immigration . . . to southern and eastern Europe, there has gone a decrease in intelligence test scores. . . . The experts . . . believe that . . . the tests give as accurate a measure of intelligence as possible. . . . The questions . . . were selected with a view to measuring innate ability. . . . had mental tests been in operation . . . over 6,000,000 aliens now living in this country . . . would never have been admitted. . . . Aliens should be required to attain a passing score of, say, the median in the Alpha test. . . .''[14]

The chairman of the Allied Patriotic Societies of New York was also a student of the science of mental testing, and at the January 5, 1924 hearing Congressman Johnson placed his letter into the record. ''. . . the bulk of the 'newer' immigration is made up of Italians, Hebrews, and Slavs. . . . During the war certain intelligence tests were made by our Army. . . . These tests threw considerable light on the mental qualities of the 'newer' . . . immigration . . . great care was taken to eliminate any advantage from speaking the English language. . . . The results . . . have been analyzed . . . particularly in the work of Prof. Carl Brigham, of Princeton . . . published by the Princeton University Press. . . . He worked under Colonel Yerkes. . . . Prof. Brigham's tables bring out certain very startling facts. . . . Professor Brigham figures out, moreover, that as many as 2,000,000 persons have been admitted . . . whose intelligence was nearer the intelligence of the average negro . . . than to the average intelligence of the American white.''[15]

Professor Brigham's tables, and those published by the National Academy of Sciences, figured prominently in the extended lecture delivered to the Johnson Committee on March 8, 1924, by Dr. Harry Laughlin. The ubiquitous Dr. Laughlin was then employed as a ''member of the scientific staff'' of the Carnegie Institution. His position as Expert Eugenics Agent of the Johnson Committee had been supplemented by ''an official appointment and credentials signed by the Secretary of Labor, authorizing me to go abroad as a United States immigration agent to Europe, to make certain scientific researches.'' Those researches concerned the biology of human migration. The chairman of the Johnson Committee carefully questioned his agent as to whether such problems ''seem capable of being attacked by purely scientific methods without recourse to politics or contention.'' To this forthright question, agent-biologist Laughlin forthrightly replied, ''Yes, sir. My province was that of a scientific investigator, and these problems were attacked in the purely scientific spirit.''[16]

Scientist Laughlin proceeded to lecture on the ''natural qualities of immigrants.'' There were, he said, some qualities which ''American stock especially prized.'' They included truth-loving, inventiveness, industry, common sense, artistic sense, love of beauty, responsibility, social instinct, and the natural sense of a square deal. ''Of course all of these elements are of a biological order. . . . It is possible to make biological studies of them. . . .''

This section of Laughlin's lecture was devoid of empirical data, and the mathematical precision and operationalism of his subsequent remarks on ''natural intelligence'' came as a refreshing contrast. The measurers of natural intelligence had obviously advanced their discipline beyond the point reached by the measurers of the natural sense of a square deal. "Many tests . . . are being developed by psychological research. Their purpose is to evaluate naked natural intelligence. . . . These examinations, as all members of the committee know, were conducted under the direction of Maj. Robert M. Yerkes. . . . The tests given were the best which the psychologists of the world had devised. . . ."

The proportions of Grade A through E men in the various countries were duly displayed in a series of charts, with appropriate credit to the National Academy of Sciences. These were supplemented by Laughlin's own tables, which equated various forms of intelligence test. The Congress was informed that those with a mental age below 9.5, or an I.Q. below 70, or a score on the Yerkes point scale or Alpha below 50, or a score on Beta below 40, or a score on Brigham's combined scale below 9.1, were D− or E men, who were described by the phrase "Cost of supervision greater than value of labor. Untrainable socially or economically." Statistician Laughlin calculated that the country already contained in its foreign-born white population 2,060,262 such men—not to mention another 4,287,573 D aliens, "Slow in adaptability; supervision needed." The number of admitted aliens deficient in a natural sense of a square deal was not calculated. Would such an estimate have been any more ludicrous than the quantifications of innate intelligence so maliciously provided to the Congress and the country by the pillars of American psychology?

The mental testers brought the facts not only to the Congress, but also to the thoughtful reading public. Their relevance to immigration policy was made entirely explicit. For example, Professor Kimball Young reported in the 1922 *Scientific Monthly*[17] that "general as well as specific abilities are transmitted by heredity" and that "special talents may actually turn out to be due to the presence of separate units in the germ plasm." The Ph.D. and M.A. theses of Terman's students at Stanford were cited to show that a group of 25 Italians had a median I.Q. of 84. Terman's student had written in her dissertation that "the tests are as accurate a judgment of the mental capacity of the low foreign element as of the American children." This conclusion was confirmed by the more massive scholarly work of a student at Columbia, who examined "500 cases each of Jewish, American, and Italian boys and 225 negro boys. . . . Italians who were thought by their teachers, principal, and neighborhood social workers to be laboring under no language handicap were found to be very inferior to the other three races." The surprisingly high performance of the blacks in this study was readily explained by Professor Young in a scholarly footnote: "The negroes were a much more highly selected group perhaps than the Italians. . . ."

The evidence, Professor Young indicated, pointed "conclusively to the fact that a continued deluge of this country of the weaker stocks of Europe will ultimately affect the average intelligence of the population. . . . these stocks are constantly sending out their tenacles [sic] into the higher biological strains. . . .

We have of course the comparable problem of preventing the continuance of inferior lines in the present population. . . . The public opinion of this country needs arousing . . . immigration should be controlled. . . . It seems to me that there is not a better piece of service for the National Research Council than an attack upon this problem. . . . True, there remains after such a program, if it is ever accepted, the entire matter, noted already, of the inferior strains in the population now present in this country.''

The Johnson-Lodge Immigration Act of 1924 was enacted after the conclusion of the congressional hearings. There had already been enacted, on a temporary basis, a 1921 law embodying the principle of ''national origin quotas.'' The number of immigrants admitted from any given country in one year had been limited to 3 percent of the number of foreign-born from that country already resident in the United States, as determined by the census of 1910. The Johnson-Lodge Act established national origin quotas as a permanent aspect of immigration policy, and it reduced the quota to 2 percent; but most important, *the quotas were to be based on the census of 1890.* The use of the 1890 census had only one purpose, acknowledged by the bill's supporters. The ''New Immigration'' had begun after 1890, and the law was designed to exclude the biologically inferior D− and E peoples of southeastern Europe. The new law made the country safe for Professor Brigham's Nordics, but it did little for the safety of Alpines and Mediterraneans. The law, for which the science of mental testing may claim substantial credit, resulted in the deaths of literally hundreds of thousands of victims of the Nazi biological theorists. The victims were denied admission to the United States because the ''German quota'' was filled, although the quotas of many other Nordic countries were vastly undersubscribed. The Nazi theoreticians ultimately concurred with biologist Laughlin's assessment that, in the case of D− and E people, ''Cost of supervision greater than value of labor.''

The biological partitioning of the European land-mass by the Congress did much to place immigration policy on a firm scientific footing. There were, however, both scientific and political loose ends to be tidied up, and they did not escape the attention of the more ardent mental testers. Dr. Nathaniel Hirsch held a National Research Council Fellowship in Psychology at Harvard, under McDougall. The results of his research endeavor were published in the 1926 *Genetic Psychology Monographs.*

The intellectual inferiority of the immigrants had already been amply documented. To demonstrate conclusively its genetic origin, Hirsch gave intelligence tests to the American-born *children* of various immigrant groups. The children were to provide a clear test of the genetic hypothesis. They had attended American schools, they spoke the English language, but they carried their parents' genes. The data indicated that, for almost all groups, the children of immigrants were intellectually inferior.

The policy implications of his contribution did not escape Dr. Hirsch. While applauding the Immigration Act of 1924, he warned in the discussion section of his scientific treatise that

> that part of the law which has to do with the non-quota immigrants should be modified. . . . All mental testing upon children of Spanish-Mexican descent has shown that the average intelligence of this group is even lower than the average intelligence of the Portuguese and Negro children . . . in this study. Yet Mexicans are flowing into the country. . . . Our immigration from Canada . . . we are getting . . . the less intelligent of working-class people. . . . the increase in the number of French Canadians is alarming. Whole New England villages and towns are filled with them. The average intelligence of the French Canadian group in our data approaches the level of the average Negro intelligence.

Professor Hirsch then quoted the lament of an earlier observer:

> I have seen gatherings of the foreign-born in which narrow and sloping foreheads were the rule. . . . In every face there was something wrong—lips thick, mouth coarse . . . chin poorly formed . . . sugar loaf heads . . . goose-bill noses . . . a set of skew-molds discarded by the Creator. . . . Immigration officials . . . report vast troubles in extracting the truth from certain brunette nationalities.[18]

Dr. Hirsch strove for and achieved a conceptual synthesis of psychological and biological principles: "The Jew is disliked primarily because despite physical, economic, and social differences among themselves, 'all Jews are Jews,' meaning that there is a psycho-biological principle that unites the most dissimilar of types of this strange, paradoxical Natio-Race."

With so masterful a grasp of psychobiology, it was perhaps inevitable that Dr. Hirsch should turn his attention to the complicated problem of estimating the precise weights of heredity and environment in the determination of I.Q. The results of this basic research, also supervised by McDougall, were published in a 1930 Harvard University Press book entitled *Twins*. Dr. Hirsch's interest in twins had been stimulated "in consequence of a suggestion made by President A. Lawrence Lowell of Harvard University." Hirsch deduced that "heredity is five times as potent" as environment. He concluded that ". . .there is no doubt that today many of the environmental agencies of civilization are contributing to 'The Decline of the West,' and that political wisdom can be garnered from a study of twins, and from other experimental studies of heredity and environment."[19]

The theme is recurrent. The academic seekers after truth pursue jointly the goals of political and scientific wisdom. Those who today investigate black-white differences in I.Q., or whose concern for The Decline of the West prompts them to brood on I.Q. and the meritocracy, might do well to remember the colloquy between Representative Johnson and Expert Eugenics Agent Laughlin:

"The Chairman: Do all of these three problems seem capable of being attacked by purely scientific methods without recourse to politics or contention?

"Doctor Laughlin: Yes, sir. My province was that of a scientific investigator, and these problems were attacked in the purely scientific spirit."

There was a lively appreciation of the relation between science and politics expressed in the 1927 address of Frank L. Babbott to the Eugenics Research Association. Mr. Babbott explained to the assembled scientists that eugenics "has made its strongest appeal to me through its influence on immigration. . . . this is an indirect result of eugenics, but it comes as the natural development of research on the part of people like yourselves. It is possible that restriction of immigration would have come without the aid of our Society, but I doubt if it would have come so soon or so permanently if it had not been for the demonstration that men, like Dr. Laughlin, have been able to make to the Committee on Immigration. . . .

"The Eugenics Research Association began its work with the House Immigration Committee in 1920, and immediately took the whole question out of politics and placed it on a scientific or biological basis. . . . It was at this juncture that Dr. Laughlin was brought into the deliberations of the Committee. As one member of the Committee has said—he became their teacher and supplied them with arguments to meet the opposition. . . ."[20]

The contribution of the mental testers toward the formulation of national policies did not end in 1924. The meeting of the Galton Society on November 4, 1927, with Carl Brigham in the chair, opened with a report by Madison Grant that the Honorable Albert Johnson had requested suggestions from the Galton Society concerning the eugenical uses which might be made of the census of 1930. The Society suggested the collection of pedigree records detailing racial and family stocks, as well as the collection of mothers' maiden names. Further, it would be useful if all persons enumerated by the census were issued an official registration card. With this public business concluded, Professor Brigham introduced Dr. Harry Laughlin, who lectured to the students of man on "The Genetics of the Thoroughbred Horse."[21]

The Society, on April 5, 1929, adopted an official statement on the maintenance of immigration control. "The Galton Society appreciates the fact that the essential character of every nation depends primarily upon the inborn racial and family endowments of its citizens." Professors Thorndike and Brigham were present; the minutes do not record any disagreement.[22]

There is a moral to be drawn from this melancholy history. The immigration debate, together with its European victims,[23] is long since dead—but only to be replaced by a curiously similar issue. The major domestic issue of our own time, as our politicians remind us, is "the welfare mess." The welfare issue, like immigration, contains within itself a tangle of the most profound racial and economic conflicts. Today's psychometricians speak with voices more cultured than that of *Genetic Psychology Monographs* in 1926. There are some, however, who are again prepared to serve as teachers to the Congress, and to supply arguments to meet the opposition. These teachers once again assert that their effort is only to remove racial and economic conflicts from politics, and to place them on a firm scientific basis.

We see today that the psychologists who provided "expert" and "scientific" teaching relevant to the immigration debate did so on the basis of pitifully inadequate data. There is probably no living psychologist who would view the World War I Army data as relevant to the heritable I.Q. of European "races." There are few who now seem much impressed by the data on "Italians in America" summarized by Rudolf Pintner in his 1923 text, *Intelligence Testing*.[24] Professor Pintner had called attention to the "remarkable agreement in the median I.Q. for the Italian children" in six separate studies. That median I.Q. was 84, a full 16 points below the average American. There is probably no psychometrician today prepared to assert that that 16-point deficit was produced by inferior Italian I.Q. genes. That does not prevent the same mental testers from pointing gravely to the possible genetic significance of Professor Jensen's recent survey of the contemporary I.Q. literature. That survey led Jensen to report: "The basic data are well known: on the average, Negroes test about 1 standard deviation (15 IQ points) below the average of the white population, and this finding is fairly uniform across the 81 different tests of intellectual ability used in these studies. . . ."[25] This kind of finding, like Goddard's earlier report that 83 percent of Jewish immigrants were feeble-minded, cannot be ignored by thoughtful citizens.

There is, of course, the theoretical possibility that the genetic theorists are correct. Perhaps I.Q. *is* highly heritable; and perhaps differences between races, as well as among individuals, are in large measure due to heredity. There are serious scholars who have assumed this, and who have labored to adduce supporting evidence. Their data ought not to be ignored, and they deserve a careful scrutiny. That scrutiny is a scientific necessity, even though the social and political policies advocated by many hereditarian theorists are in no sense compelled or justified by the facts which they assert to be true.

The remaining chapters of this book are not primarily concerned with questions of social policy. They ask, instead, whether the policy recommendations of today's mental testers are any more surely grounded in scientific knowledge than were those of their predecessors in the 1920's. What kind of evidence in fact supports the wide-spread assertion that I.Q. test scores are heritable? That is a straightforward scientific question, one which can be answered by a logical analysis of the data. The following chapters attempt such an analysis, and are concerned with the merit and quality of the actual I.Q. data, and with their logical interpretation. The social functions served by the data do not in principle affect their scientific validity. The social history of I.Q. testing has told us something about psychologists, and science, and society; but only the data can tell us the truth about I.Q. The following chapters deal successively with the major types of evidence which have been asserted to demonstrate that I.Q. test scores are heritable.

NOTES TO CHAPTER TWO

1. K. Young, "Intelligence Tests of Certain Immigrant Groups," *Scientific Monthly*, 15, (1922), 434.

2. H. H. Goddard, "The Binet Tests in Relation to Immigration," *Journal of Psycho-Asthenics*, 18, (1913), 105–107.
3. H. H. Goddard, "Mental Tests and the Immigrant," *Journal of Delinquency*, 2, (1917), 271.
4. *Eugenical News*, 2, (1917), 22.
5. *Psychological Examining in the United States Army*, ed. R. M. Yerkes (Washington, Memoirs of the National Academy of Sciences, 15, 1921).
6. Yerkes, *Psychological Examining*, p. 699. There are, at various points in the volume, references to the possibility that language handicaps *might* have depressed the scores of the foreign-born (e.g., p. 704).
7. M. Grant to H. F. Osborn, March 9, 1918, Davenport MSS, American Philosophical Society, Philadelphia.
8. C. C. Brigham, *A Study of American Intelligence*, (Princeton, Princeton University Press, 1923). The Brigham research project supported by the National Research Council was devoted to the development of an "internationalized" test, presumably free of cultural and language bias. Whatever private reservations the NRC committee entertained about the fairness of the wartime tests, these were not expressed publicly, and did not influence the debate on the immigration law.
9. Ibid, p. 100.
10. Ibid, p. 210.
11. *Journal of Educational Psychology*, 14, (1923), 184–185.
12. *Hearing before the Committee on Immigration, United States Senate, February 20, 1923*, (Washington, Government Printing Office, 1923), pp. 80–81.
13. *Hearings before the Committee on Immigration and Naturalization, House of Representatives, January 3, 4, 5, 22, and 24, 1923*, (Washington, Government Printing Office, 1923), pp. 589–594.
14. *Hearings before the Committee on Immigration and Naturalization, House of Representatives, December 26, 27, and 31, 1923, and January 2, 3, 4, 5, 7, 8, 10 and 19, 1924*, (Washington, Government Printing Office, 1924), p. 837.
15. Ibid, p. 580.
16. *Hearings before the Committee on Immigration and Naturalization, House of Representatives, March 8, 1924*, (Washington, Government Printing Office, 1924), pp. 1231–1284.
17. Young, *Tests*, pp. 418–425.
18. N. D. Hirsch, "A Study of Natio-Racial Mental Differences," *Genetic Psychology Monographs*, 1, (1926), 394–397.
19. N. D. Hirsch, *Twins: Heredity and Environment*, (Cambridge, Harvard University Press, 1930), pp. 148–149.
20. *Eugenical News*, 12, (1927), 93.
21. Ibid, 172–173.
22. *Eugenical News*, 14, (1929), 71.

23. A. D. Morse, *While Six Million Died: A Chronicle of American Apathy,* (New York, Random House, 1968).
24. R. Pintner, *Intelligence Testing: Methods and Results,* (New York, Holt, 1923), pp. 351 – 352.
25. A. R. Jensen, "How Much Can We Boost I.Q. and Scholastic Achievement?", *Harvard Educational Review,* 39, (1969), 81.

3
SEPARATED IDENTICAL TWINS

Political wisdom can be garnered from a study of twins.

−Professor N. D. M. Hirsch, 1930[1]

Probably the best known evidence supporting the idea that I.Q. scores are inherited comes from observations made on separated identical twins. That evidence seems especially powerful, because it is based on fewer—and simpler—arbitrary assumptions than must be made to interpret other forms of data. There are two very different types of twins. When a single sperm fertilizes a single ovum, it sometimes happens that two different individuals develop. These individuals are identical, or monozygotic (MZ), twins. They presumably have identical genes. They are necessarily of the same sex, and their physical similarities are typically very striking. The other type of twin pair occurs when two different sperms fertilize two different ova at about the same time. The mother will then bear two different individuals, known as fraternal, or dizygotic (DZ), twins. Though born at the same time, these two individuals will be no more genetically alike than are ordinary brothers and sisters. They will have in common, on average, only half their genes. They may be same-sexed or opposite-sexed, and may be very dissimilar physically.

The MZ twin pairs seem uniquely equipped to serve as subjects in experiments concerned with heredity. They are the only paired individuals who exist with identical genes. That means that any differences which exist between a pair of MZ twins must be exclusively of nongenetic origin. To experiment upon heredity, it would be logical, though immoral, deliberately to subject members of an MZ twin

33

pair to vastly different environments. We would then expect that if a trait were much influenced by environment, the twins would not be much alike for that trait. The fact that MZ twins who have been reared in the same home resemble one another for a given trait does *not* indicate that the trait has been determined by their genes. The MZ twins have experienced very similar environments—probably more similar than those experienced by any other types of individuals.

There exists a kind of natural experiment with MZ twins. There are occasions when a pair of MZ twins is separated very early in infancy and brought up in separate households. This may occur because the mother has died, or is ill or incompetent, or cannot provide for two additional children. Whatever the reason, psychologists have found it theoretically relevant to administer I.Q. tests to sets of MZ twins who were separated in infancy. We might expect, if I.Q. were entirely inherited, and if it were measured without error, that the I.Q. resemblance between separated MZs would be perfect. That is, the I.Q. correlation for a set of such separated pairs might be 1.00. There is nobody, however, who asserts that I.Q. is *entirely* inherited, or perfectly measured. Thus, even under a genetic hypothesis, the correlation should be less than 1.00, but it should be very substantial. There should, under an environmental hypothesis, be no I.Q. resemblance between MZ twins who have been reared in truly different environments. That means that the I.Q. correlation among a set of such twins should be .00, *if* the environments in which members of a pair have been reared are not related to each other. The fact is, however, that separated twins are not assigned to foster families by a lottery. The parents may, for example, place one of the infants with their own relatives, or with family friends. There will certainly be, in the real world, some correlation between the environments into which two separated twins are placed. To the degree that the environments of a pair resemble each other, the I.Q. resemblance between them may be environmentally produced. Thus, from an environmentalist viewpoint, it is only necessary that the I.Q. correlation not be "too large" for whatever degree of environmental similarity is involved.

The heritability of a trait is defined as the proportion of the total variance in that trait attributable to genetic factors, in a particular population at a particular point in time. The heritability, like the correlation coefficient, can vary between .00 and 1.00. The intraclass I.Q. correlation[2] of separated MZ twin pairs would in fact be an estimate of the heritability of I.Q. *if* some key assumptions were made. First, the twins would have to be a representative sample, genetically, of the population in which we are interested. Then, the range of environments to which the twins have been exposed would have to be fairly representative of the range of environmental variation in the population. Third, and perhaps most critical, there must be no tendency for the environments in which twin pair members were reared to be systematically correlated. There is little reason to suppose that these assumptions hold for any of the studies that have been made of separated twins. The results of the studies are nevertheless of great interest, even if the observed I.Q. correlation cannot be used to estimate precisely I.Q. heritability.

There have been only four statistically analyzed studies of separated MZ twins, and the basic data reported by their authors are conveyed in Table 1. There are numerical discrepancies between the I.Q. correlations reported by different authors, but all studies agree that the correlation is very substantial. That substantial correlation is the strongest single piece of evidence we have supporting the idea that I.Q. scores are heritable. The purpose of this chapter is to analyze the four separated twin studies in detail. The apparent evidence for I.Q. heritability will evaporate to nothing.

THE WORK OF CYRIL BURT

Probably the most influential of the four studies has been that of the late Sir Cyril Burt. Professor Burt's scholarly labors were rewarded not only by an English title, but also, in 1971, by the Edward Lee Thorndike Award of the American Psychological Association. The Burt study is impressive on several counts. First, it involved more twin pairs than any of the other studies. Then too, it reported the largest observed I.Q. correlation. The most important feature of the Burt study, however, is its purported demonstration that the environments in which twins were reared were not at all correlated. The Burt study is unique among the four in providing quantitative data about this critical matter.

Professor Burt's work during a lengthy lifetime has had a major impact on all facets of the study of I.Q. heritability. There are, for example, various categories of kinship for which the only existing I.Q. correlations have been provided in Burt's publications. Those publications, and those of his colleagues and students, are almost limitless in number. They furnish us with a veritable treasure of I.Q. data. To appreciate fully Burt's contribution to the study of separated twins it will be necessary to acquaint ourselves first with the general style of his work. The following paragraphs are not to be construed as a digression from our discussion of separated twins. The meaning of Burt's twin data cannot be grasped without a consideration of the rest of his work.

The fact is that the various papers published by Burt often contain mutually contradictory data, purportedly derived from the same study. These contradic-

TABLE 1

I.Q. Correlations in Four Studies of Separated MZ Twins

Study	Test	Correlation	Number of pairs
Burt	"Individual Test"	.86	53
Shields	Dominoes + 2 × Mill Hill	.77	37
Newman et al.	Stanford-Binet	.67	19
Juel-Nielsen	Wechsler	.62	12

tions, however, are more than compensated for by some remarkable consistencies which occur repeatedly in his published works. The first examples that we shall cite do not involve his study of separated twins, but later examples will do so.

The papers of Professor Burt, it must be reported, are often remarkably lacking in precise descriptions of the procedures and methods that he employed in his I.Q. testing. The first major summary of his kinship studies, a 1943 paper, presents a large number of I.Q. correlations, but virtually nothing is said of when or to whom tests were administered, or of what tests were employed. The reader is told, "Some of the inquiries have been published in L. C. C. reports or elsewhere; but the majority remain buried in typed memoranda or degree theses."[3]

The 1943 paper, among many other findings, reported a correlation of .32 "between children's intelligence and economic status." There was no clear indication of how intelligence had been measured, but the data had been "obtained during surveys carried out for the London County Council and the National Institute of Industrial Psychology." The correlation was said to be based on a "composite group of 343 cases, chosen so that the several proportions in each category should correspond with those in the population at large." Parenthetically, the mean I.Q. of children of "higher professional" parents was given as 120.3. That is peculiar, since as Burt later indicated in 1961, only three-tenths of one percent of parents of English children are "higher professionals."[4] Thus, in a composite sample of 343, only one child of a higher professional should have been included. The actual numbers of children on which mean I.Q.'s for categories were based were not provided by Burt.

The main point, however, is that Burt carefully distinguished *economic* status, which he had measured, from *cultural* status. The paper noted that other investigators had reported correlations larger than .32, but those investigators, unlike Burt, had correlated intelligence "with cultural status rather than economic." The very same survey was later cited by Burt and Howard in 1956.[5] They at that time reported that, for 253 families, the correlation between "ratings of socio-economic status" and "the adjusted assessments [of intelligence]" was .315. That figure, rounded to the second decimal, had been reported in the 1943 paper, which they cited. The socioeconomic ratings were now said to correlate .453 with "crude test-results." That is, we are first explicitly told 13 years after the fact that the correlation reported in 1943 had *not* been based on "crude" I.Q. test results, but on something called an "adjusted assessment." We shall shortly discuss Burt's procedure for adjusting the crude numbers produced by his I.Q. tests. We note now that the sample of 343 children described in 1943 obviously contained many sib pairs. We note also that by 1956 the clear distinction between economic and cultural status is blurred by the term "socio-economic."

The very same survey was again cited by Burt and Howard in 1957. They now reported correlations for both crude test marks and adjusted assessments. Further, it now developed that the survey had included ratings for "(a) the material (i.e., financial and hygienic) conditions of each family, and (b) the cultural (i.e., educational and motivational) background.''[6] The correlation between adjusted assessments and *cultural* environment was now said to be .315; for material environment, an entirely new correlation of .226 was reported. The same rather low correlation of .315, which 14 years earlier had been explained to be low because it involved economic rather than cultural status, now turns out to involve ''cultural'' as opposed to ''material'' conditions. When and how were the ratings of material and cultural conditions made? Where was the very low correlation for ''financial and hygienic'' status in 1943, when Burt carefully distinguished—to reconcile his own data with others'—between ''economic'' and ''cultural''? The possibility that Burt and Howard may have rated the homes retrospectively in 1957 is unsettling, since a 1959 paper by Burt's associate Conway[7] makes clear for the first time that the I.Q. data were collected in London between 1922 and 1927.

Throughout a lengthy research career, Burt continued to accumulate intelligence data for numerous categories of biological relatives. The correlations for each category were intermittently reported in a number of publications, based on a gradually increasing sample size. The reports contain virtually no information about the methods employed in testing I.Q., but the correlations were usually reported to three decimal places. They were astonishingly stable, seeming scarcely to fluctuate as the sample size was changed. Two forms of such stability are illustrated in Table 2, which reproduces data contained in Burt's 1955[8] and 1966[9] reports.

The intelligence correlations were reported in three forms: for ''group test,'' for ''individual test,'' and for ''final assessment.'' There is, as we shall see, much

TABLE 2

Correlations Reported by Burt

	Siblings reared apart		DZs reared together	
	1955 (N = 131)	1966 (N = 151)	1955 (N = 172)	1966 (N = 127)
Intelligence				
Group test	.441	.412	.542	.552
Individual test	.463	.423	.526	.527
Final assessment	.517	.438	.551	.453
School attainment				
Reading, spelling	.490	.490	.915	.919
Arithmetic	.563	.563	.748	.748
General	.526	.526	.831	.831
Physical				
Height	.536	.536	.472	.472
Weight	.427	.427	.586	.586

Note.—N refers to number of pairs, as reported by Burt.

ambiguity concerning what these terms mean. There were also correlations reported for various measures of "school attainment" and for physical traits. The table indicates that, for the category siblings reared apart, Burt managed to locate an additional 20 cases between 1955 and 1966. The addition of those cases did have some effect on the intelligence correlations, but three correlations for school attainments, plus those for height and weight, remained identical to the third decimal place. That seems highly improbable, to say the least, but it is possible that Burt simply failed to measure school attainments or physical traits in the added 20 subjects. That same reasoning will not do for the category of DZ twins reared together. Within that category, 45 pairs have mysteriously disappeared between 1955 and 1966. The shrinking sample size cannot be attributed to a typographical transposition of two digits, since all the intelligence correlations, and one for school attainment, were somewhat changed. The other correlations remained identical. Professor Burt's data seem remarkably insensitive to changes, up or down, in the sizes of his samples.[10]

This remarkable stability also characterized the unknown "group test" of intelligence which Burt administered to his separated MZ twins. Table 3 reproduces the correlations reported by Burt on that test for MZ twins reared apart, and for MZ twins reared together. The table includes data from a 1958 paper by Burt[11] and a 1958 paper by Conway[12], as well as from the 1955 and 1966 papers. The sample sizes increased over time by 32 pairs for MZs reared apart, and 12 pairs for MZs reared together. There is a minor perturbation which simultaneously afflicted both correlations in late 1958, but a benign Providence appears to have smiled upon Professor Burt's labors. When he concluded his work in 1966, his three decimal place correlations were back to where they had been in the beginning. The 1943 paper had contained his first reference to separated MZs. Then, for 15 pairs, the correlation had been reported as .77.

We have already noted that Burt, often without specific acknowledgment, employed "adjusted assessments" of I.Q. rather than raw test scores. The reader must be sharp-eyed to detect this on occasion. The 1956 Burt and Howard paper

TABLE 3

Correlations for MZ Twins, "Group Test" of Intelligence

Source	Twins reared apart	Twins reared together
Burt, 1955	.771	.944
	(N = 21)	(N = 83)
Burt, 1958	.771	.944
	(N = "over 30")	(N = ?)
Conway, 1958	.778	.936
	(N = 42)	(N = ?)
Burt, 1966	.771	.944
	(N = 53)	(N = 95)

reported correlations for "assessments of intelligence" for 963 parent-child pairs, 321 grandparent-grandchild pairs, 375 uncle-nephew pairs, etc. The term "assessments" was not defined, and the description of procedure is characteristic of Burt: "The sources for the latter [assessments], the procedures employed, and the results obtained have already been described in previous publications (Burt, 1955, and refs)."[13] The Burt and Howard paper, which has been very widely read and cited, goes on to fit a mathematical-genetic model of inheritance to the reported correlations. The fit is excellent.

The reader who troubles to refer to the 1955 paper will discover that many of the 1956 results were not reported there, and he will also discover that the entire description of procedure is contained in a footnote. The footnote includes the following sentence: "For the assessments of the parents we relied chiefly on personal interviews; but in doubtful or borderline cases an open or a camouflaged test was employed."[14] That sentence bears pondering. The scores of children, on the other hand, were "based primarily on verbal and non-verbal tests of intelligence . . . transformed into standard scores . . . for each age . . . converted to terms of an I.Q. scale. . . ." Whatever ambiguity exists in the case of children, clearly the intelligence of adults was simply guessed at in the course of a personal interview. The spectacle of Professor Burt administering a camouflaged test of intelligence to a London grandparent has considerable comic merit, but it does not inspire scientific confidence. The only reported I.Q. correlation between uncle and nephew in the entire scientific literature appears to be Burt's, obtained in this survey in this way.

The same survey was cited by Burt and Howard in 1957, who in reply to a critic stressed that "in each of our surveys, assessments were individually obtained for a representative sample of parents, checked, for purposes of standardization, by tests of the usual type."[15] The 1955 footnote is cited. There is some ambiguity in the meaning of "for purposes of standardization"; but it is entirely clear that over two years Professor Burt's memory had magically transmuted "doubtful or borderline cases" to "a representative sample of parents." The "open or a camouflaged test" of 1955 had become by 1957 "tests of the usual type." Professor Burt, we may conclude, was not always precise in his use of language.

There are numerous brief references in Burt's writings to the "adjusted assessments" applied to test scores of children, but no adequate description of what rules were followed. For example, Burt wrote in 1958 that "The final assessments for the children were obtained by submitting the marks from the group tests to the judgment of the teachers . . . where the teacher disagreed with the verdict of the marks, the child was interviewed personally, and subjected to further tests, often on several successive occasions."[16]

The fullest rationale for this unorthodox procedure was provided by Burt and Howard in 1957. Their interest, they explained, lay in testing the goodness-of-fit of I.Q. correlations to their model of polygenic I.Q. inheritance. To test the theory, they reasoned, it was advisable to use the most accurate available measure of "genotypic" intelligence. That was *not* the raw I.Q. score: "We . . . are perfectly willing to admit that, as a means of estimating genotypic differences, even the most carefully constructed tests are highly fallible instruments, and that their verdicts are *far less trustworthy* than the judgments of the pupil's own teachers . . . [italics added]."[17]

That represents a considerable faith in the ability of teachers to detect camouflaged genotypes, but Burt had not always expressed that view. He had written in 1943: "But in regard to innate general ability there can be no question: the unaided judgments even of the most experienced teachers, shrewd as they are in many cases, are nevertheless *far less trustworthy* in the long run than the results obtained with properly applied intelligence tests [italics added]."[18] The 1943 paper argued that in post-war Britain the genetically most gifted students should be steered at an early age into a university-bound stream. For such an important practical purpose, Burt reasoned, the nonscientific judgments of teachers could not be trusted; only the science of mental testing could reliably detect the superior genotypes. The teachers, however, could evidently be trusted to adjust Burt's test scores to conform with his genetic theory.

Though Burt sometimes writes of "crude test results," it is by no means clear that raw test scores, or determinate transformations of them, ever entered into his correlations. What is to be made of his 1955 statement that the inquiry on children "was based primarily on verbal and non-verbal tests of intelligence . . . transformed into standard scores . . . for each age. . . "? What tests were given? How were the scores on different tests combined? Were some children given one test, while "doubtful and borderline cases" were given two, three, or four? There is nowhere in Burt an explicit statement that any correlation was ever based on a single, standardized administration of the same test to an entire group of subjects. The few remarks about his procedure that he does provide make it reasonable to suppose that this may never have been done.

The procedural ambiguities are no less marked in the case of Burt's 53 pairs of separated MZ twins. These cases had been gradually accumulated over a period of some 45 years. The most explicit and extended discussion of the twin data was given in Burt's 1966 paper.[19] That paper indicates that all the twins had been separated before the age of 6 months, but it contains no information about the extent or duration of separation. There is no information about the sexes of the twin pairs, nor is their age at testing indicated. They were all, however, "children," and except in three cases "the tests were applied in school." Three very early cases had been dropped from the sample because of a relatively late age of separation. There were, "in the initial survey," some children outside London "originally tested by the local teacher or school doctor; but these have all been since re-tested by Miss Conway." We are not told whether Miss Conway's test results corresponded to the teachers', nor whether discrepancies were averaged, or handled in some other way.

There is no way of knowing what tests were in fact administered to the twins. The correlations are reported under three separate headings: group test, individual test, and final assessment. The description of the tests was as follows: "The tests employed have been fully described elsewhere (Burt, 1921, 1933). . . . They consisted of (i) a group test of intelligence containing both non-verbal and verbal items, (ii) an individual test (the London Revision of the Terman-Binet Scale) used primarily for standardization, and for doubtful cases (iii) a set of performance tests, based on the Pintner-Paterson tests and standardized by Miss Gaw (1925). The test-results, which generally covered other children in the school as well, were submitted to the teachers for comment or criticism; and, wherever any question arose, the child was re-examined. . . . The reliability of the group test of intelligence was 0.97; of the Stanford-Binet 0.95; of the performance tests 0.87."[20]

We consider first the "group test of intelligence." The same test, with its reliability of .97, was evidently used over a 45-year period. The test produced a twin correlation of .77, repeatedly, whether cases were dropped from or added to the sample. We cannot, however, locate the test. The two references provided by Burt will not help. The 1933 source[21] contains no group tests of intelligence. The 1921 source[22] contains no fewer than seven. Those seven tests, however, each contain exclusively verbal items; either these were not used, or one or more of them was somehow combined with unspecified "non-verbal" tests for one or more twins. With regard to the seven group tests published in his 1921 text, Burt wrote: "complete tables of age-norms would be unnecessary or even misleading. . . . I give only rough averages calculated regardless of sex. . . . I have not thought it worth the necessary time and space to elaborate and print a set of standardized instructions as to procedure or marking."[23] When applied to MZ twins—who are necessarily of the same age and sex—the age and sex standardization of a test are absolutely critical matters, since improper standardization may grossly inflate the twin correlation. We shall discuss this point in detail in connection with other studies of twins. There is no sense in discussing it in connection with Burt, who does not provide the data that would make analysis possible. We can only note that there is no way of knowing what test(s) he used, how well they were standardized, or how test scores might have been combined. We do not know what was correlated with what in order to produce the coefficient of .77.

The situation with respect to "individual test" is no better. The 1966 description of procedure appears to imply that all twins were given a Binet Scale, but a close reading fails to explicate the meaning of "used primarily for standardization." We again find a reference to "doubtful cases," who were given "performance tests." There is, however, no correlation reported for performance test, only for "individual test." That correlation was .86. The situation is further confused by Burt's reply to a critic in 1958. The critic had noted that the twin correlation at that time reported by Burt under the heading "individual test" differed substantially from one earlier reported by Newman, Freeman, and Holzinger, using the Stanford-Binet test. Burt replied, with very specific reference to the correlation given for "individual test," that "the figures he quotes from our own research were based on non-verbal tests of the performance type."[24]

The 1966 paper strongly implies that the correlation for "individual test" was based on the Binet; the 1958 paper just as strongly implies that it was based on performance tests. Were both tests given to all twins and the scores in some way averaged? The 1966 report indicates that this was not the case. Were the performance tests given as a supplement only to "doubtful cases"? With doubtful cases, were the performance tests added to, or did they take the place of, the Binet scores when "individual test" correlations were computed? There is, as is often the case with Burt, no way of knowing what in fact lies behind his three decimal places. The only possible way out of this morass might be to examine Burt's raw data. That was recently attempted by Professor Jensen, but he has indicated: ". . . alas, nothing remained of Burt's possessions . . . unfortunately, the original data are lost, and all that remains are the results of the statistical analyses. . ."[25]

We have rather more information on the set of performance tests standardized by Miss Gaw in 1925.[26] The standardization sample consisted of "100 pupils in London schools," none of them "of scholarship or central school ability." There were "striking" differences between the sexes in test scores. We have already noted that, in an MZ sample containing both sexes, such differences must inflate the observed correlation. The intercorrelations of several of the individual tests were negative. The reliability of the battery of 13 performance tests was reported as .76 for boys and .54 for girls. The reliability of the tests in the hands of Professor Burt rose to .87.

There is, as usual, no precise information on how test scores were adjusted, on the basis of teachers' criticisms, to provide "final assessments." The correlation for final assessments was given by Burt as .87. The final assessments, however, do not appear to have been really final. The "I.Q.'s" of the two brightest twins had been given as 137 and 136 in 1958,[27] and in 1966.[28] They were changed to 132 and 131 in a list of I.Q. scores later privately circulated by Burt and published by Professor Jensen.[29] The 137 I.Q. reported for a twin named Llewellyn in 1958 and in 1966 was clearly not the result of a Binet test, since his "reading, and his verbal abilities generally, were those of a child of barely eleven."[30] When Llewellyn was tested he was already a young farmer, and his twin—presumably of the same age—had already obtained a university degree. The twins were described in 1966 as "two scholarship winners," suggesting that reading and verbal abilities are not heavily weighted in the English school system. The two dullest twins were reported to have I.Q.'s of 66 in 1966. The list later circulated by Burt gave them I.Q.'s of 68 and 63.

The complete set of I.Q. scores had never been published, but they were published by Jensen in 1970, as given to him by Burt. They were at that time erroneously described by Jensen as I.Q.'s "obtained from an individual test, the

English adaptation of the Stanford-Binet.''[31] The numbers circulated by Burt were in fact a belated version of his ''final assessments.''[32] The numbers were used by Jensen to estimate the heritability of I.Q. The heritability of a trait, it will be recalled, is defined as the proportion of its phenotypic variance not attributable to environmental factors. This is a rare moment of high comedy in the heritability literature. The *purpose* of changing test scores into ''assessments,'' as described by Burt and Howard in 1957, was to ''reduce the disturbing effects of environment to relatively slight proportions.''[33]

Professor Jensen has very kindly provided me with a copy of the list of raw scores sent to him by Burt. The ''IQ's'' (i.e., assessments) of all twins are tabulated together with the ''social class'' of the homes in which they were reared. The Burt list indicates that in each case one member of a pair was reared in ''own home'' and the other in ''foster home.'' That was not literally so; in 1966 Burt had indicated that in ''the vast majority'' of cases one twin had been reared by his own parents. For the ''few remaining cases,'' the twin who had been reared by a ''relative'' or ''the better type of foster-parent'' was regarded as having been reared in ''own home.'' The ''social class'' of each home was ranked on a six-point scale of occupational categories of the parents. Thus, Social Class 1 consisted of ''Higher professional, etc.,'' while Social Class 6 consisted of ''Unskilled.'' Perhaps the most astonishing aspect of Burt's data is that the social classes of the twins' homes, defined in this way, correlated −.04. ''These figures,'' Burt wrote, ''should dispose of one of the commonest explanations advanced by thoroughgoing environmentalists—namely, that the high correlations for the separated twins is due to the way the foster-parents were chosen.''[34] Professor Jensen, who had reported the social class correlation to be close to zero, pointed out that ''virtually none of the correlation between twins' IQ is attributable to similarities in their home environments when these are classified by *SES* in terms of the parents' occupation.''[35] Professor Herrnstein had similarly emphasized that only one of the four studies (Burt's) had reported quantitative social class data, and that the correlation of social class between separated twins had been zero. Thus, in at least the Burt study, the correlation in I.Q. between twins could not be attributed to a social class correlation between foster homes.[36] The I.Q. correlation between separated twins, calculated from Burt's list, was .88. The case for environmentalism seems bleak.

The I.Q. and social class data tell an almost incredible tale of the potency of heredity. For the twin individuals reared in ''own home,'' the correlation between I.Q. and social class was a significant .31. The higher the social class, the higher was the child's I.Q.[37] That is not to be interpreted as an environmental effect. For the children reared in foster homes, the correlation between I.Q. and foster home social class was −.01. These data are marvelously consistent with the hereditarian thesis. The high I.Q. of an upper-class child reared in his own home is evidently a consequence of the superior I.Q. genes he has inherited from his successful parent. The influence of home environment alone, as seen in foster homes, is literally nil.

There are, however, some peculiarities in Burt's data, which appear readily upon analysis. The six social classes fall naturally into two groupings. The upper three classes consist of higher professional, lower professional, and clerical workers. The lower three classes consist of skilled, semiskilled, and unskilled workers. We shall label Classes 1–3 "upper class," and Classes 4–6 "lower class." The twin pairs each consist of one child reared in own home and one child reared in foster home. That gives us four groups of children to analyze, and we shall label them conveniently. There are 19 Upper-Own children (Classes 1–3, reared in own home), 34 Lower-Own children, 14 Upper-Foster children, and 32 Lower-Foster children. The social class designation, it should be noted, refers to the home in which the child was *reared*. There were also seven foster children reared in "residential institutions"; for analyses involving the six-point social class scale, their data cannot be used.

The Upper-Own children, as we might deduce from the correlation, had significantly higher I.Q.'s than the Lower-Own children. The mean I.Q.'s were 102.1 and 94.7. The Upper-Foster children had a mean I.Q. of only 95.6, less (though not significantly) than the 99.9 of Lower-Foster children. That, however, is the smallest part of the story. The I.Q. standard deviation of the Upper-Foster children was only 9.5, compared to 17.4 for the Lower-Foster group. Thus the two variances *differed significantly*. That is a most peculiar effect, and no comparable phenomenon was noted among children reared in their own homes. For the two "Own" groups, the respective standard deviations were 16.4 and 13.1 I.Q. points. There appears to be a force at work which causes children reared in upper-class foster homes to have relatively low I.Q.'s, with remarkably little variance.

We can now ask whether the very low variance in the Upper-Foster group was *produced* by the upper-class foster homes, or whether it was also shown by the twins of the Upper-Foster children. The twins of the Upper-Foster children, though reared in considerably lower-class (own) homes, had a mean I.Q. virtually as high (94.9). Their standard deviation was only 7.6 I.Q. points. That is remarkable. The mean social class of these selected children was identical to that of other children reared in their own homes, whose standard deviation was 17.4 points. There is no obvious reason why children whose *twins* are adopted by upper-class families should show such little variation in I.Q. We can note, however, that if they had shown a normal amount of I.Q. variation, the I.Q. correlation between twins would have been reduced. The unidentified force at work on these data seems to be striving mightily to preserve a very high I.Q. correlation between twins. That force could conceivably be the genotypes. Why then are the genotypes of twin pairs, one member of which is adopted by an upper-class family, so strikingly unvariable? That effect is very large in magnitude. The "genotype" can in theory best be estimated by the mean I.Q. of a twin pair. The standard deviations of the two sets of "genotypes" are 7.4 and 17.0. That is, the variances of the two sets of genotypes differ by a factor of more than 5. That result would occur by chance about 1 time in 500. The result is a stable one. When we regard only twin pairs in which "own home" was lower class, the "genotypic" standard deviation of pairs in which the foster child was lower class was 16.3; when the foster child was upper class, it was 7.4. When we now consider twin pairs in which "own home" was upper class, the corresponding standard deviations were 16.4 and 7.6. The force at work on these data, a reasonable man might speculate, is Professor Burt's method of making "assessments."

There is no plausible way of attributing these different variances to a policy of selective adoption. Possibly, it might be argued, upper-class parents refuse to adopt children whom they regard as genetically inferior; but it would be absurd to argue that they also refuse to accept children whom they recognize as genetically superior. We can suggest at least two obvious and plausible interpretations of these data. The first is that, to preserve the I.Q. correlation between twins, the I.Q.'s of children adopted into upper-class homes have been systematically underassessed. The second is that, to present the appearance of uncorrelated environments, the social class status of some foster homes has been systematically overrated. These two interpretations are not mutually exclusive; and it is of course not necessary to assume that any such systematic effects were consciously produced.

There are many other oddities in the data. We note briefly that, among upper-class children reared in their own home, the social-class–I.Q. correlation was a significant .61, despite the very severe restriction of social class range. For lower-class children reared in own homes, the class-I.Q. correlation was −.04, significantly different. That might be plausible, but among children reared in adoptive homes the picture was entirely reversed. For upper-class adopted children, the class-I.Q. correlation was a modest .12; for lower-class adopted children, it was a significant .34. These data, if taken seriously, would suggest that home environment makes a difference only within the range of working-class homes. Further, we would conclude that the gene pools are sharply differentiated between the various strata of white-collar workers, but not among the strata of manual workers and ne'er-do-wells. There is no good reason to take these data seriously. The calculational effort we have expended on them was prompted only because these data have been so repeatedly cited by major theoreticians of heritability.

We must comment, finally, on the reliability of Burt's social class data. When only 42 separated twin pairs were available, Conway, in 1959, clearly indicated that *at least* four children of "professional" parents had been reared in "orphanages."[38] The 1966 Burt paper presented social class data indicating, in flat contradiction, that only two children of such parents had been reared in "residential institutions." The sample size had meanwhile increased to 53 pairs. The social class data published for the 53 pairs in 1966 *do not agree* with the social class data that Burt later provided to Jensen and to others. The marginal totals of his 1966 table make it clear that in at least six cases the social class of a twin was changed *after* 1966.

The twin data were collected by Burt over a period of almost 50 years, and it seems quite possible that assessments both of intelligence and social class were subjected throughout to a continuing process of revision and refinement. The arithmetical contradictions aside, there appears to have been some arbitrariness in Burt's assessments of social class. The 1958 Conway paper describes the two brightest twins, George and Llewellyn. They were said to be the children of an Oxford don who died before their birth. George remained with his mother, who was "unable with her slender purse to bring up two boys."[39] The social class of George, as described in a Burt letter to Professor Shockley,[40] was 1, "higher professional, etc." Poor Llewellyn was brought up by an elderly Welsh couple "on an isolated farm in North Wales." The home was assigned to Social Class 4, since the foster parents were "an uneducated type, but in moderately comfortable circumstances, that is, they belonged to the lowest cultural, though not to the lowest economic class."[41] Why comfortable farmers should rank three whole classes below the slender-pursed and unmaternal widows of deceased dons is not entirely clear.

The matter of social class appears to have greatly interested Professor Burt, and it is conceivable that his social biases might have affected his ratings of social class. Those biases may be detected, faintly, in his Bingham Memorial Lecture of 1957. There he observed that "the able children from the working classes, even when they have obtained free places or scholarships at secondary schools of the 'grammar' type, frequently fail to stay the course: by the time they are sixteen the attractions of high wages and of cheap entertainment during leisure hours prove stronger than their desire for further knowledge and skill." That was not wholly bad, Professor Burt reasoned, since "it would surely be a misfortune were all the brightest youngsters to forsake the social class into which they were born. Their continued presence there must help, not only to elevate its tone, but also (a point too often overlooked) to prevent its genetic constitution from being wholly depleted of its better elements."[42]

Professor Burt went on to quote a schoolmaster—perhaps one who had criticized and adjusted I.Q. scores for him—on the characteristics of working-class students. Their "chief interest in life," the schoolmaster reported, "is television, Hollywood films, football pools, 'the dogs,' and 'the girls.' " Those lamentable interests, none of which appear to have been shared by the master, had "not improved the tone of my school." The High Master of St. Paul's, on the other hand, described a different class of student: "The parents are themselves imbued with four traditional ideals which they hand on to their posterity: self-discipline, a community spirit, the Christian religion, and a readiness to accept social responsibility. . . ."

Professor Burt mused over these contrasting characteristics of the upper and lower classes in the following language: "Underlying all these differences in outlook I myself am tempted to suspect an innate and transmissible difference in temperamental stability and in character, or in the neurophysiological basis on which such temperamental and moral differences tend to be built up." The polygenes of the upper class appear to be pleiotropic for high I.Q. and committed Christianity.

The class biases implicit in Sir Cyril's remarks might conceivably have affected the way in which he collected and analyzed his I.Q. data. The first serious Burt paper on twins was the work of a 72-year-old gentleman with strong opinions. The majority of the cases described in his final report were collected between that time and his 83rd year. The revised lists of I.Q.'s and social class ratings were being dispatched around the globe in his 88th year.

The conclusion seems not to require further documentation, which exists in abundance. The absence of procedural description in Burt's reports vitiates their scientific utility. The frequent arithmetical inconsistencies and mutually contradictory descriptions cast doubt upon the entire body of his later work. The marvelous consistency of his data supporting the hereditarian position often taxes credibility; and on analysis, the data are found to contain implausible effects consistent with an effort to prove the hereditarian case. The conclusion cannot be avoided: The numbers left behind by Professor Burt are simply not worthy of our current scientific attention. We pass on now to the more serious work.

THE SHIELDS STUDY

The second large scale study of separated MZs was reported by Shields in 1962.[43] That study, like Burt's, was performed in England. The Shields report, unlike Burt's, contains a marvelously detailed appendix. The appendix presents detailed case studies of each twin, together with raw data. That makes possible a type of analysis that cannot be performed on Burt's unfortunately mislaid data.

The Shields data in some respects seem even more supportive of a strong hereditarian position than do Burt's. For 37 pairs of separated MZs Shields reported a "total intelligence score" correlation of .77. The same tests given to 34 pairs of normal, nonseparated MZs produced a correlation of only .76. Finally, for 7 pairs of DZ twins, the correlation was .51. There thus seemed to be literally no effect of separation on genetically identical individuals. The moderate correlation for DZ twins, virtually identical to that normally found for ordinary sibs, "confirmed the importance of genetical factors for intelligence."[44] That particular confirmation, however, is not convincing and need not detain us for long. The appendix reveals that, for DZ twins, Shields pooled into a single group four pairs of separated and three pairs of nonseparated twins. The correlation for separated DZs can be calculated as .05, and that for DZs reared together as .70.

The "intelligence tests" used by Shields pose some problems. There were two separate tests. The Dominoes, a 20-minute nonverbal test, had been employed in the British Army. There are no standardization data for female civilians, who make up two-thirds of Shields' sample. The median age of the separated MZs was 40, with a range from 8 to 59, and there are no data concerning age effects on the

Dominoes test. For the twins reared together, although not for the twins reared apart, males had a significantly higher Dominoes score than females. The failure to observe a sex difference among the separated twins may be due to the fact that their Dominoes scores were significantly lower than those of the nonseparated twins. There are no obvious effects of age in the Shields sample, but it is conceivable that with MZ twins in this age range shared effects of aging could to some degree inflate the between-twin correlation.

The second test used by Shields was a *part* of the Mill Hill Vocabulary Scale. That test had been standardized on a civilian population, although the instruction manual kindly made available by Shields indicates that the standardization sample consisted of "2,300 men." The standardization in any event refers to the *entire* test. The manual indicates a significant effect of age on total test score. There is no way of knowing the magnitude of the age effect on the test portion used by Shields, but his raw data do not indicate any obvious effect either of age or sex. The separated twins, however, have a significantly lower vocabulary score, and a significantly greater variance, than the nonseparated twins. For both tests used by Shields, the mean score of separated twins — but not of twins reared together — was lower than the "population" mean. The relatively restricted vocabulary score variance among twins reared together can only serve to attenuate the correlation among them. There is no way to know whether their variance is lower than the population variance, or whether the separated twins' variance is higher than the population's, or whether both are lower. The standard deviation of twins reared together was 4.0, and that of twins reared apart was 5.7. The latter figure has been used by Jensen[45] to compute "IQ's" for the separated twins; but Jinks and Fulker,[46] in still another analysis, have estimated the population standard deviation to be 7.89! The choice of standard deviation will radically affect any transformation of raw scores into "IQ's." The raw scores are in addition very negatively skewed. There seems to be no satisfactory way of transforming them into I.Q.'s, and Shields quite properly did not attempt to do so.

The intelligence measure used by Shields in his analysis was derived by adding, for each subject, his raw scores on the two tests. The Mill Hill standard deviation in the sample was about half of the Dominoes standard deviation, however, so Shields doubled the Mill Hill score before computing the subject's "total intelligence score." That was supposed to give roughly equal weight to each of the two tests. The analysis from this point on will follow Shields; it is primarily concerned with total intelligence scores.

The painstakingly scrupulous appendix indicates that the tests were, in fact, given to 40 pairs of separated MZ twins.[47] For 35 pairs, Shields personally gave the tests to each twin — sometimes simultaneously, and sometimes consecutively. For the remaining 5 pairs, two *different* examiners (one usually Shields) tested the two twins. This conscientiously described procedure enables us to ask the following question: Do twins tested by the same psychologist resemble one another more than do twins tested by different psychologists? That is a way of asking whether the theoretical predilections of the examiner might unconsciously bias his administration and/or scoring of the tests so as to maximize the resemblance of twins. The standard procedure in separated twin studies has been for the same examiner to test both twins, and the incidental data provided by the Shields appendix are thus unique.

For the 5 pairs tested by different psychologists, the mean difference in total intelligence score between twins was 22.4. For the 35 pairs tested by Shields, the mean score difference was only 8.5. These two figures, despite the very small size of one sample, differ to a statistically significant degree. The intelligence correlation for the small sample was a mere .11, compared to .84 for the sample tested exclusively by Shields. These two intraclass correlation coefficients differ significantly. Though this effect is suggested by the vocabulary data, it occurs primarily in the Dominoes test. For that test the correlation among twins tested independently was −.27; for twins tested by Shields, it was .82. The probability of so large a discrepancy arising by chance, even with such small samples, is less than .025. There is clearly a strong suggestion that unconscious experimenter expectation may have influenced these results.*

The D-48 Test, a French translation of the experimental Dominoes test used in the British Army, was reviewed in the 1965 edition of Buros' *Mental Measurements Yearbook*.[48] The "non-verbal" test in each version begins with the examiner delivering instructions, and working out with the testee some specimen problems. The two independent reviewers in Buros' volume each felt impelled to comment on the instructions. The first spoke of "the extensive verbal directions and the importance of the testee's *understanding* the samples and requirements of the test." The second reviewer indicated that "The directions for administration allow great freedom to the examiner. He is told that it is his responsibility to see that the testee understands all four examples." This procedure obviously allows considerable scope for unconscious bias. The procedure characteristically employed by Shields appears to have been to explain the Dominoes test simultaneously to both members of a twin pair.[49] The Buros reviews indicated that the test-retest reliability of the D-48, with a 2-month interval between successive testings of the *same* individuals, was only .69. That did not prevent Shields from obtaining a .82 correlation for 35 pairs of separated twins whom he had examined. The consistency between twins appears to be considerably larger than the consistency within a single individual.

With full recognition that the correlations are likely to be inflated, it is nevertheless instructive to make some further analyses of Shields' total intelligence scores. The appendix reveals that 27 pairs of separated twins were reared in related

*The point has been made by an early reader of this manuscript that the five twin pairs tested by different examiners include some who were very widely separated geographically. Thus, the absence of correlation in these cases may reflect the effects of very different environments, rather than unconscious experimenter bias. In either event, the potency of the genes seems minimal, and independent testing of members of a twin pair seems methodologically desirable.

branches of the parents' families. The most common pattern was for one twin to be reared by the mother, and the other twin by the maternal grandmother or aunt. There were 13 pairs of twins who were raised in unrelated families. For twins reared in related families, the score correlation was .83. For those reared in unrelated families, it was .51. These two correlations differ significantly. The genes within each pair are of course identical, so this is *very* powerful evidence for the role of environment in determining intelligence test scores. The twins in the pooled sample resemble one another to the degree that they have been reared in similar environments. The fact that twins reared in "unrelated" families correlated .51 should not be taken as an unambiguous indication of any role for heredity. The majority of children reared in unrelated families had been given to family friends of the mother, and another pair were reared in different cottages of the same orphanage. Thus, the correlation between identical twins assigned at random to truly uncorrelated environments might well have been zero.

The Shields appendix provides detailed understanding of what may be meant by the phrase "separated twins." The rule adopted by Shields was explicit: "Without exception they were brought up in different homes for at least five years during childhood."[50] Thus the following not wholly atypical cases were included in the study. Benjamin and Ronald had been separated at 9 months: "Both brought up in the same fruit-growing village, Ben by the parents, Ron by the grandmother, Father and grandfather were both small market gardeners. . . . They were at school together. . . . They have continued to live in the same village. . . . They used to truant together and smoke cigarettes on the sly." Ben and Ron were 52 years old when tested in London by Shields. They had similarly poor vocabularies, presumably caused by their identical genes.

Jessie and Winifred were separated at 3 months: "Brought up within a few hundred yards of one another. . . . Told they were twins after girls discovered it for themselves, having gravitated to one another at school at the age of 5. . . . They play together quite a lot. . . . Jessie often goes to tea with Winifred. . . . They were never apart, wanted to sit at the same desk. . . . One is reminded of the finding with cattle twins!" These girls were 8 years old when tested by Shields. They have been included, in the previous analysis, among twins reared in *unrelated* families. They are the only case in which Shields presents some intelligence data for the foster mothers of two separated twins.[51] The Mill Hill raw scores of the two foster mothers were 12 and 11, each at about the 20th percentile. The twins' scores were 11 and 12.

Bertram and Christopher were separated at *birth*. "The paternal aunts decided to take one twin each and they have brought them up amicably, living next door to one another in the same Midlands colliery village. . . . They are constantly in and out of each other's houses." Odette and Fanny were separated from birth until the age of 12. The conditions of their separation seem to have been worked out by a specialist in experimental design. From the age of 3 until the age of 8 the twins were rotated every 6 months, one going to the maternal grandmother and the other to the mother. Joan and Dinah were separated at birth, but "reunited at about 5." Their entire school careers were spent together in a "small country town." They were tested at age 40. Joanna and Isobel were similarly "separated from birth to 5 years," and then "went to private schools together." When tested at age 50, their scores were virtually identical, and much higher than any other scores in the entire sample. Adeline and Gwendolen were not separated until their mother's death, when they were 9½. Gwendolen then moved to the maternal aunt's house, "at the other end of the village," and they continued their work "at the village school."

The 7 cases just described have been selected as the most striking examples of correlated environments in Shields' sample, but they only exaggerate a condition evident among all twin pairs. Twins in the real world are not randomly deposited on doorsteps for the convenience of mental testers, who must make do with what they find. For the 7 cases just described, the intelligence correlation is .99. That seems incredible. Tests are never that reliable, nor are *nonseparated* twins so highly correlated. The 33 remaining cases correlated .66. The difference between the two correlations is very highly significant. The most reasonable interpretation is that an unconscious experimenter bias has inflated both correlations equally, preserving a difference due to different degrees of environmental similarity. The F ratio between the within-twin pair variances of these two samples is significant beyond the .001 level.[52] That is a clear illustration of the potency of environment, even when the range of environmental differences is rather small across the two samples.

The appendix suggests that in only 10 of the 40 cases had members of a pair never attended the same school, nor been reared by related families. For those 10 pairs the correlation was .47, not a very powerful testimonial to identical genes. Within those 10 pairs 6 individuals were given to family friends to be reared, 5 saw their twins during childhood, and in at least 3 cases, the twins lived in the same town, meeting one another in their homes; but Valerie had to take "a fourpenny bus ride" to meet her twin.

The genetic significance of Shields' findings is not much illuminated by another peculiarity observed in his data. For the 80 individuals in his separated MZ sample, the correlation between Dominoes and Mill Hill scores was .62. For the 70 individuals in his MZ reared-together sample, the same correlation was .37. The two correlations differ significantly. This might, however, largely reflect the different Mill Hill variances in the two samples.

We have, of course, incomparably more information about Shields' twins than about Burt's. We know that the Shields twins were volunteers responding to a television appeal, and we know their sexes and ages. We have seen in detail what the conditions of their separation were. We have no analogous information from Burt, who has informed us only that the twins were "separated" before 6 months of age. The "separation" of Shields' twins is assuredly not what is imagined by most readers of textbooks when they are informed that separated twins have similar I.Q.'s. There is little exaggeration in Shields' comment that "Large differences in social class do not occur often.''[53] The only information we have from Burt on the possibility of correlated environments is a skeletal table indicating no correlation between the occupational categories of homes in which members of a pair were reared. We have seen that the data in that table contradict other data reported by Burt. The Shields testing procedure, and his scoring rules, are a model of explicitness; we do not know what tests Burt used, or how. There can be no question as to which set of data carries more force as evidence. The Shields data have the enormous merit of allowing the reader to make his own judgments.

The Shields data demonstrate powerfully the role of environment in establishing I.Q. differences between genetically identical individuals, even when environmental differences seem relatively small. We have seen that even a very partial control for correlated environments reduces the separated MZ correlation to about .50. That figure *would* estimate the heritability of I.Q. *if* a number of assumptions — including *no* correlation of environments — were met. The data, in fact, provide no evidence damaging to the assumption that, with uncorrelated environments, the I.Q. correlation of separated MZ's would be zero. The data strongly suggest that, in twin studies, experimenter bias may unconsciously inflate correlations. That possibility is of course especially relevant to Burt's procedure of ''adjusting'' his ''assessments.''

THE NEWMAN, FREEMAN, AND HOLZINGER STUDY

There remain two smaller-scale studies of separated MZs, to which we now turn. The only American study was reported in 1937 by Newman, Freeman, and Holzinger.[54] For brevity's sake, we shall refer to it as NFH. Their study, like Shields', is replete with detailed raw numerical data and with case histories. They studied 19 pairs of separated MZs, 12 female and 7 male. The twins ranged in age from 11 to 59, with a median of 26. They used the 1916 Stanford-Binet test. That test included scales for normal and superior adults, but its I.Q. measure had been designed primarily for children in the age range of 5 to 14.

The basic NFH finding was an I.Q. correlation of .67 for separated MZ twins. They also reported correlations of .91 for 50 pairs of MZs reared together, and of .64 for 50 pairs of DZ twins reared together. There is not much point, however, in comparing the separated MZs to the other twin samples. The two other samples were children located in the Chicago school system, with an age range of 8 to 18. The separated MZs, mostly adults, had responded to newspaper and radio appeals for volunteers, and they came from across the country. The process of recruiting volunteers introduced an interesting bias into the sample, frankly acknowledged by NFH. They, like Shields, were very much concerned with establishing the zygosity of the twins through finger prints, physical measurements, etc. The study was conducted in Chicago during the Great Depression, and the separated twins had to be brought to, and lodged in, the city at considerable expense. The authors therefore rejected volunteers who, on examination, might well be discovered to be

DZs rather than MZs. Potential volunteers were not accepted unless they indicated, in response to mailed questions, that they were "so strikingly similar that even your friends or relatives have confused you." They were required also to state their belief that they were "far more alike than any pair of brothers or sisters," and they were required to send photographs.[55]

The 19 twin pairs finally invited to the NFH laboratory were in fact all MZs. They "constitute a selected group, from which any doubtful cases have been excluded. . . . One case was excluded because the twins wrote: 'A good many people think we are identical twins, but we ourselves do not think we are so very much alike.' Another case failed to meet our requirements because one of the twins wrote that, while they look very much alike so that they were sometimes mistaken for each other, they were 'as different as can be in disposition. . . .' "[56] These twins, and other rejections, might well have been monozygotes. The exclusion of even a very few dissimilar separated MZs from such a small sample could radically affect the correlation. The separated twins collected by NFH were, in short, deliberately selected to be very much like one another — and quite clearly from the examples, not only physically. There is also in all such studies the possibility that the only twins who volunteer in the first instance are those who markedly resemble each other. The deliberate exclusion of dissimilar pairs, in any event, could only serve to exaggerate the observed I.Q. correlation. The study of this biased sample may yield interesting information, but it seems foolhardy to estimate heritability in the population from such a sample. The NFH data, pooled with those of Burt, Shields, and Juel-Nielsen, have been used by Professor Jensen to estimate heritability of I.Q. in the "English, Danish, and North American Caucasian populations."[57]

There appears to have been more actual separation, and less correlated environments, among the NFH twins than among Shields'. The NFH case histories, however, are less detailed and systematic about these points than are Shields', and there are some instances of puzzling inconsistencies. For example, Ed and Fred's separation is at one point in the text described as "complete until their first meeting at 24 years of age." Further, "they lived without knowledge of each other's existence for twenty-five years."[58] Their genes, during this period, appear to have impelled them to remarkably similar experiences. They each worked as electrical repair men for the telephone company, and each owned a fox terrier named Trixie. The case study, however, reports that "They even went to the same school for a time, but never knew that they were twin brothers. They had even noticed the remarkable resemblance between them, but they were not close companions. When the twins were about eight years old, their families were permanently separated."[59] This simply does not square with the earlier account of no knowledge of each other's existence for 25 years. There appears to have been some difficulty in eliciting detailed information from the twins: "There is evidence that Edwin had more continuous and better instruction, though the actual facts are difficult to obtain."

The case study includes a photograph of the twins side-by-side "at the time of their first meeting." The photograph was "reproduced by permission of *The American Weekly*." The twins are remarkably alike in appearance. They are wearing identical pin-striped suits, and identical striped ties. These, of course, might have been bought "at the time of their first meeting." Perhaps it is relevant to note that Fred was unemployed at the time of the NFH study.

The NFH twins were rewarded with considerable newspaper and magazine publicity; one threatened a legal suit because a magazine had described her as intellectually inferior to her twin. There was also a very tangible inducement offered to all twins by NFH. They were treated to a visit at the Century of Progress Exposition then being held in Chicago. "Pair after pair, who had previously been unmoved by appeals to the effect that they owed it to science and society to permit us to study them, could not resist the offer of a free, all-expenses-paid trip to the Chicago Fair."[60] To qualify for this reward, the twins had to attest to the fact that they had been separated, and that they were remarkably alike.

This raises a very serious issue. The facts about separation, in all the twin studies, depend heavily upon the verbal accounts of the twins themselves. When there are not tangible inducements, the twins are exhorted to make themselves available in the name of science. They receive free medical examinations, and enormous amounts of detailed individual attention from distinguished scientists. They could scarcely be blamed if, in a misguided effort to cooperate with science, or to bolster a sense of their unique worth, they were to stretch a fact or two. The report that "actual facts" concerning schooling were "difficult to obtain" does little to allay anxiety on this score.

The twins Kenneth and Jerry were adopted by two different families at the age of 3 weeks and their separation was described as "complete for 13 years." The two different sets of adoptive parents displayed some curious resemblances. Kenneth's foster father was "a city fireman with a very limited education." Jerry's foster father was "also a city fireman with only fourth-grade education." When the boys were 5 years old, and until they were 7, they lived in the same "medium-sized Michigan city," where their fathers were firemen, but "they were unaware of the fact." These twins were thus adopted by unrelated families and were completely separated. There nevertheless appears to be a possible correlation between the environments to which the random processes of fate have exposed their identical genotypes. Though Harold and Holden were separated, they were each adopted by family relatives. They lived 3 miles apart and attended the same school. The majority of the NFH twin pairs saw each other at least occasionally during childhood, and others had lived together for extended periods as adults before being tested. The occasional childhood visits could conceivably tend to produce some resemblance between the twins. The photograph of Richard and Raymond at 10 was presumably taken during one of their "almost annual visits." The children had been adopted at one month of age by apparently unrelated families. The side-by-side photograph shows them wearing identical striped shirts and identical checkered knickers. The foster parents evidently felt it appropriate to purchase identical clothing for the twins. They could, of course, have purchased identical books and home encyclopedias for them as well. We can raise no serious objection to NFH's assertion that "It is also probable that the effective environmental differences for some of the separated cases were not much greater than for those reared together."[61]

There is still another factor in the NFH study which serves to inflate the apparent resemblance between at least some of their twins. The 1916 Stanford-Binet had been constructed primarily for children, and the NFH scoring procedure inappropriately penalized bright or well-educated adults. The original scoring procedure suggested by Terman was to assign all adults a chronological age of 16 when calculating the I.Q. The highest mental age possible was 19.5, achieved by answering all questions on the scales. Thus the highest possible I.Q. for an individual 16 years or older was 122. That I.Q. is 17 points lower than the I.Q. which would have been assigned to the same individual at age 14, had he answered the same questions in exactly the same way. To eliminate this absurd artifact, Terman had suggested a revised scoring scheme for adults, crediting extra months of "mental age" according to the number of test items successfully answered.[62] That, of course, increases the scored I.Q. The failure to use the revised scoring procedure has an interesting effect on a twin study. When one member of an adult pair answers nearly all questions, and her twin does not, an artificial upper limit is placed on the brighter twin's I.Q. That reduces the discrepancy between the twins' I.Q.'s which would have appeared with a more appropriate scoring procedure.

This scoring artifact had a major effect on at least one NFH twin pair. The case of Gladys (I.Q. 92) and Helen (I.Q. 116) is repeatedly cited in reviews of the separated twin literature. The mean I.Q. difference between twins in the NFH study was 8.21 I.Q. points. The 24 point difference between Gladys and Helen was the largest observed. The raw data and scoring rules make it entirely clear that, appropriately calculated by Terman's procedure, Helen's I.Q. was in fact 125, producing a 33 point difference from her twin. This might be related to the fact that these two women with identical genotypes had different educational experiences. Though Helen graduated from college, Gladys, reared in the isolated Rocky Mountains, received only two years of primary school education. Professor Jensen, however, has stressed that "They had markedly different health histories as children; Gladys suffered a number of severe illnesses, one being nearly fatal, while Helen enjoyed unusually good health."[63] The NFH case study of Helen indicates in fact that "Helen claims to have been very healthy as a child." The near-fatal illness suffered by Gladys was a severe attack of measles. The NFH report indicates that "she seems a very healthy, robust woman."

We shall in any event accept the numbers provided by NFH as valid I.Q.'s for our continuing analysis. The reported twin correlation of .67 might, under the untenable assumptions outlined earlier in this chapter, be taken as an estimate of the heritability of I.Q. in "the population." The correlation at the least suggests that there is a very substantial I.Q. resemblance between genetically identical individuals reared in "different" environments. There is an easy tendency if one ignores the fact of correlated environments to assume that the resemblance is attributable to the identical genes. Without regard to correlated environments, however, there is another major artifact in the data, one with profound theoretical significance.

Twins and the Age-I.Q. Confound

The I.Q. tests, according to those who market them, have been "standardized" to produce a mean I.Q. of 100 for individuals of any chronological age. Thus, ideally, the average individual should have an I.Q. of 100 whether tested at age 10, 15, or 50. There is always the possibility, however, that the tests have not been accurately standardized. The questions asked at one age level may be too easy, while those asked at another age level may be too hard. That would mean that people's I.Q.'s would fluctuate, depending upon their age when tested. Twins, of course, are of exactly the same age, so their I.Q.'s would fluctuate together. Thus, if a set of twin pairs are tested at a given point in time, and if the pairs vary in age, the correlation for the set of twin pairs might in theory be *largely attributable to a defective age standardization of the I.Q. test.* There is also the possibility that the I.Q. test produces different scores, at different ages, for the two sexes. When the twins being tested are MZs, and both males and females are included in the sample, the members of each pair are of course of the same sex. That also could inflate the correlation. Without an assurance that the test scores are not confounded with age and sex, there is absolutely no ground on which to attribute an observed correlation to genetic factors.[64]

The fact is that the 1916 Stanford-Binet, used by NFH, was repeatedly shown to be negatively correlated with age during childhood. The documentation for this observation, well known among testers, is provided in Chapter 5. The infrequent use of the test with adults, however, means that there are no comparable data relating adult I.Q. on this test to age. There are data within the NFH monograph amply confirming the confound of age and I.Q. They presented, it will be recalled, some data for *nonseparated* twins of school age — 50 pairs of MZs and 50 pairs of DZs. For the MZs, the correlation of I.Q. with age was reported as a robust −.49, a highly significant effect. That is, the older the child, the stupider the I.Q. test declared him to be. For the DZs, the correlation was only −.16, significantly different than for the MZs, though pointing in the same direction. The difference might be attributable to very slight differences in the age distributions of the school children making up the two samples. The basic negative correlation for children in that age range is in any event clear. There was no age-I.Q. correlation calculated by NFH for their *separated* MZs. The bulk of that sample consisted of adults.

To make comparisons between their *nonseparated* MZs and DZs, each sample with a mean age of about 13, NFH employed the technique of "partial correlation." The partial correlation technique "corrects" statistically for the confounding of two correlated variables with still a third variable. The procedure in the present instance is supposed to provide an estimate of what the correlation between twins' I.Q.'s *would* be if all twins were of the same age. For the two samples of school children, the partial correlation "correction" had only trivial effects on the raw correlations. The separated MZ correlation was not "partialled" by NFH, presumably because of considerations similar to those outlined in the next paragraph.

To "control" for age effects with partial correlation it is necessary to assume, among other things, that the correlation between age and measured I.Q. is linear throughout the range of ages being studied. That is a wildly implausible assumption. We suppose, for example, that the test is so standardized that the mean I.Q. in the population drops from 100 to 98 between the ages of 11 and 12. The use of partial correlation in a sample composed of children and adults would be based on the assumption that the mean I.Q. at age 59 should have plummeted to 4. With a very small sample, of course, it will be impossible to disprove the assumption of linearity between the ages of 11 and 59.

These considerations did not deter McNemar,[65] who in 1938 applied a heavy dosage of statistical correction to the NFH data. For the 38 individuals comprising the 19 pairs of separated MZ twins, the correlation between age and I.Q. can be computed to be $-.22$. Partial correlation pure and simple would thus have reduced the observed I.Q. correlation for separated MZs from .67 to .65. That is not, however, what McNemar did. The correlation was given a *double* correction — for age, and for restriction of range. The I.Q. variances for all three NFH samples were first "adjusted" by removing the proportion of variance theoretically attributable to age in each sample. This was done despite the fact that the age-I.Q. correlation differed significantly between two samples covering the same age range. That left McNemar with three "partial trait variances (age constant) for Binet I.Q." for the three NFH samples. He now observed that the variance for separated MZs looked smaller than that for nonseparated DZs. The difference, however, was not statistically significant. That did not prevent McNemar from using the adjusted variance of the DZs as the basis of a further "correction" of the separated MZ correlation for restriction of range. This chain of procedures enabled him to conclude that the true correlation for separated MZs was .77. That in turn enabled him to assert that the separated MZ correlation did not differ significantly from the nonseparated MZ correlation, which had been adjusted downwards by his double correction "for age and range." That had evidently been the point of the entire exercise. To accomplish this end, McNemar assumed that the adjusted sample variance of a group of children was a better estimate of the "population" variance of adults than that provided by the adult sample variance itself.

The exercise seems an impressive testimonial to McNemar's commitment to a hereditarian position, but it also seems arbitrary in the extreme. The assumptions are piled one on top of another. We can, however, thoroughly agree with

McNemar's observation that "the assumption underlying correction for the range of ability, i.e., equal correlation throughout the range, is in this case as tenable as and no more hazardous than some of the assumptions involved in the h^2 technique." The h^2 technique is purported to measure heritability. The moral to be drawn seems obvious. The corrections and adjustments and assumptions and partial correlations tend to be made when and if the outcome pleases the statistician's theoretical fancy. The apparent meaning of data can be completely reversed by a statistical adjustment based on a false assumption. We might note that McNemar's arbitrary conversion of the separated MZ correlation to .77 appears in the great majority of introductory psychology textbooks, without explanation, and is presented as if it were the correlation reported by NFH. The two corrections by McNemar were not, however, sufficient for Professor Jensen, who further inflated the correlation to .81. That was accomplished by adding a third correction, this time for test unreliability.[66]

Whatever the demerits of partial correlation and other statistical corrections may be, we are left with the problem that the confounding of age and I.Q. seriously contaminates the I.Q. correlation between twins. With small sample sizes, and with a considerable range of ages, it is difficult to estimate the age-I.Q. correlation appropriately. There is good reason to suppose that its magnitude will differ over different age ranges. For example, we would not expect the Stanford-Binet scores of adults to deteriorate as rapidly between the ages of 20 and 40 as they do between the ages of 40 and 60. The scoring procedure virtually guarantees a negative correlation between the ages 14 and 16, but the correlation could conceivably be positive at even lower age ranges. Whatever the peaks and valleys of mean I.Q. scores over the age range, a correlation between twins will inevitably be inflated by any confounding of age and I.Q. score. That will occur even if, extending over the full range of ages, the linear correlation between age and I.Q. is zero. The only way in which it would not occur would be if the test had been *perfectly* standardized on a large sample, with mean I.Q.'s of 100 (and equal variances) at each age for each sex. Then, of course, it would also be necessary for the twin sample to be fairly representative of the "population" from which the standardization sample had been drawn.

There are a number of observable effects in the NFH twin data that suggest either faulty standardization of the Stanford-Binet (a known fact) or, alternatively, that the twin sample was not drawn from the same population as the standardization sample (also a known fact). The original adult standardization sample, for example, contained no women![67] The NFH data, like those of Shields and of Juel-Nielsen, are preponderantly based on female twins. There are clear suggestions of a sex difference in the I.Q.'s of NFH's separated MZs. The variance of the female sample is considerably larger, and the difference borders on statistical significance ($p \cong .06$). The I.Q. standard deviation for the females is 15.1; for the males, 9.0. There was only 1 of the 14 males with an I.Q. below 90, while 11 of the 24 females had such low I.Q.'s. That effect is statistically significant. This apparent sex difference will play a role in our subsequent analysis.

We would like somehow to remove the contaminating effects of age from the observed I.Q. correlation among separated MZ twins. There is no easy and elegant way to do this. The technique of partial correlation will not serve, since it is based upon assumptions that are more than likely to be false. We shall first demonstrate that the assumptions do not hold for the NFH data. We shall then propose a crude and *ad hoc* procedure for estimating the effect of age on the observed I.Q. correlation.

The use of partial correlation assumes that the age-I.Q. relation is linear across the entire range of ages. The procedure also assumes, when both sexes are represented in a sample, that the age-I.Q. relation is the same for each sex. We note that, for the entire sample of 38 individuals, the age-I.Q. correlation was only −.22. For the 14 males, however, it was −.78; for the 24 females, it was −.11. The correlations differed significantly between the two sexes. This apparent sex effect, however, is itself very largely confounded with age. The male pairs averaged 20.3 years of age (ranging from 13.5 to 27), while the female pairs averaged 29.8 years (ranging from 11.4 to 59.2). The age variance of the female pairs was significantly greater than that of the males. With the 1916 Stanford-Binet, it is entirely possible that the regressions of I.Q. on age vary, for different sectors of the age range, in sign as well as in slope. Though the sample size is embarrassingly small, it seems prudent to examine the age-I.Q. correlation among females in different age ranges.

There were seven female pairs *older* than the eldest male. The age-I.Q. correlation among them was −.27. There were two female pairs *younger* than the youngest male. Though it seems ludicrous to calculate it, the age-I.Q. "correlation" for these four individuals was .99. There were, finally, three female pairs whose ages fell within the range covered by the males. The age-I.Q. correlation for them was −.60. That value seems reasonably close to the significant −.78 correlation observed among males in the same age range. Thus it may be reasonable, for some analyses, to pool these female subjects with the males. We shall, however, regard both the "elderly" and "juvenile" females as separate samples.

Whether the significantly different age-I.Q. correlations are attributable to sex or to age differences, partial correlation is clearly inappropriate. The only alternative method of attempting to remove the age bias which has occurred to me is extraordinarily inelegant, but it may serve at least some illustrative function. We shall refer to it as the "pseudopairing procedure." The normal method of calculating the intraclass correlation of twins' I.Q.'s is to set down in two columns the paired I.Q.'s of each set of twins. The I.Q. of either twin may be set down in the X column; the I.Q. of his mate is entered in the Y column. The intraclass correlation depends upon an analysis of variance contrasting between-family with within-family variances.

The pseudopairing procedure, exemplified in Table 4, first sets down the scores of all twin pairs, with the order of entry corresponding exactly to the ages of the twins. The twins are then divided into clusters, each cluster consisting of two twin sets immediately adjacent in age. (When the number of twin pairs in the sample is odd, the set midmost in age enters into two clusters — one with the next oldest and one with the next youngest set.)[68] Then, a new set of pseudopairings is made. There are four pseudopairings formed out of each cluster. They consist of pairings of each score within a cluster with each other score in the cluster — *except that* pairings of the scores of actual twins are *omitted*. Finally, the intraclass correlation is computed in the normal fashion for the pseudopairings.

The columns of pseudopairings, it will be noted, contain precisely the same numbers as do the columns of true pairings, but each number appears twice among the pseudopairings. The virtue of the pseudopairing procedure is this: All genetic effects are removed from the correlation, and the only systematic bias introduced is that all pseudopairings involve individuals close together in age.

The correlation computed from the pseudopairings cannot be assessed for statistical significance, but it does provide — without the assumptions underlying partial correlation — an estimate of the resemblance to be expected between twins solely on the basis of their shared age. The estimate is conservatively biased, since pseudopaired individuals are not exactly of the same age. We can now apply the pseudopairing technique to the NFH data. We begin with the 7 male pairs. The observed I.Q. correlation among them is .58. The pseudopairing procedure produces a correlation of .67. For the males, at least, we can predict an individual's I.Q. just as well from knowing his age as from knowing his twin's

TABLE 4

Illustration of Pseudopairing Procedure

Pairs	Age	True Pairings		Pseudopairings	
		IQ	IQ	IQ	IQ
Pair A,	13.5	105	106	105	115
				106	105
Pair B,	13.9	115	105	106	115
				105	105
Pair C,	19.0	94	95	94	102
				95	96
Pair D,	19.3	102	96	95	102
				94	96
		etc.		etc.	

Note.—Twin pairs are NFH males, entered in order of age. Pairs A and B form the first cluster. Pairs C and D the second cluster, etc. The intraclass correlation is calculated from the pseudopairings, as from the true pairings.

I.Q.! The genetic identity of the twins, in this example, literally contributes nothing to prediction. The correlation between twins' I.Q.'s may be entirely due to their identical ages, rather than to their identical genes.

We might, as previously indicated, pool the three equivalently aged female pairs with the males. When we do so, we obtain an I.Q. correlation of .65. The pseudopairing procedure produces a correlation of .47. We see again that at least a substantial proportion of the I.Q. correlation appears to be attributable to age. We can also examine the seven pairs of elderly females. The observed I.Q. correlation among them is .48. The pseudopairing procedure produces a value of .06. That clearly suggests that not all of the I.Q. correlation between twins can be attributed to age. The very high I.Q. correlations appearing in some samples, however, seem very likely to be spuriously inflated by the age effect. We shall soon see independent evidence of this in new data. The relatively moderate I.Q. correlation between twins which cannot be attributed to age need not, of course, be due to genes. We would expect, as in Shields' data, that the correlated environments of "separated" twins would produce some I.Q. correlation quite independent of age. The pseudopairing procedure is inapplicable to the remaining "sample" of two juvenile female pairs. We can reasonably conclude that the .67 correlation reported for separated MZs by NFH was to some considerable extent inflated by an age bias. That conclusion did not flow from McNemar's "correction."

THE JUEL-NIELSEN STUDY: AGE AND I.Q. AGAIN

The final study of separated MZs was performed in Denmark by Juel-Nielsen.[69] The study was very small-scale, involving only 12 twin pairs. There were nine female and three male pairs; like the Shields and NFH studies, there was a preponderance of women. In the three studies combined, 46 female and 25 male pairs were observed, a statistically significant effect. The I.Q. test employed by Juel-Nielsen was a Danish adaptation of the Wechsler Adult Intelligence Scale. The translated test, as Juel-Nielsen scrupulously indicated, had never been standardized on a Danish population. The WAIS test in principle expects a decline in raw scores as adults advance in age. The test scoring procedure had been supposedly standardized on an American white adult population so as to produce a mean I.Q. of 100 at every age. There is no particular reason to suppose that the standardization would survive intact when a translated version of the test is administered to adult Danes.

The study, like Shields and NFH, contains detailed case histories of the twins. The material, however, provides no really quantitative information about correlated environments, and the verbal descriptions are at times strikingly inconsistent. For example, in a summary of the similarities between the home environments of separated pairs, it is said of Peter and Palle that "the standard of the homes in different parts of Copenhagen were socially very different."[70] The case study of the *same* pair of twins asserts that "Their homes do not seem to have differed particularly as regards social and economic status, housing conditions or general cultural influences, but their childhood environments were otherwise very different."[71] This sort of contradiction makes it very difficult to regard the verbal descriptions of some twin investigators as having serious scientific merit. The verbal descriptions, however, are probably preferable to the mutually contradictory "numbers" provided by Burt to quantify occupational status.

There is reason to suppose that the environments of the Juel-Nielsen twins may have been correlated. For example, Ingegard and Monika were cared for by relatives until age 7, but then lived with their mother until age 14. "They were usually dressed alike and very often confused by strangers, at school, and sometimes also by their step-father. . . . The twins always kept together when children, they played only with each other and were treated as a unit by their environment, but their attitude toward their surroundings and particularly toward their mother were different from an early age." The reader is asked to reflect on the fact that the I.Q. correlation between such "separated" twins is said to estimate the heritability of I.Q. in the Caucasian population. Those who write in this way cannot have read the original sources with an open or critical mind. We shall pass over such facts as that Maren and Jensine were reared six miles apart by paternal aunts each married to farmers, or that the adoptive fathers of Peter and Palle were both described as drunkards. The picture by now should be clear enough.

The I.Q. data for Juel-Nielsen's twins seem to reflect the lack of standardization of the test. The mean I.Q. of the 24 individuals in the sample was a rather high 105.5, considerably higher than that observed for other separated MZ twins. The standard deviation was a very low 9.6. The mean I.Q. of the males was 113.2, compared to 103 for the females, a statistically significant difference. The 9 female pairs averaged 52.6 years of age, ranging from 35 to 72. The 3 male pairs averaged 48, ranging from 22 to 77. There is again, with a different test in a different country, a very clear correlation between age and I.Q. For the 18 females, the correlation was a significant .61. For the 6 males, the correlation was also significant, −.82, with a reversed sign![72] Two of the male pairs, it should be noted, lay entirely outside the range of female ages, one at each extreme. The apparent sex difference here is again in part confounded with age.

The I.Q. correlation reported for the entire sample by Juel-Nielsen was .62, but that correlation has clearly been influenced by age effects in the Wechsler test. We can apply the pseudopairing procedure to the female sample. For those 9 pairs, the intraclass I.Q. correlation was .59. The pseudopairing procedure produced an identical correlation of .59. We observe once again that an I.Q. correlation attributed to identical genes may logically be attributed to the identical ages of subjects administered, in this instance, a wholly unstandardized test. There seems no question but that, at least for some samples of separated MZ twins, the correlation between I.Q. score and age contributes mightily to the reported I.Q. resemblance of twins.

There are fragments of other data that suggest that the age-I.Q. confound is not limited to a few studies of separated twins, conducted with old-fashioned or wholly unstandardized I.Q. tests. To test for the presence of this confounding, we require raw data that provide both I.Q. scores and chronological ages of tested subjects. Two such sets of relatively recent data were provided by Babson et al.[73] in 1964 and by Willerman and Churchill[74] in 1967. Their studies were concerned with a possible relation between birth weight and I.Q. in twins. They did not calculate the I.Q. correlation between twin pairs, nor did they calculate the age-I.Q. correlation. Their raw data, however, make such computations possible. The Babson et al. study, in Oregon, utilized a recent version of the Stanford-Binet. The Willerman and Churchill study, in Michigan, employed a recent Wechsler test for children. The I.Q.'s for the verbal and performance sections of the Wechsler were presented separately, without full-scale I.Q.'s. We have utilized the Verbal I.Q.'s in all subsequent comparisons. Though the Babson et al. subjects had been selected for low birth weight, they were very comparable to the Willerman and Churchill twins in terms both of I.Q. and of age. The comparative statistics are entered in Table 5, together with the data for a small group of DZ twins reported by Babson et al. The twins in these studies, of course, had been reared together.

The mean ages of the two MZ samples (8.5 years) were identical, and the range of ages covered was very similar. The intraclass I.Q. correlation between MZ twins was strikingly similar in each sample, .83 in one case and .82 in the other. The positive and statistically significant correlations between age and I.Q. agreed even more strikingly, .59 in each case. For this age range, and in these two different modern I.Q. tests, we discover that I.Q. *increases* with age. This phenomenon does not appear to be limited to MZ twins. The age-I.Q. correlation of .77 in the small DZ sample is also statistically significant. The effect of age is not a trivial one. The table indicates that in all three samples, children aged 8.5 or

TABLE 5

Data from Babson et al. (1964) and Willerman and Churchill (1967)

	Willerman and Churchill	Babson et al.	
	14 MZs	9 MZs	7 DZs
I.Q. correlation	.82	.83	.65
Age × I.Q. correlation	.59	.59	.77
Mean age, in years	8.5	8.5	8.3
Range of ages	5.3–13.0	4.4–10.9	5.1–10.8
Mean I.Q., age 8.5 or more	107.9	106.6	112.5
Mean I.Q., age under 8.5	87.6	82.7	92.3

older had mean I.Q.'s at least 20 points higher than did the younger children. Pooling all 60 individuals represented in the table, the correlation between age and I.Q. is .60.

The age-I.Q. confound, of course, again contributes to the observed I.Q. resemblance between twins. For the pooled sample of 23 MZ pairs reared together, the intraclass correlation between twins' I.Q.'s was .82. The pseudopairing procedure produces a correlation of .64. For the small sample of seven DZ pairs, the observed I.Q. correlation was .65. The pseudopairing procedure produces .41. Thus, again, pairing individuals on the basis of age alone produces very substantial I.Q. resemblances.

The age problem has obviously contaminated twin data for a considerable period of time. For example, a classic study by Merriman in 1924[75] presented raw Stanford-Binet I.Q. data for various types of twins. The I.Q. correlation for opposite-sexed DZs was .52, very close to the "genetic expectation." The 38 twin pairs ranged in age from 6 to 17 years. For the female members of the twin pairs, the age-I.Q. correlation was a significant −.50. For the male members, it was −.21. Though suggestive, the difference between the two correlations was not statistically significant. The strong effect of age on female I.Q. scores reflects itself in the I.Q. correlations. For the 19 eldest pairs of DZ twins, the I.Q. correlation was only .26. For the 19 youngest pairs, it was .71. The difference was at the borderline of significance ($p \cong .06$). Which of these two correlations best describes the I.Q. resemblance of opposite-sexed DZ twins? The evidence indicates that had Merriman restricted the age range of his sample, very different answers — each contradicting the genetic expectation — would have been obtained. The majority of twin studies, unfortunately, do not present the raw data that make such computations possible.

The most obvious way to circumvent the contaminating effect of age on twin I.Q. resemblances, one might suppose, is to study only twins of the same age. There are, however, perils even in such an enterprise. The age-I.Q. correlation exists over very limited age ranges. The 1949 study of adopted children by Skodak and Skeels contains a splendidly detailed appendix, with raw I.Q. data and chronological ages of 100 singleton children.[76] The children had been given the same Stanford-Binet tests on four successive occasions during infancy and childhood. The appendix indicates that 53 of the children were 6 years old at the time of the third test administration. The chronological ages are given in months, and the 53 6-year-olds ranged from 6 years, 0 months to 6 years, 10 months. Within this very restricted range of ages, the correlation between age and I.Q. was a significant −.35. For 24 boys, the correlation was −.34; for 29 girls, it was −.35. This stable and significant correlation was clearly an artifact built into the Stanford-Binet test. When the same 53 children were tested 6.5 years later, at an average age of 13, the correlation between age and I.Q. was literally .00. The negative correlation between age and I.Q. was, however, then demonstrated in another way. The mean I.Q. of the children had dropped a significant 7.2 points during the

6.5 year interval. That drop obviously reflected the tendency of the old Stanford-Binet to be negatively correlated with age over the span of 6 to 13 years and beyond. The temporary age-I.Q. correlation observed at age 6, over a range of just 10 months, may be due to the fact that the divisor in calculating Stanford-Binet I.Q.'s was the child's chronological age in months. When the child is very young, a couple of months of "extra" age can make a large difference. Those who use I.Q. scores to stream young school children into "ability" groupings might fruitfully ponder these data.

We do not know whether the rather strong age-I.Q. relation we have observed in twin samples is larger than the same correlation among singletons. The data seem to indicate, however, either that our leading I.Q. tests are very badly standardized, or that general population norms do not apply to twins, or that the twin samples studied by psychologists are bizarre — or all three.

SOME CONCLUSIONS

The discussion of the effects of age on I.Q. is now completed, and we return to our survey of the four separated MZ twin studies. The observed I.Q. correlation between separated MZs would in theory be illuminated by comparing it to certain other twin correlations. First, of course, one can ask whether it is as large as the correlation between MZs reared together. From an exclusively genetic standpoint, these two correlations should be identical. To the degree that the separated twins have been placed into effectively different environments, an environmentalist view would obviously expect the correlation between them to be reduced. There is, however, another theoretical anchoring point. The environmentalist will assert that the positive correlation between separated MZs merely reflects their correlated environments. That assertion raises an interesting question about the I.Q. correlation of *DZ* twins reared *together*. They, of course, have highly correlated environments, without genetic identity. The environmentalist would find it awkward, though not impossible, to suppose that the environments of so-called separated MZs are more highly correlated than those of DZs reared together. From this point of view, under an exclusively environmentalist interpretation, the I.Q. correlation of DZs reared together should set something like an upper limit on the I.Q. correlation to be expected between separated MZ's.

The relevant comparisons can be made appropriately only if the same investigator, using the same tests, has studied each of the various kinship categories. Further, the samples of MZs and DZs reared together must be matched to the separated MZ sample in terms of age and sex. The Juel-Nielsen study, using a translated Wechsler, reports no data other than those for separated MZs. The remaining three studies purport to provide the relevant comparative data.

With Burt's data, as usual, genetics carries the day. For his "group test" of intelligence, MZs reared together correlated .94; MZs reared apart correlated .77. That does suggest some effect of environment, but the effect scarcely survives

Burt's scientific adjustments. For "final assessments" the two correlations were .93 and .87. The last two correlations do not differ significantly. The comparison between MZs reared apart and DZs reared together is even more disastrous for an environmentalist view. For group test, the correlations were .77 and .55. That in itself is bad enough, but the final assessments managed simultaneously to raise MZs apart to .87, while lowering DZs together to .45.

The Shields data, taken as presented, provide similarly bad news for the environmentalist. The separated MZs had a (nonsignificantly) higher I.Q. correlation than the MZs reared together: .77 vs. .76! These virtually identical correlations were contrasted by Shields with a .51 correlation for DZs. There could scarcely be a more perfect demonstration of the potency of the genes, since the .51 correlation of DZs is very close to the genetic expectation for ordinary sibs. We have seen, however, in the Shields appendix, that his 7 DZ pairs are a *pooling* of pairs reared together and pairs reared separately. The DZ pairs reared together correlated .70. Thus, taken as they stand, the Shields correlations seem to suggest that *nothing* makes much difference — neither separation, nor full vs. half genetic identity. To be sure, separation does appear to affect (nonsignificantly) DZ twins. The DZ twins reared apart correlated only .05. This is all nonsense; the pooling of two tiny DZ samples in the Shields study is not defensible, and the separate samples are trivially small.

We have seen that for the seven Shields separated MZ pairs selected as having the most obviously correlated environments, the I.Q. correlation was .99. For the 10 pairs reared in nonrelated families, and apparently attending different schools, the correlation was a significantly lower .47. These results are profoundly embarrassing to a genetic interpretation. The difference between the two correlations indicates a very large effect of correlated environments. The .99 correlation for separated MZs reared in highly correlated environments is no less embarrassing, since it is vastly larger than that observed in MZs reared together.

The NFH data indicated a correlation of .67 for separated MZs, and a significantly larger correlation of .91 for MZs reared together. Further, a DZ sample correlated .64, a considerably larger value than that normally observed for sibs, and about the same as that found for separated MZs. The MZ and DZ reared-together groups are not, however, really comparable to the separated MZs. The first two groups were school children. We have also seen that even within those two groups the age-I.Q. correlations differed significantly.

The four separated MZ twin studies reviewed in this chapter led Professor Jensen to conclude: "The overall intraclass correlation . . . .824 . . . may be interpreted as an upper-bound estimate of the heritability of I.Q. in the English, Danish, and North American Caucasian populations sampled in these studies."[77] The conclusion of our own review is vastly different. We have seen that Burt's data, reporting by far the strongest hereditarian effects, are riddled with arithmetical inconsistencies and verbal contradictions. The few descriptions of how the data were collected are mutually inconsistent, as are the descriptions of the "tests" employed. The "assessments" of I.Q. are tainted with subjectivity. The utter failure to provide information about procedural detail can only be described as cavalier. There can be no science that accepts such data as its base.

The remaining three studies provide considerable information. The degree to which the environments of "separated" twins are correlated cannot be imagined by reading secondary sources, but the case studies provided by the authors are rich in detail. The Shields study provides clear evidence that the degree of I.Q. resemblance between separated twins is profoundly influenced by the degree of resemblance of their environments. The study also contains data suggesting that the theoretical expectation of the tester may unconsciously bias the I.Q. measurements of twins. We have also recognized another possible source of bias in depending on the twins themselves to provide detailed information about the degree of their separation. The reward structure of the experimenter-subject relation may exert strong pressures on the twins to exaggerate the degree of separation. The Newman et al. and Juel-Nielsen studies provide graphic illustrations of how the I.Q. correlation between twins may be spuriously inflated by the confounding of I.Q. score with age. The correlations they report, even with this inflation, and even with correlated environments of the twins, are relatively modest. We cannot guess with confidence from the available data what the I.Q. correlation would be among a set of MZ twins who, at birth, had been randomly sprinkled across the full range of environments provided for the English, Danish, and North American Caucasian populations. We have good reason to suppose that it would be much less than the .47 observed in the Shields twins who had been reared in "unrelated" families and had attended different schools. There is no compelling reason to suppose that it would be larger than the nothing which remained for the NFH men and Juel-Nielsen women after the effect of the age-I.Q. confound was removed.

To the degree that the case for a genetic influence on I.Q. scores rests on the celebrated studies of separated twins, we can justifiably conclude that there is no reason to reject the hypothesis that I.Q. is simply not heritable. The hereditarians assert, however, that other kinds of more indirect evidence support their position. The subsequent chapters will examine these conceptually more difficult types of evidence.

NOTES TO CHAPTER THREE

1. N. D. Hirsch, *Twins: Heredity and Environment*, (Cambridge, Harvard University Press, 1930), p. 149.
2. The intraclass correlation coefficient is a necessity with twin data, since there is no rational reason to place one twin, rather than the other, into the "X" or "Y" column of a correlational table. The total score variance is partitioned into between-class (B) and within-class (W) components, with each twin pair constituting a class. Then mean squares are computed for B and for W. The correlation is expressed by dividing B-minus-W by B-plus-W. The result obtained is essentially identical to that produced by the "double entry"

Pearsonian procedure, in which each twin pair's scores are included twice, reversing column entries. The intraclass procedure is preferable, since it appropriately subtracts a degree of freedom from the between-class variance.

3. C. Burt, "Ability and Income," *British Journal of Psychology,* 13, (1943), 89.
4. C. Burt, "Intelligence and Social Mobility," *British Journal of Statistical Psychology,* 14, (1961), 11.
5. C. Burt and M. Howard, "The Multifactorial Theory of Inheritance and its Application to Intelligence," *British Journal of Statistical Psychology,* 9, (1956), 127 – 128.
6. C. Burt and M. Howard, "The Relative Influence of Heredity and Environment on Assessments of Intelligence," *British Journal of Statistical Psychology,* 10, (1957), 103.
7. J. Conway, "Class Differences in General Intelligence: II," *British Journal of Statistical Psychology,* 12, (1959), 11.
8. C. Burt, "The Evidence for the Concept of Intelligence," *British Journal of Educational Psychology,* 25, (1955), 167–168.
9. C. Burt, "The Genetic Determination of Differences in Intelligence: A Study of Monozygotic Twins Reared Together and Apart," *British Journal of Psychology,* 57, (1966), 146.
10. The 1966 Burt paper (p. 149) contains a disquieting couple of sentences: "We have endeavoured to select the individuals composing the group so that they should, as far as possible, be genuinely representative of the population as a whole. With the smaller groups this has not been easy: but for all of them the standard deviations, which range from just under 14 to a little over 16 I.Q. points, are much the same." I have preferred not to believe that the shrinking sample sizes are explained by one possible reading of those sentences.
11. C. Burt, "The Inheritance of Mental Ability," *American Psychologist,* 13, (1958), 6–7.
12. J. Conway, "The Inheritance of Intelligence and its Social Implications," *British Journal of Statistical Psychology,* 11, (1958), 187.
13. Burt and Howard, *Multifactorial,* p. 118.
14. Burt, *Evidence,* p. 172.
15. Burt and Howard, *Heredity and Intelligence,* p. 51.
16. Burt, *Inheritance,* p. 8.
17. Burt and Howard, *Heredity and Intelligence,* p. 39.
18. C. Burt, "The Education of the Young Adolescent: The Psychological Implications of the Norwood Report," *British Journal of Educational Psychology,* 13, (1943), 136.
19. Burt, *Genetic Determination,* pp. 140 – 141.
20. Ibid, p. 140.
21. C. Burt, *Handbook of Tests for Use in Schools,* (London, Staples, 1933).
22. C. Burt, *Mental and Scholastic Tests,* (London, King, 1921), pp. 221–235.

23. Ibid, p. 227.
24. C. Burt, "A Note on the Theory of Intelligence," *British Journal of Educational Psychology,* 28, (1958), 287.
25. A. R. Jensen, "Kinship Correlations Reported by Sir Cyril Burt," *Behavior Genetics,* 4, (1974), 24 – 25.
26. F. Gaw, "A Study of Performance Tests," *British Journal of Psychology,* 15, (1925), 379 – 384.
27. Conway, *Inheritance,* p. 186.
28. Burt, *Genetic Determination,* p. 144.
29. A. R. Jensen, "IQ's of Identical Twins Reared Apart," *Behavior Genetics,* 2, (1970), 136.
30. Conway, *Inheritance,* p. 186.
31. Jensen, *Identical Twins,* p. 135.
32. This has been acknowledged by Jensen in a revised version of his paper printed in his book *Genetics and Education,* (New York, Harper & Row, 1972), p. 310. The final assessments and social classes of all the twins have been reproduced in Jensen, *Kinship Correlations,* p. 15.
33. Burt and Howard, *Heredity and Intelligence,* p. 39.
34. Burt, *Genetic Determination,* p. 143.
35. Jensen, *Identical Twins,* p. 139.
36. R. J. Herrnstein, *I.Q. in the Meritocracy,* (Boston, Atlantic Monthly Press, 1973), p. 159.
37. In computing these correlations, I have, hoping to reduce confusion, assigned a high numerical value to the "upper" class. That is, I have tipped Burt's 1-through-6 scale upside down, so that 6 represents upper-class and 1 lower-class. This does not, of course, affect the numerical value of the correlations, but it does change the sign.
38. Conway, *Class Differences,* p. 8.
39. Conway, *Inheritance,* p. 186.
40. W. Shockley, "Dysgenics, Geneticity, Raceology: A Challenge to the Intellectual Responsibility of Educators," *Phi Delta Kappan,* January, 1972, p. 300.
41. Conway, *Class Differences,* p. 9.
42. Burt, *Inheritance,* p. 12.
43. J. Shields, *Monozygotic Twins Brought Up Apart and Brought Up Together,* (London, Oxford University Press, 1962).
44. Ibid, p. 64.
45. Jensen, *Identical Twins,* pp. 135 – 136.
46. J. L. Jinks and D. W. Fulker, "Comparison of the Biometrical Genetical, MAVA, and Classical Approaches to the Analysis of Human Behavior," *Psychological Bulletin,* 73, (1970), 335.
47. The correlations reported by Shields were based on only 37 of these 40 twin pairs. Two pairs were discarded by Shields because one twin had a raw score

of only 1 in the Dominoes test, and a third pair for psychiatric reasons. Full details are provided in the Shields appendix. In my own calculations, I have utilized the scores of all tested individuals. The exclusion of very low scorers is arbitrary. For example, Joyce scored 1 on the Dominoes, and her twin scored 27. That is a difference of three standard deviations. Shields writes that "Joyce evidently did not understand the instructions of the Dominoes . . . she did not give an impression of low intelligence, and, as in other pairs where a subject gave a score of only 1, the Dominoes scores have been excluded from statistical analysis." These twins may be contrasted to Olwen and Gwladys, who scored 4 and 2 on the Dominoes. That is, each twin was close to three standard deviations below the mean. Their scores were included by Shields in his analysis: "Both twins are naturally Welsh speaking, but this does not explain their low score on the Dominoes which is in keeping with the impression on interview of low intelligence." My own impression suggests that low scores of people who speak a foreign language might well be excluded from statistical analysis. It seems safer, however, to take the test scores as they stand, rather than to be guided by impressions.

48. *The Sixth Mental Measurements Yearbook*, ed. O. K. Buros, (Highland Park, N.J., Gryphon Press, 1965), 724 – 725.
49. Shields, *Monozygotic Twins*, p. 24.
50. Ibid, p. 27.
51. Ibid, p. 190. The failure of separated MZ twin investigators to test the step-sibs and step-parents of adopted twins seems astonishing, considering what a unique and precious resource such twin pairs are supposed to be. The assertion that the separated twins have been brought up in uncorrelated environments implies that there would be no correlation between the I.Q.'s of members of the households in which the two twins were reared. This seems obviously worth investigating, but the idea does not seem to have occurred to any of the separated-twin investigators.
52. The *F* ratio between the within-pair variances of MZ and DZ twins has been employed as an index of a trait's heritability, on the false assumption that within-family environmental variance is identical in the two types of families. The *F* ratio in the present instance cannot possibly reflect a genetic effect, so it here serves as an index of "environmentability." The argument is made in Chapter 4 that, in the case of MZ vs. DZ comparisons, the *F* ratio may have precisely the same meaning.
53. Shields, *Monozygotic Twins*, p. 48.
54. H. H. Newman, F. N. Freeman, and K. J. Holzinger, *Twins: A Study of Heredity and Environment*, (Chicago, University of Chicago Press, 1937).
55. Ibid, p. 135.
56. Ibid, p. 136.
57. Jensen, *Identical Twins*, p. 146.
58. Newman, Freeman, and Holzinger, *Twins*, p. 147.
59. Ibid, p. 281.

60. Ibid, p. 134.
61. Ibid, p. 343.
62. L. M. Terman, *Genetic Studies of Genius, Volume I, Mental and Physical Traits of a Thousand Gifted Children,* (Stanford, Stanford University Press, 1925), pp. 42–43.
63. Jensen, *Identical Twins,* p. 142.
64. That is not to say that sex is not genetically determined! That kind of genetic variance, however, is not what is meant when heritability estimates are calculated for populations. There would of course be no adequate ground to assign any male-female difference in test scores to genetic factors directly, unless one could demonstrate that cultural differences in the treatment of the sexes were not responsible.
65. Q. McNemar, "Newman, Freeman, and Holzinger's Twins: A Study of Heredity and Environment," *Psychological Bulletin,* 35, (1938), 247–248.
66. A. R. Jensen, "How Much Can We Boost IQ and Scholastic Achievement?", *Harvard Educational Review,* 39, (1969), 52.
67. L. M. Terman, *The Measurement of Intelligence,* (Boston, Houghton Mifflin, 1916), p. 54.
68. With a reasonably large sample, another alternative is simply to discard the mid-most set. With very small samples, it seems preferable to utilize all available information.
69. N. Juel-Nielsen, "Individual and Environment: A Psychiatric-Psychological Investigation of Monozygotic Twins Reared Apart," *Acta Psychiatrica et Neurologica Scandinavica,* (1965), Monograph Supplement 183.
70. Ibid, p. 98.
71. Ibid, p. 33.
72. The data for the three males afford an eerie experience to one who calculates the correlation. The *means* of the three twin pairs' I.Q.'s literally correlate −1.00 with their ages. That, even with only one degree of freedom, is significant. Throughout, I have followed the practice in the twin literature of regarding each twin's score as an independent entry when calculating correlations. The correlations of twin-pair I.Q. means with age are invariably higher than those reported in the text.
73. S. G. Babson, J. Kangas, N. Young, and J. L. Bramhall, "Growth and Development of Twins of Dissimilar Size at Birth," *Pediatrics,* 33, (1964), 329–330.
74. L. Willerman and J. A. Churchill, "Intelligence and Birth Weight in Identical Twins," *Child Development,* 38, (1967), 626.
75. C. Merriman, "The Intellectual Resemblance of Twins," *Psychological Monographs,* 33, (1924), 50–58. Whole Number 152.
76. M. Skodak and H. M. Skeels, "A Final Follow-Up Study of One Hundred Adopted Children," *Journal of Genetic Psychology,* 75, (1949), 122–124.
77. Jensen, *Identical Twins,* p. 146.

4

KINSHIP CORRELATIONS

*He married III, 2, licentious in youth and alcoholic,
who bore him eight children (IV, 2, 3, 6, 8, 10, 11, 13,
15) all of Nam Hollow. The first, IV, 2, was a suspicious,
causationless, alcoholic harlot who married a cousin (IV,
1) . . . equipped with a good memory but of no initiative
or reasoning power. . . . The progeny . . . were all
typical Nams, indolent and unable to learn at school, the
men alcoholic and the women harlots.*

*The next, IV, 3, was an indolent, inefficient, alcoholic,
illiterate man, who . . . had by IV, 4, a harlot who died of
tuberculosis in 1893, two children. . . . Their mother's
fraternity, of Canadian origin, was not without mechani-
cal ability, but full of licentiousness. . . . The other
woman, IV, 5, was a cousin . . . alcoholic, and a harlot.
She . . . cohabited with an Italian in New York. . . .
This belongs to one of the worst strains of the Nams. . . .
The ten-year old son of this pair, V, 47, is a stubborn,
uncontrollable mischief-maker who ran away from the
orphan asylum where he had been placed. . . .
The next child is V, 29. . . . His principal wife, (V,
31), was active, busy, orderly, neat, good-natured,
neither loquacious nor taciturn, but a harlot. . . . The 13
year old son is doing fair work in school, is taciturn and
unambitious. His sex instincts have not yet broken into
flame.*

—Dr. A. H. Estabrook, 1912[1]

When a trait is inherited, persons who are biologically related will of course resemble one another with respect to that trait. The closer the degree of biological relatedness, the closer the resemblance will be. The trait is determined by the genes, and close relatives have many genes in common. This obvious logic has led hereditarians to explore the I.Q. correlations of pairs of individuals of varying degrees of relatedness. The demonstration that kinfolk resemble one another — that a trait "runs in families" — cannot in itself establish that the trait is genetically determined. The difficulty is that relatives share more than common genes. They also share a basically similar familial environment. The rich and well-educated parent tends to produce, not necessarily via genetic mechanisms, rich and well-educated children. To be rich and well-educated might conceivably affect I.Q. scores. Further, it seems entirely reasonable to assume that the more closely two people are related genetically, the more similar are the environments to which they have been exposed.

This obvious confounding of genetic and environmental factors poses fundamental difficulties for the interpretation of kinship correlations in I.Q. The hereditarians point to the asserted fact that the I.Q. correlations for various types of relatives correspond quite closely to what would be expected on the basis of the number of shared genes. That, if it is a fact, would not establish the genetic determination of I.Q. — not so long as shared genes are associated with shared environments. The observation that a genetic model more or less fits a set of data does not mean that a different, environmental model could not fit the data just as well. To be sure, if all kinship correlations in I.Q. correspond fairly exactly to predictions made on *a priori* genetic grounds, that would be a very strong point in favor of a genetic model — if we believed that the reported correlations had not been influenced by the theoretical predilections of those who calculated them.

We shall therefore review the kinship data with several questions in mind. First, what do we in fact know about the I.Q. correlations between different types of relatives? Do we have sufficiently reliable data from which to make reasonable estimates of the correlations between, for example, grandparents and grandchildren, or between cousins? Then we shall have to ask how "genetic models" make theoretical predictions about kinship correlations. Particularly, are such predictions made on independent genetic grounds, without reference to the correlations that are to be predicted? Further, are the assumptions on which genetic models are based reasonable ones? The plan of this chapter is first simply to review the empirical evidence on kinship correlations. We shall then examine the relation between genetic models and the data. The chapter concludes with an examination of the comparative study of MZ and DZ twins, and the way in which estimates of I.Q. "heritability" are derived from such studies.

.

THE ERLENMEYER-KIMLING AND JARVIK FIGURE

The major summary of the existing kinship data was provided in a brief paper published by Erlenmeyer-Kimling and Jarvik.[2] For the sake of brevity, we shall

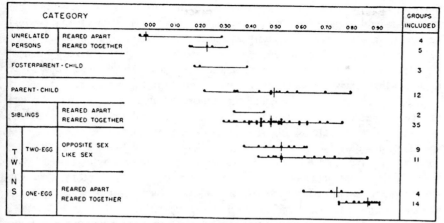

FIG. 2. Correlation coefficients for ''intelligence'' test scores from 52 studies. Reproduced with permission of the publisher from L. Erlenmeyer-Kimling and L. F. Jarvik, ''Genetics and Intelligence: A Review,'' *Science,* 142, (1963), 1477–1479. Copyright 1963 by the American Association for the Advancement of Science.

refer to this work as ''EKJ.'' The EKJ figure has been reproduced in countless psychology and genetics textbooks, and is here reproduced as Fig. 2. The influence of the EKJ paper is difficult to exaggerate. Professor Vandenberg has called it ''a paper that condensed in a few pages and one figure probably more information than any other publication in the history of psychology.''[3] The sheer quantity of the information conveyed is indeed impressive. Professor Burt quotes EKJ to the effect that the figure is based on ''over 30,000 correlational pairings from 8 countries in 4 continents.''[4] Professor Jensen cites the same ''30,000 correlational pairings,'' adding that they were obtained over a period of more than two generations,[5] and the same ''30,000 correlation pairs'' are cited by Professor Herrnstein.[6]

Thirty-thousand correlation pairs cannot, evidently, be wrong. The quantitative force of this argument, however, can easily be reduced by approximately one-half. There is a footnote in the EKJ paper which explains that 15,086 of the pairings involve unrelated individuals living apart. The I.Q. correlation for such individuals, under the laws both of nature and of nurture, ought not to deviate very far from zero, and are thus of no interest.

The EKJ paper reported that their survey had covered 52 separate studies. Though EKJ suggested that some of the surveyed studies might be vulnerable to methodological criticisms, they stressed the ''orderliness'' of the results that emerged. That apparent orderliness had occurred despite the contrasting views about heredity said to be held by the various individual investigators, who had used different ethnic and socioeconomic samples.[7]

The argument here is that the emergence of a clear signal from such a noisy background constitutes particularly impressive evidence. The ''orderliness'' of the results lies in the median values obtained for the kinship categories—not in the very considerable dispersion around the medians. The impressiveness of the signal derived from this welter of data will depend upon our conviction that the "noise" is in fact random, and uninfluenced by repeated and systematic biases. We shall need to look carefully at the empirical studies summarized by EKJ, and at the way in which they excerpted correlation coefficients from those studies.

The 1963 paper by EKJ indicated that a more detailed presentation of the data was being prepared for subsequent publication. That publication, however, has not occurred in the intervening years, and the original paper did not list the 52 studies from which data had been extracted. Thus it seems likely that some of the writers who have cited EKJ have done so in relative ignorance of the actual data base. The original paper did indicate, however, that detailed information was available upon request from the authors, and Dr. Jarvik has very kindly made available to me a list of the 52 studies.

Without offering a quantitative proof, I can report that rumors about the contrasting views regarding the importance of heredity of these 52 investigators have been considerably exaggerated. The great majority of the original studies were conducted by committed hereditarians, but that does not, of course, invalidate the data.* Perusal of the studies produces some perplexities concerning precisely what data have been extracted by EKJ. The studies often include, for the same kinship category, a considerable number of correlations. The same report may contain a raw correlation, one corrected for test unreliability, one corrected for restricted range, and one corrected for a confounding with age. For the same kinship category, significantly different correlations are sometimes reported for as many as three distinct samples, together with a still different correlation obtained by pooling the samples. The EKJ paper is for the most part silent with respect to the rules employed in selecting coefficients for inclusion in the figure. For the parent-child category, however, it does indicate that the midparent-child correlation was used when available, in preference to the mother-child correlation.

There is a bit more information in a subsequent paper by Jarvik and Erlenmeyer-Kimling, published in 1967. That paper expanded slightly on the original figure and was based upon 56 studies. "The values plotted are those considered the best estimate by the original investigator in reports where corrections (for age, attenuation, etc.) were made."[8] This provides little useful guidance in the case of a large number of studies, such as that of Thorndike in 1944.[9] For 409 pairs of brothers who had attended Columbia University, Thorndike reported a correlation of .41. The students had of course been highly selected, and, after a number of statistical corrections, Thorndike estimated that the actual sib correlation in the population was .73. We have no way of knowing which of these vastly different coefficients found its way into the EKJ figure.

*The differences in points of view about heredity among the authors of these studies seem roughly equivalent to the range in attitudes toward extrasensory perception found among investigators of that phenomenon. The possibility of large apparent effects resulting from the cumulation of minor systematic biases ought not to be discounted in either case.

KINSHIP CORRELATIONS   77

The difficulties in EKJ's procedure can be most clearly illuminated by examining in detail the category for which the least data are provided. That is the case of siblings reared apart, for which only two correlations were reported. The studies that provided those two correlations can be easily identified from EKJ's footnote, which indicates that the sibs reared-apart data were based on 125 pairs plus 131 individuals. There were in fact 125 such pairs reported upon by Freeman, Holzinger, and Mitchell in 1928;[10] and Burt, in 1955, reported correlations for "984 siblings, of whom 131 were reared apart."[11] The fact that 131 is an odd number—and the context of the quotation — suggests that Burt is in fact referring to 131 *pairings* of sibs reared apart; but as is often the case with Burt, one cannot know. The sample could have included sibships larger than two.

The Freeman et al. report calculated correlations by two separate procedures: "age entry," which segregates the scores of elder sibs in a single column of the correlational table, and "double entry," which is logically equivalent to Fisher's intraclass correlation.[12] For the 125 separated pairs, the correlation was reported as .34 by age entry, and as .25 by double entry. The Burt paper provides three separate correlations for siblings reared apart, each calculated by intraclass correlation. For "group test" the coefficient was .44; for "individual test," .46; and for "final assessment" — clearly regarded by Burt as the "best estimate" — .52. The EKJ figure indicates by inspection that Burt's "best estimate" was *not* entered. This cannot have been due to a reluctance to use data with a subjective taint; for the mother-child category, EKJ did employ Honzik's 1957 study in which mother's I.Q. was estimated by the "rating" of a social worker.[13] The EKJ figure also indicates that, for the Freeman et al. study, they used the .34 figure derived by the age-entry procedure. That figure is more consistent with a genetic hypothesis, but if the correlation is to be compared to Burt's, it is more appropriate to use the .25 figure, derived by a calculational procedure logically equivalent to Burt's. The correlations actually utilized by EKJ suggest a median for the category sibs reared apart of just about .40. Perhaps a preferable procedure would have been to use in each case the correlation based on an individual test and similarly calculated. Those figures — .46 for Burt, .25 for Freeman et al. — produce a median of .36, which is after all not very different from EKJ's, though slightly less suggestive of genetic determination.

The list of references from which EKJ culled their data, however, contained a *third* study with data for sibs reared apart. The study was published by Hildreth in 1925[14] and was evidently used by EKJ for its data on normal, nonseparated sibs. (For three quite large and very distinct samples of ordinary sibs, correlations of .63, .27, and .32 were reported; for a lumping of all three samples, the correlation was .68. Partial correlation was then employed to correct for age. That yielded correlations of .47, .08, and .13 for the three samples, and .42 for the lump. We had been forewarned that some of the 52 studies were subject to methodological criticism. We have no way of knowing which of Hildreth's figures for sibs reared together entered the EKJ data pool, but we are straying from the point.) For 78 pairs of sibs reared apart, Hildreth reported a correlation of only .23. The I.Q.'s of the sibs, however, were said to exhibit "curtailed range," and the correlation was statistically corrected for this deficiency. The correction boosted the correlation to a remarkable .50, but only as a result of Hildreth's mathematical operations. The correction, if it is to be performed, would in fact boost the correlation to only .28, but there was no significant curtailment of range among the separated sibs. The sensible value to include in the EKJ figure would be the uncorrected .23. The addition of this third and overlooked value would change the EKJ median from the reported .40 to .25. That change profoundly affects the theoretical interpretation. The median value for sibs reared together is close to .50. To assume a median of .40 for sibs reared apart suggests that I.Q. is very largely genetically determined. To assume a median of .25 is wholly compatible with the probability that "separated" sibs have been reared in correlated environments, and that there is no genetic effect. The effect of correlated environments is distinctly suggested by an observation reported by Freeman et al., which is in no way reflected in the EKJ graphic summary of their data. For the half of the separated sib pairs reared in "the more similar homes," the I.Q. correlation was .30; for the half reared in "widely different homes," it was .19.

This overlooking by EKJ of a single separated sib study was more than compensated for by Professor Burt, whose 1966 paper incorporated the EKJ data, but added to it some of his own. The additional data were said to come from "a number of studies, chiefly British, which do not appear in the American collection."[15] The table published by Burt indicated that the median correlation for separated sibs was .47 — based upon no fewer than 33 investigations! There were, unfortunately, no references cited for the 31 studies which Burt's search of the British literature had added to the humble beginnings of EKJ. This oversight did not prevent Professor Jensen, or Professor Vandenberg, or the writers of many textbooks, from informing their audiences that the median correlation in 33 studies of separated sibs had been found to be .47. There can have been few environmentalist readers whose dogmatism was so blind as to withstand empirical evidence of this quantity.

There has been a recent recognition that something may be, if not rotten, at least inaccurate in the state of England. Professor Jensen has recently reported that "Burt gives the 'number of investigations' of siblings reared apart as 33; I questioned this to Burt and he said it was a misprint—the correct number is 3."[16] Professor Jensen has of late, in his own reproductions of Burt's table, conscientiously corrected the "number of studies" to 3.[17] The median correlation is *still* given as .47. Professor Jensen evidently rejects Hildreth's .23 value, but he has not informed us *which* study has been added to the work of Burt and of Freeman et al. to produce this remarkable median.

The Burt error seems to have been independently noted by Jencks, who indicated that "One of the tables in Burt, . . . which has been widely reproduced, reports the existence of forty-two studies of siblings reared apart. This is a typographical error. So far as we can discover, there are only two studies other than Burt's."[18] The Jencks error attributes to Burt nine more fictitious studies than Burt had in fact claimed. We begin to imagine that other errors might lurk in the complex calculations that underlie the quantitatively exact "heritability estimates" pervading the literature.

To return to the EKJ figure, more complex problems are encountered in grappling with the medians reported for the parent-child and sibling correlations. The 52 studies provide a multitude of possible permutations and combinations of such correlations which might have been selected for inclusion in the figure. There are also, for these kinship categories, studies *not* cited by EKJ, and it is by no means clear that they were methodologically inferior to those included. For example, Pintner reported, in 1918, a correlation of only .22 for 180 pairs of siblings.[19] The EKJ figure very clearly does not include this data point. The exclusion cannot be attributed to a bias against old studies, since their references do include studies published in 1912 and in 1919. The 1939 study by Pintner, Folano, and Freedman[20] *is* included in EKJ. They reported a correlation of .38 for 378 pairs of sibs. They also reported that, for sibs differing by less than 18 months in age, the correlation was .48; for those differing in age by 36 months or more, it was .22. We can only guess which number(s) entered the EKJ figure.

The 52 references also include a 1932 study by Carter,[21] who gave both a vocabulary and an arithmetic test to parents and to children. The midparent-child correlations were .17 for vocabularly and .19 for arithmetic. The EKJ figure does not appear to include any value this low for parent-child. The Carter study also included sib pairs, for whom the vocabulary correlation was .34 and the arithmetic correlation .21. The lowest EKJ entry for siblings is close to .30, suggesting that, since Carter's study was utilized, the vocabulary test was taken as a more valid index of I.Q. than the arithmetic test.

We can extract from the morass of data presented (or not presented) in the EKJ figure two facts about the parent–child and sibling correlations. First, the reported correlations based on various "mental tests" differ very widely from study to study, and even within single studies. But second, the medians of all such studies conducted—for whatever such information is worth—are probably somewhere in the neighborhood of .50. The median correlations of about .50 do not in themselves tell us anything about the relative importance of heredity and environment in determining I.Q. The difficulties of interpretation are very nicely exemplified within one of the 52 studies on which the EKJ figure is based.

The study was reported by Verner Sims of the University of Alabama in 1931, and it contains some elegant logic.[22] The work took place in a school system, where Sims found an I.Q. correlation of .40 for 203 pairs of sibs. This finding provoked the following thoughtful observation in Sims — one that has eluded many research workers and textbook writers. "Presumably children paired at random would show no resemblance, but one cannot compare paired siblings with random pairs and account for the differences in terms of inheritance. It is only when environmental differences are equal that comparisons have meaning." The trick, Sims reasoned, was to find pairs of unrelated individuals who, like the siblings, shared common environments. The appropriate question could then be asked: Is the I.Q. correlation any higher among pairs who share a common environment *plus* common genes than it is among pairs who share only a common environment?

To obtain pairs who shared only a common environment, Sims selected another 203 pairs of entirely unrelated children from the same school system. These new children were formed into pairs on the basis of as close a matching as possible to the true sibs with regard to "home background," age, and school attended. The I.Q. correlation for these 203 pairs of "unrelated individuals reared apart" was a significant .29. That correlation was not significantly lower than the .40 observed among true sibs. To guard against the possibility that a confounding of age and I.Q. was reponsible for these data, Sims next formed 203 entirely new pairs of unrelated individuals, matched to the true sibs only in terms of age. The correlation for these pairs was only .04. The impeccable logic that guided Sims throughout this study prompted him to observe that the social class questionnaire which measured "home background" could not really produce unrelated pairs with environments as wholly similar as those shared by sibs. Therefore, the nonsignificant difference in correlations between the true sibs and the unrelated pairs must exaggerate the influence of heredity. The conclusion of Sims' impressive research report was modest: "The interpretation that one may give the findings is a personal matter, but the indications are that intelligence, so far as we are today able to measure it, is greatly influenced by environment." This sophisticated and elegant study has simply disappeared from contemporary reference lists. The inclusion of the study in the EKJ figure affects neither the median for siblings, nor that for "unrelated persons reared apart."

The determined hereditarian, of course, can raise a logical objection to Sims' careful and ingenious procedure. When unrelated individuals are matched for social class and other home background variables, it is conceivable that they are being matched for genetic constitution as well. This would follow from Professor Herrnstein's thesis that good genes propel people to the upper social classes. To interpret the Sims data in this way, however, seems to imply a truly extraordinary genetic stratification of the white social classes of Alabama in 1931. These various considerations thus indicate that the median sib correlation reported by EKJ is of ambiguous significance. Their median for the DZ twin correlation, on the other hand, seems positively misleading.

The correlation for DZ twins has a special theoretical interest, particularly when it is compared to the correlation for ordinary sibs. From a purely genetic standpoint, the two correlations ought to be identical, since for each type of kinship paired individuals, on average, have half their genes in common. From an environmental point of view, however, it is logical to suppose that DZs would be more highly correlated than ordinary sibs. Twins, after all, must share more similar environments than do siblings who are born years apart.

This is in fact a fairly critical matter for an environmental theorist. The EKJ figure reflects the well-documented fact that MZ twins resemble each other in I.Q. much more than do DZ twins. For an environmentalist, this indicates that MZ twins share more similar environments than do DZs. There is ample evidence for this, as will be indicated later in this chapter. The environmentalist, however, cannot comfortably assert that MZs have much more similar environments than DZs without simultaneously recognizing that DZs have more similar environments than do ordinary sibs. The environmentalist view thus seems to require a substantially larger correlation for DZs than for sibs.

The EKJ figure appears to contradict this environmentalist expectation. The median correlation for DZs is reported as .53, whether the twins are like-sex (11 studies) or opposite-sex (9 studies). This is scarcely different from the reported median for ordinary sibs (.49, based on 35 studies). There are, however, reasons to question the validity of this comparison. Though the EKJ figure includes many studies of sibs, and many of DZ twins, it includes only three studies in which data for *both* DZs and sibs were simultaneously reported; and one of these, unfortunately, is Burt's.[23] The DZ-sib comparison can obviously be made much more sensitively if the same investigator, studying the same population with the same test, calculates the two correlations. The relevant data from the three studies are presented in Table 6.

The pattern of correlations reported by Burt, it will be seen, differs very substantially from that reported by other investigators. For the Burt data only, there is no detectable difference between DZs and ordinary sibs—a very comforting outcome for the hereditarian. The studies by Herrman and Hogben,[24] and by Tabah and Sutter,[25] agree in reporting a substantially larger correlation for DZs than for sibs. The Herrman and Hogben data indicate a surprisingly low correlation for sibs, but this English finding is not wholly atypical. The entire child population of an English rural community was studied by Matthews et al. in 1937.[26] They used the Otis test, as did Herrman and Hogben, and found a sib correlation of only .30 for 276 pairs. The Otis appears not to have measured the genotypes of English school children with anything like the precision of Burt's final assessments.

TABLE 6

Comparative I.Q. Correlations

Study	Test	Like-sexed DZs	Opposite-sexed DZs	Sibs
Herrman and Hogben (1933)	Otis	.47 ($N = 96$)	.51 ($N = 138$)	.32 ($N = 103$)
Tabah and Sutter (1954)	Gille mosaic	—	.58 ($N = 62$)	.45 ($N = 1244$)
Burt (1966)	Final assessment	.55 ($N = 71$)	.52 ($N = 56$)	.53 ($N = 264$)

The preceding analysis emphasizes a danger inherent to the EKJ procedure of tabulating medians for different kinship categories, when different sets of categories have been studied by different investigators using different tests and procedures. The EKJ medians for DZs are based on a much smaller number of studies than their median for sibs. Thus, any procedural peculiarities tending to lower the DZ correlation in a particular study will tend to affect the DZ median. The same study will probably not have included sibs, and its procedural peculiarities thus will not affect the sib median. But even if sibs had been included, the much larger number of sib studies would buffer any effect on the sib median.

There are in fact a number of procedural peculiarities that afflict the relatively few DZ studies summarized by EKJ. For example, the lowest reported correlation for opposite-sexed DZs is that of Byrns and Healy—.44 for 105 pairs.[27] The same study, however, also reports by far the lowest correlation for same-sexed twins (a pooling of undiagnosed MZ and DZ pairs). The latter correlation is only .59 for 307 pairs. The reason for these low correlations is not far to seek. The investigators correlated *percentile* scores on the Henmon-Nelson test. The statistical consequence of this is that two individuals with I.Q.'s of 96 and 104 are regarded as no more different than two individuals with I.Q.'s of 61 and 90; the difference for each pair is 20 percentiles. The study did not include sibs; we can be certain that had it done so, the sib correlation reported would have been low. The lowest reported correlation for same-sexed DZs is that of Blewett;[28] depending upon which of four measures was used, 26 DZ pairs yielded correlations ranging from .37 to .44. The Blewett study, however, also reported the lowest obtained correlation for MZ twins—ranging between only .58 and .76, again for 26 pairs. The Blewett study similarly did not include sibs; with the same tests, the sib correlation would doubtless have been low.

The EKJ figure is thus systematically biased in a way that reduces the discrepancy between the median correlations of sibs and of DZs. This bias is further exaggerated by the inclusion of a number of sib studies (about 7) reporting correlations between about .60 and .80. Those studies—some performed in the 1910's and 1920's, before genetic theory had clarified what the sib correlation ought to be—did *not* observe DZ twins. They would presumably have found high DZ correlations had they done so.

The idea that the DZ correlation is very close to .50 has been perpetuated in tables similar to EKJ's, published by various hereditarian theorists. The table published by Burt in 1966, for example, reported .49 as the median correlation found for opposite-sexed DZs by six (unnamed) "other investigators."[29] The table published by Jensen, in 1969, also reported .49 as the median correlation for opposite-sexed DZs, but now based on nine (unnamed) "studies."[30] This seems to be an error. There do not appear to be nine studies of opposite-sexed DZs that produce a median correlation of .49. The .49 figure, however, has been republished by such authorities as Herrnstein[31] and Vandenberg, [32] with references to how closely the data fit a genetic model. The fact is that the "orderliness" of the

EKJ figure, and of the "supplemented" tables based on it, in large measure reflects a strong and systematic bias on the part of the compilers. The plausibility of the genetic hypothesis to many psychologists and textbook writers has been so great that the arbitrary "medians" of those figures and tables have been routinely accepted, with no rude questions about where they came from. This has represented, I believe, a serious abnegation of the responsibilities of scientists. The reference list has been an accepted convention of science for some time, and the publication of "medians" culled from arbitrary and unreferenced sets of studies seems a dubious practice.

What then is the "real" correlation between DZs? The incredible fact is that we have no very sure basis for making an estimate. Presumably, we should give extra weight to those studies that include a large number of subjects and constitute a representative sample. The most nearly representative sample was that of Mehrota and Maxwell, who studied almost all Scottish 11-year-olds.[33] Their study included 182 pairs of opposite-sexed (and thus DZ) twins, for whom the I.Q. correlation was .63. The correlation for same-sexed DZs might, of course, have been higher. Probably the best sample of same-sexed DZs was that of Husen, who studied Swedish males reporting for possible military induction.[34] For 416 DZ pairs, Husen reported a correlation of .70. This value is very close to that of another large Swedish sample studied by Wictorin. For 141 same-sexed DZ pairs, Wictorin reported correlations of .70 and .73 on two different I.Q. tests.[35] The largest single sample of same-sexed DZs was studied in the United States by Nichols.[36] For 482 pairs, he reported a correlation of .63. This study, however, is beset by sampling problems. The Newman, Freeman, and Holzinger study of same-sexed DZs, though only 50 pairs were observed, seems to have involved a reasonably good sample of the Chicago school system.[37] They reported correlations of .64 and .62 on two different tests. The Wictorin and Nichols studies were not included by EKJ. They did include the Shields study, with data for 7 same-sexed DZ pairs, four of which had been separated.[38] We can conclude that the large-scale and representative studies give a fairer idea of the DZ correlation than do the various published "medians." The evidence clearly suggests that the actual DZ correlation is very substantially larger than that predicted by a genetic theory.

There are still further problems with the EKJ figure, but perhaps enough has been said. The skeptical may be led to wonder whether there exists another branch of science in which it would be asserted that an analogous paper "condensed in a few pages and one figure probably more information than any other publication in the history" of the discipline.

There is a special form of kinship correlation that might warrant intensive study, one that is in no way reflected in the EKJ figure. For EKJ, as for all genetic theorists, a sib is a sib. That is, sibs are defined by the brute fact that their common parentage endows them, on the average, with half of their genes in common. The singleton sib of a pair of twins, however, is an especially interesting case. When a pair is formed of *one* of the twins plus the singleton sib, the two paired individuals are genetically sibs. Thus, on genetic grounds, one would expect the correlation for such pairs to be equal to that usually reported for ordinary sibs. From an environmental view, however, it could well be that the correlation for such twin-sib pairs would be low. The twins, presumably, spend a considerable amount of time with each other, and thus come to resemble each other. To the degree that the odd singleton sib is excluded from this small "society of twins," he might conceivably fail to display the normally substantial sib resemblance to his twin sibs.

The EKJ reference list includes only one study that reports the relevant correlations, plus one study from which such correlations can be calculated. The scores on the Iowa Basic Skills Vocabulary Test—described as "a measure of intelligence"—of Iowa school twins were analyzed by Snider.[39] The score of a singleton sib tested at the same grade level was also included whenever available. The score of the singleton sib was paired randomly with the score of *one* of his twin sibs. For 329 such twin-sib pairings, the correlation was only .26. When the twin was MZ, the correlation was only .19; when the twin was DZ, the correlation was .32. These values are, of course, substantially lower than the traditionally observed sib correlation of about .50. The Snider study did not include ordinary sib pairs, but it reported a DZ correlation of precisely .50, and an MZ correlation of .79.

The twin study by Stocks and Karn[40] includes an appendix with raw Stanford-Binet I.Q.'s of a number of singleton sibs of the twins. Thus it is possible to calculate a twin-sib correlation based on 104 pairings. The correlation is only .12. The same study reported correlations of .65 for DZs and .84 for MZs.

There are at least two studies published since EKJ's survey which also contain relevant data. Partanen et al.[41] formed 90 twin-sib pairs and found correlations of .41 and .34 on two separate tests of verbal abilities. For their verbal comprehension test, the MZ and DZ correlations were .75 and .51, respectively. For their word fluency test, the same two correlations were .81 and .54. Thus, again, the twin-sib correlation appears perceptibly smaller than expected on genetic grounds in a study that reports quite traditional values for MZs and DZs. There is also a report by Huntley,[42] who gave a composite vocabulary ("intelligence") test to English children. The Huntley data, however, are quite different. For 108 twin-sib pairs, the correlation was reported as .58. The values for MZs and DZs were .83 and .58.

The available data are thus only suggestive. Probably most weight should be given to the Snider study, which contained by far the largest number of twin-sib pairings. That study, like Partanen et al., employed only one member of a pair of twins—and only one singleton sib in a family—in forming pairs. Thus there is a real suggestion that singleton sibs may resemble their sib-twins much less than, according to a genetic view, they ought to. Perhaps the major point to be made is merely that analyses of this sort are rarely undertaken by investigators whose major aim is to demonstrate that the "sib" correlation is close to the value predicted by genetic theory.

To obtain information about kinship categories other than sibs, parent-child, and twins, we must turn to authorities other than EKJ. Their figure does summarize data on the effects of separation and adoption, but it makes no reference to the more remote degrees of kinship. The genetic model is of course supposed to predict I.Q. correlations for all degrees of kinship. The median correlations for more distant relatives were included in an expanded version of the EKJ summary published by Burt in 1966. The Burt table was said to supplement EKJ's "American collection" with a "list" of "chiefly British" studies. The Burt table, with its typographical error asserting the existence of 33 studies of separated sibs, has been very widely reproduced. The Burt data, together with those of EKJ, formed the basis of a very similar table published by Jensen.[43] Professor Jensen explained that his own table had been based primarily on EKJ's figures, but he had "supplemented these with certain kinship correlations not included in their survey. . . ." There are, unfortunately, no references provided by Jensen for these supplementations; neither has Burt's "list" appeared in print.

The Jensen table is here reproduced as our Table 7. For the remote kinship categories, Jensen has simply copied Burt's "medians." For two such categories

TABLE 7[a]

Correlations for Intellectual Ability: Obtained and Theoretical Values

Correlations between	Number of Studies	Obtained Median r*	Theoretical Value[1]	Theoretical Value[2]
Unrelated Persons				
Children reared apart	4	−.01	.00	.00
Foster parent and child	3	.20	.00	.00
Children reared together	5	.24	.00	.00
Collaterals				
Second Cousins	1	.16	.14	.063
First Cousins	3	.26	.18	.125
Uncle (or aunt) and nephew (or niece)	1	.34	.31	.25
Siblings, reared apart	3	.47	.52	.50
Siblings, reared together	36	.55	.52	.50
Dizygotic twins, different sex	9	.49	.50	.50
Dizygotic twins, same sex	11	.56	.54	.50
Monozygotic twins, reared apart	4	.75	1.00	1.00
Monozygotic twins, reared together	14	.87	1.00	1.00
Direct Line				
Grandparent and grandchild	3	.27	.31	.25
Parent (as adult) and child	13	.50	.49	.50
Parent (as child) and child	1	.56	.49	.50

*Correlations not corrected for attenuation (unreliability).

[1]Assuming assortative mating and partial dominance.

[2]Assuming random mating and only additive genes, i.e., the simplest possible polygenic model.

[a]Reproduced with permission of the publisher from Arthur R. Jensen, "How Much Can We Boost IQ and Scholastic Achievement?", *Harvard Educational Review*, 39, Winter 1969. Copyright © 1969 by President and Fellows of Harvard College.

— uncle-nephew and second cousins — there is only a single study and a single correlation. The study is in each case Burt's, and the correlations are based on Burt's "assessments," doubtless occasionally checked by camouflaged I.Q. tests. We thus have no real idea of what the I.Q. test score correlation is for these kinship categories. For grandparent-grandchild and for first cousins Jensen presents medians said to be based on three studies in each case. For each of these categories, Burt presented his own correlation together with a median said to be based on two "other" investigations. For grandparent-grandchild, I have not been able to find any other study than Burt's, but perhaps Professor Jensen has. Without identification of such other studies, we must question whether we have any real idea of the grandparent-grandchild I.Q. correlation.

The situation with first cousins is not much better. The value given by Burt for his own research is .28, with a median of .26 attributed to two other investigators. Professor Jensen gives .26 as the median of three studies. There have in fact been at least two British studies, other than Burt's, of first cousins. The 1933 paper by Gray and Moshinsky[44] reported a correlation of .16, about half as large as Burt's. Their paper cited a .34 correlation reported in 1907 by Elderton,[45] "based upon arbitrary standards of assessment which antedated the more modern methods of testing." They also cited a 1924 American correlation of .22, reported by Dexter,[46] but "the methods employed do not satisfy the requirements of modern technique in the testing of intelligence." We have no way of knowing whether Burt's .28 or Gray and Moshinsky's .16 is a closer approximation to the truth. The difference might be of some consequence, since two alternate sets of "theoretical values" presented by Jensen predict correlations of .18 and .125, respectively. There are not many areas of scientific endeavor in which such an impoverished and confused data base is used to assess the goodness-of-fit of theoretical models. The mathematical elegance and power of quantitative genetics can in no way compensate for the inadequacies of the kinship data. The shop argot of computer technicians seems wholly appropriate here: garbage in, garbage out.

For kinship categories that *had* been included in the EKJ survey, Jensen's table is a confused combination of the EKJ values and those tabled by Burt. The "observed" correlations published by Jensen are the medians attributed by Burt to unnamed "other investigators." The "number of studies" on which Jensen alleges each median to be based is, however, usually taken from EKJ. This unorthodox practice leads to some confusion. For example, EKJ had reported median correlations of .53 both for same-sexed and opposite-sexed DZ twins. Those correlations were said to be based on 11 and 9 studies, respectively. The correlations given in the Jensen table are .56 and .49. They are said by Jensen to be derived from 11 and 9 studies. The medians given by Jensen, however, are in fact those given by Burt, who had said that they were based on 8 and 6 studies.

Professor Burt had indicated that his own table had been supplemented with studies called to his attention by EKJ, so it is possible to deduce what most likely happened. Professor Burt obviously found that 3 same-sexed and 3 opposite-sexed studies listed by EKJ did not meet his own high standards of methodological rigor, and so he rejected them. Professor Jensen, after a careful weighing of the evidence, concurred in Burt's assessment of those unnamed defective studies and also rejected them. The confusion arises only because Professor Jensen forgot to subtract the defective studies from his "number of studies" column. With the category siblings reared apart, however, Jensen at that time seems to have preferred Burt's "number of studies," 33, to EKJ's modest 2. Professor Herrnstein has reprinted Jensen's tabulated medians, referring to them as "obtained average correlation."[47] The Herrnstein version does not indicate upon how many studies each median is based, but the reader is informed that "This table almost certainly summarizes more sheer data, over a broader range of conditions, than any other chart in the field of quantitative psychology."

PREDICTED KINSHIP CORRELATIONS AND GENETIC MODELS

The point of the Jensen table, in any event, is to indicate that its empirical kinship correlations correspond reasonably closely to "theoretical values" that are somehow derived from genetic theory. The median empirical correlations are given for a wide range of kinship categories. The table includes, for comparative purposes, two different sets of theoretical values, derived from two very different "genetic models." The reader is not informed as to how the theoretical values were generated by the two models, but this is a critical matter.

We examine first the genetic model represented in the last column of Jensen's table. The theoretical values produced by that simple model assume that there is literally no effect of environment on kinship correlations. That model also assumes, as Jensen indicates, that there is no genetic dominance and that mating is random with respect to I.Q. The assumption of random mating, at least, is known to be grossly false. Thus, as Burt has correctly indicated, comparisons of empirical correlations to theoretical values that make no allowance for assortative mating and dominance "are really fallacious and may be seriously misleading."[48] The fact is that the theoretical effect of assortative mating is large enough so that, if empirical correlations correspond very closely to the theoretical values of the simple model, this would be evidence *against* the heritability of I.Q.

We shall shortly examine the second, more complicated model in some detail, but we begin with an overview. For the moment we note that the theoretical values generated by this model are hypothetically the summation of four additive effects. The model assumes additive genetic variance, genetic variance produced by assortative mating, genetic variance produced by dominance, and variance produced by "random" environmental effects. This model cannot generate theoretical values for kinship correlations until it has in hand estimates of the effects of assortative mating, dominance, and environment. There is in principle no problem in obtaining an estimate for assortative mating. The model simply uses the phenotypic I.Q. correlation of husband and wife. Though Jensen's table does not indicate this fact, the theoretical values generated by this model depend upon Burt's reported correlation of .38 for husband and wife.

To obtain estimates of the effects of dominance and environment is a more complicated process. The model uses two further empirical correlations to estimate these effects. The simple effect of assortative mating would be to increase the correlations for parent-child and for siblings. The effect of dominance, and of random environmental fluctuations, would be to reduce both of these correlations. There is no independent way of knowing how much dominance might exist for I.Q., nor, of course, can the effect of environment be specified on purely theoretical grounds. The model thus uses the empirical parent-child and sib correlations to estimate the effects of dominance and environment. The failure of the empirical parent-child correlation to be as high as would have been predicted solely on the basis of assortative mating provides an indication of the *joint* effects of dominance and environment. The random effects of environment are assumed to be the same for all kinship categories, but on Mendelian grounds it can be shown that dominance if present does not reduce the sib correlation as much as it reduces the parent-child correlation. Thus the model can now use the empirical sib correlation, compared to the empirical parent-child correlation, to separate the hypothetical effect of dominance from that of environment. This procedure has the following consequences. The hypothetical effects of dominance and of environment are "traded off" against each other. For a given degree of assortative mating, dominance can play a major role only if the random effects of environment are relatively small, and vice versa. The *joint* action of dominance and environment is necessary to offset the theoretical effects of assortative mating. But the reciprocally determined *separate* estimates of dominance and environmental effects will depend critically on very minor sampling fluctuations in the *empirical* parent-child and sib correlations. The model, in short, can be no better than the caliber of the empirical correlations *from which the "theoretical values" have been deduced.*

The model's estimates and theoretical values will not only be influenced by sampling fluctuations in the data base from which they are generated, but they will also be influenced by the *type* of empirical correlation used to provide the data base. The full development of this model was described in a 1956 paper by Burt and Howard.[49] We must recognize that Burt's data base, by his deliberate choice, was of a very unorthodox type. The "empirical" correlations used by Burt were not based upon raw I.Q. test scores. They were instead based on Burt's "adjusted assessments." The purpose of adjusting raw test scores was explicitly to remove most of the "disturbing effects of environment." The Burt data were thus subjected to a deliberate and systematic bias, justified by Burt's faith that he could intuitively detect the genotypic value behind the raw test score. The theoretical values generated on the basis of Burt's adjusted assessments thus have no general applicability. They apply only to adjusted assessments made by Burt. To quote Burt, "Nor were we concerned with any specific observable trait, but with differences in a hypothetical innate general factor."[50]

The Burt model can, however, be based upon and applied to real-world empirical data. The Burt procedure merely applies to intelligence a model first developed by R. A. Fisher, who employed it with unadjusted measurements of height and other physical traits. To see how the Burt model fits actual I.Q. data, we can apply it to the EKJ medians reproduced in Jensen's table. The values assigned to environment, dominance, and assortative mating might, when derived from actual I.Q. scores, be vastly different from those based upon Burt's idiosyncratic adjusted assessments. The EKJ medians contain all the necessary empirical correlations but one — that for husband and wife. We need not, however, search far for a suitable empirical assortative mating correlation. The same Jensen paper that presents the table of Burt's theoretical values includes the following: "The I.Q., interestingly enough, shows a higher degree of assortative mating than any other measurable human characteristic. I have surveyed the literature on this point, based on studies in Europe and North America, and find that the correlations between spouses' intelligence scores average close to .60."[51] There is no reason to suppose that Jensen's literature search was less precise than EKJ's, so we shall use his average value of .60 for the husband-wife correlation.

The Burt model applied to the median empirical kinship correlations produces the following impressive result. (The formulas necessary to reach these conclusions are lucidly derived and explicated by Burt.)[52] The I.Q. variance in the population is divided into the following three genetic components: additive genetic 39.1 percent, assortative mating 23.4 percent, and dominance a full 24.1 percent. Thus the broad heritability of I.Q. scores in the population is 86.6 percent, and random environmental effects contribute a very modest 13.4 percent to the variance. That is the impressive result produced when the model is applied to the results of over 30,000 correlational pairings from 8 countries in 4 continents over 2 generations in 52 studies. The model of course "fits" the parent-child and sib correlations; it must do so because it takes these as givens in order to derive parameter estimates. The structure of the model, as we shall soon see, is such that even when it employs impossible parameter estimates it generates theoretical values for lesser degrees of biological relatedness which are scarcely distinguishable from those predicted on the basis of Burt's adjusted scores. For example, based on the EKJ medians, the model "predicts" a correlation of .32 for uncle-nephew. When based on Burt's adjusted scores, it predicts .31.

To appreciate the Burt model, and to understand in detail how it produces theoretical kinship correlations, it will now be necessary to work our way through a few formulas. That seems especially appropriate, since Professor Herrnstein has warned that "In some polemics against intelligence testing . . . the statistical approach is denigrated to the advantage of less quantitative efforts, which are doubtless more accessible to the layman's intuition. It is not hard, and it is usually rewarding to the critic, to fan the untrained reader's latent hostilities towards incomprehensible mathematical formulas." Professor Herrnstein specifies in particular "the highly quantitative analyses of, for example, Cyril Burt."[53] We shall now review Burt's model in detail.

The mathematical work of Fisher[54] had demonstrated that, for a trait determined by polygenes, predicted phenotypic correlations for all kinships could be obtained if one had estimates of three parameters. The first expresses the random effects of environment, the second expresses the degree of dominance, and the third expresses the effects of assortative mating. The genetic phenomenon of dominance refers to the tendency, observable in some traits, for heterozygotes to resemble phenotypically one form of homozygote more than the other. The Fisher model allows the phenotypic value of heterozygotes to be intermediate at any level between those of homozygotes, or to fall entirely outside their range. The term "assortative mating" refers to the tendency of individuals to mate with people whom they resemble genotypically.

The geneticist working with animals or plants, it should be noted, does not need to "estimate" these parameters in a similar way. The experimental control over breeding can guarantee random mating or the mating of pure-bred lines, thus obviating the need to make guesses about the degree of assortative mating. With assortative mating controlled, it is a relatively simple matter to determine whether or not dominance is present; the experimenter counts and measures the phenotypes of the offspring of controlled matings. The effect of environment can be directly observed by manipulating the range of environments to which known genotypes are exposed.

The situation is incomparably more complex in human population genetics. The parameters must themselves be estimated from the data that they are to explain. The simultaneous existence of three unknowns allows for a certain flexibility. To indicate the way in which the model works, we shall present here, without derivations, only those formulas necessary to understand the model's basic structure. The full mathematical development is given by Burt and Howard.

The parameter that expresses random environmental effects is C_1, and its maximum possible value is 1.[55] The larger the effect of environment, the *smaller* will be the value of this parameter. The parameter expressing degree of dominance is C_2, with limits of .5 and 1. When, averaged across the set of polygenes, there is no dominance, C_2 has a value of 1; when there is maximum dominance, the value of C_2 is .5. The parameter for assortative mating is derived from M, the observed correlation between spouses, with a theoretical limit of 1.

The starting place for the model is the correlation between parent and child. That correlation is expressed by the following theoretical formula:

$$r_{po} = C_1 \, C_2 \, \frac{1 + M}{2}$$

The correlation between parent and child, r_{po}, is the multiplicative product of three unknowns. Thus, if we knew the values of C_1, C_2, and M, we could predict the correlation. We in fact know — as did Burt and Howard — that the actual empirical value of r_{po} is something reasonably close to .50. Therefore, once we know the value of M, we shall know the approximate value of the product $C_1 C_2$.

The value of M is simply the empirical correlation between spouses. That correlation was reported by Burt and Howard to be .386—"a figure which we are inclined to think a little too high." The .386 figure implies that the value of C_1C_2 will be about .72; Jensen's .60 figure for assortative mating implies a C_1C_2 of about .625. The next step, in any event, is to break down the product C_1C_2 into its components, C_1 and C_2. These two parameters are reciprocally related. With any given value of assortative mating, a high C_1 necessarily produces a low C_2. That is how the model "trades off" environment against dominance. The more dominance one postulates, the less effect one attributes to environment. There is no independent way of discovering the amount of dominance for I.Q. The alternatives are either to guess, or to estimate it from the data that are to be explained— while simultaneously estimating the effect of environment.

The Burt and Howard paper first merely guesses the dominance parameter: "let us suppose that the different genes vary between complete dominance and complete absence of dominance, and so put C_2 midway at 0.75." Further, from "conclusions already reached with physical measurements," C_1 was guessed to be .95. These two shrewd guesses produced a C_1C_2 of .7125. Placed into the formula for the parent-child correlation, together with the .386 value for assortative mating, these guesses "predict" a correlation of .494. The empirical parent-child correlation, according to Burt, was .489. The match is not bad at all.

For this prediction—as for all predictions involving relatives in a direct line of descent—it was not in fact necessary to have separate estimates of C_1 and C_2. The formula involves only their product. The separate estimates, however, are required for collateral relatives, such as siblings. The theoretical formula for the correlation between siblings is as follows:

$$r_{oo} = 1/4 \ (C_1 + C_1C_2 + 2C_1^2C_2^2M)$$

By placing the Burt and Howard guesses into the sibling formula, the predicted correlation is .514. The observed correlation was reported to be .507, again not a bad match. The aspirations of Burt and Howard toward perfection seem extraordinary. They remark that "in both cases the theoretical estimates are rather too high." We can note, though, that other shrewd guesses also predict the observed correlations tolerably well. For example, a guess of .7056 for C_1 and of 1 for C_2 would predict perfectly the parent-child correlation of .489. Those guesses, unlike Burt's and Howard's, assert a total *absence* of dominance, and a considerable effect of environment. The new guesses do not do quite so well with the sib correlation, for which they predict a value of .449. The Burt and Howard guesses, on the other hand, would have fared rather poorly if they had been used in conjunction with Jensen's .60 estimate of assortative mating. They would then have predicted correlations of .570 for parent-child, and .568 for sibs.

We will not get far with this guessing game, and as Burt and Howard observe, it is "more satisfactory" to obtain "*empirical* estimates for C_1 and C_2 deduced directly from the paternal and fraternal correlations actually observed." That is done in the following way. First, with the aid of the empirical correlation for assortative mating, the value of C_1C_2 is deduced from the formula for the parent-child correlation, using the *observed value* of the parent-child correlation. Then, in a similar manner, the value for C_1C_2 is placed into the formula for the sib correlation, which is solved for C_1. We then, of course, can also calculate the value of C_2. This means that the values we obtain for C_1 and C_2 will depend critically on quite minor fluctuations in the *empirical* values that we use for the two critical kinship correlations. The process is illustrated by Table 8, which gives the estimates of C_1 and C_2 that would be derived from various sets of entirely plausible empirical kinship correlations. The estimates of C_1 and C_2 are given for each set of observed correlations, first assuming Burt's .386 value for assortative mating and then assuming Jensen's .60 value. The value of C_1, it will be recalled, cannot in theory exceed 1, and the value of C_2 must in theory fall between .5 and 1.

The table makes clear that the model can successfully accommodate a limited set of empirical correlations which are close to .50. The mechanisms that are postulated to account for the data, however, differ vastly. For example, if the parent–child correlation is found to be .52, and the sib correlation .48, Burt and Howard would "explain" these data by postulating a total absence of dominance together with a substantial effect of environment. But if the parent–child correlation is found to be .48, and the sib correlation .52, Burt and Howard would now assume a very large degree of dominance, and no effect of environment. The reciprocal relation between C_1 and C_2 means that, if the empirical sib correlation is only a trifle larger than the empirical parent–child correlation, the model will assert that environment has virtually no effect. To be able to assert that, it will conveniently postulate a large amount of dominance. When the parent–child

TABLE 8

Empirical Estimates of Environmental and Dominance Parameters, Given Certain Sets of Observed Parent-Child and Sib Correlations

Parent-child correlation	Sib-sib correlation	Assortative mating = .386		Assortative mating = .60	
		Environment (C_1)	Dominance (C_2)	Environment (C_1)	Dominance (C_2)
.54	.46	.59	1.31	.62	1.09
.53	.47	.66	1.16	.69	.96
.52	.48	.73	1.02	.76	.85
.51	.49	.81	.91	.83	.76
.50	.50	.88	.82	.91	.69
.49	.51	.95	.75	.98	.63
.48	.52	1.02	.68	1.05	.57
.47	.53	1.09	.62	1.12	.53
.46	.54	1.16	.57	1.19	.48

correlation is found to be a little larger than the sib correlation, the postulate of dominance is abandoned *in toto,* and environment is allowed some role.

What we have so far seen is that the model, as it was designed to do, will accommodate empirical parent–child and sib correlations close to .50. The reciprocal values it assigns to environment and dominance will be heavily influenced by minor perturbations in those two empirical correlations. The material reviewed in the first part of this chapter indicates that we do not in fact know whether one or the other of these two correlations is a little larger. That is to say, the model cannot realistically tell us anything about the relative weights of dominance and environment. The weights we get will depend on the precise empirical values of the parent–child and sib correlations that we happen to use in estimating C_1 and C_2. The model does not *predict* the parent-child and sib correlations; instead it uses those two correlations to estimate C_1 and C_2. What then is the use of the model? Theoretically — in the happy event that the estimates of C_1 and C_2 are permissible — they can be checked by using them to predict correlations for still other categories of kinship. The goodness-of-fit of the C_1 and C_2 estimates could thus in principle be tested. There are, however, problems.

First, for relatives in a direct line of descent, it literally makes no difference what the separate values of C_1 and C_2 are estimated to be. That is so because the formulas for these correlations always involve the product of C_1 and C_2, and never either term in isolation. Thus, the prediction for grandparent-grandchild depends only upon the observed parent-child and assortative mating correlations. With an observed parent-child correlation of .50, assortative mating of .386 predicts a grandparent-grandchild correlation of .320. The prediction if assortative mating is .60 is .358. The two predictions are very similar, and there are no data with which to test them except for Burt's "assessments." The model at this point has no perceptible advantage over an environmental view which simply asserts that, with decreasingly common environments, the correlations between relatives will become lower.

For collateral relatives, it is necessary to estimate C_1 and C_2 separately. The formulas for remote collaterals, however, involve increasingly higher powers of decimal quantities. Thus in practice the predictions are very insensitive to gross changes in the estimates of C_1 and C_2. We now assume parent-child and sib correlations of .50, and inquire what correlation the model predicts for first cousins. With assortative mating of .386, the prediction is .192. With assortative mating of .60, the correlation predicted is .205. The predictions are in practice indistinguishable, and the actual data on first cousins are very scanty and contradictory. The same basic prediction for first cousins may be made on the basis of very dissimilar estimates of the amount of dominance (C_2). For example, if we now fix $r_{po} = .50$, and $M = .60$, an observed sib correlation of .523 would mean that $C_1 = 1$, and $C_2 = .63$. These parameter estimates would be completely reversed if the observed sib correlation were .43. The model would then tell us that $C_1 = .63$, and $C_2 = 1$. The two examples imply (*a*) no effect of environment (coupled with very substantial dominance), or (*b*) a very substantial effect of environment (coupled with the total absence of dominance). These very different assumed mechanisms do not perceptibly affect the model's predictions of the correlation to be observed between cousins. They are .203 in the first example and .205 in the second. The appeal to a hypothetical mechanism of dominance is either made or not made, exclusively on the basis of the values that happen to be chosen as empirical estimates of r_{po} and r_{oo} (and, of course, of M). When predicting correlations for more remote kinship categories, it makes no real difference whether or not the model postulates dominance. The model in practice predicts nothing much more testable than that the correlations should diminish as the degree of relationship diminishes. The environmentalist can predict this just as well by postulating that the communality of environment diminishes for more remote relatives. There is nothing more hypothetical about that—indeed, a good deal less—than about postulating dominance. The caliber of actual I.Q. data is such that the apparent numerical precision of the genetic model's predictions is specious. That, of course, is not a comment about the model's mathematical elegance.

The elegance of the model—or perhaps its incomprehensible mathematical formulas—appears to have dazzled Professor Herrnstein. The Burt theoretical values were said by him to provide "the correlations that would be expected if I.Q. were entirely genetic and transmitted according to certain plausible assumptions."[56] The details were not fully spelled out: "If intelligence were purely genetic, the I.Q.'s of second cousins would correlate by .14 and that of first cousins by .18 (the reasons for those peculiar percentages are well beyond the scope of this discussion, so they are offered without proof)."

Professor Herrnstein does not denigrate what he describes as "highly quantitative" work, but he fails to explicate it adequately for his readers. The theoretical correlations published by Burt not only assume a hypothetical innate intelligence, but also a specific quantitative effect of environment (C_1) on the adjusted assessments employed by the model. The magnitude of that effect cannot be estimated without simultaneously influencing the estimate of genetic dominance (C_2). Thus the model does not and cannot predict "pure" effects of the genes, derived from a prior knowledge of genetic mechanisms. The "purely genetic" mechanisms are postulated on the basis of the same phenotypic correlations which they are said to predict. To eliminate environmental effects from Burt's model is to fix the value of C_1 at 1. That postulate, combined with Burt's guess of .75 for C_2 and Jensen's .60 for M, would predict a theoretical "purely genetic" correlation for first cousins of .29, not .18.

The quantitative details, however, seem not really to interest Professor Herrnstein. Thus, he indicates that "the predicted correlation between parent and child, by genes alone, is .49, whereas the actual correlation is .50 using the parents' adult I.Q.'s and .56 using the parents' childhood I.Q.'s—in either case too small a difference to quibble about." This minor quibble, however, is worth lingering over. Professor Herrnstein fails to inform his readers that the "obtained average correlation" of .56 between child's I.Q. and parent's childhood I.Q. is derived from a single study — Burt's, using adjusted assessments. Professor Herrnstein similarly fails to inform his readers that Burt's model does not "predict" the parent-child correlation, but uses it as a starting point from which to estimate C_1 and C_2. This last point poses an interesting paradox. To estimate C_1 and C_2, and then to predict the more remote kinship correlations, should Burt use the .56 correlation he found between parent-as-child and child, or the .49 correlation he found between parent-as-adult and child? Will the arbitrary choice of one of these two empirical correlations make a difference, or is this merely a quibble?

The empirical correlation in fact used by Burt to generate his 1966 theoretical values was the .492 for parent-as-adult and child. This was used in conjunction with empirical correlations of .379 for husband and wife and .531 for siblings.[57] Though Burt does not mention this fact, these correlations produce a C_1 of 1.02 and a C_2 of .70. These estimates inform us that 31% of I.Q. variance in the population is attributable to dominance, and that the broad heritability of I.Q. is 102.4%. The environment accounts for an impossible -2.4% of I.Q. variance. The results would have been rather different if Burt had used the .56 correlation between parent-as-child and child. Then C_1 would be .81, and C_2 would be 1.00. These estimates would mean that there is *no* dominance variance. The broad heritability of I.Q. is now estimated as 81.2%, with environment accounting for 18.8%. These two very different outcomes, as we might expect, have relatively minor effects on predicted correlations for more remote kinship categories. For example, use of the parent-as-child correlation would change Burt's prediction for grandparent-grandchild from .31 to .37. The prediction for first cousins would change from .18 to .23.

The reprinting by Jensen and Herrnstein, without explanation, of Burt's "theoretical values" implies to the reader that the theoretical values spring full-blown out of iron genetic laws. That is emphatically not the case. The theoretical values are themselves derived from the observed data, and they will vary, depending upon what part of whose data is employed. The Burt model does not in fact predict parent-child or sib correlations, and its predictions for more remote kinships are relatively insensitive to grossly different assumptions about the hypothesized genetic mechanisms. There are no adequate data with which to test these predictions. To speak about the "genes alone" and to cite "incomprehensible mathematical formulas" while chastising those who denigrate the deeper mysteries of quantitative methods does the reader no service. The appeal "without proof" to mathematics seems more threatening to the integrity of science than is any assault by an uninformed polemicist. The moral here is repetitious, but important. We see again that the aura of numbers surrounding much work on I.Q. heritability is in large measure specious.

MZ AND DZ TWINS

We shall conclude our discussion of kinship correlations with an examination of a very special type of kinship data. The argument has been made that a comparison of the correlations shown by MZ and same-sexed DZ twins can in itself demonstrate the heritability of a trait and can provide an estimate of the degree of heritability. The empirical and theoretical approaches are exemplified by the work of Vandenberg, particularly in the often cited Michigan and Louisville twin studies.[58,59] The basic procedure is to give batteries of mental tests to samples of MZ and like-sexed DZ twins. The emphasis is not upon correlations as such, but upon analysis of variance. For each test, the score variance of each twin sample is partitioned into two components. There is "between-family" variance, derived from the scatter of twin-pair means, and there is "within-family" variance, derived from the distribution of co-twin difference scores. The focus of analysis is the within-family variance. That variance, in the case of MZ twins, must be exclusively nongenetic in origin. With DZ twins, who differ genetically, the within-family variance is said to consist of the environmental component *plus* a genetic component. Thus, *on the assumption that within-family environmental variance is the same for MZ and DZ twins,* a genetic model predicts that the within-family I.Q. variance should be larger for DZs than for MZs. This prediction can be tested appropriately by the familiar F test. The detection of a significant F, granted the assumption made above, would indicate that the heritability of I.Q. is significantly different from zero,[60] but it would not provide an estimate of the degree of heritability.

The Vandenberg papers provide dozens of such significant F ratios, purporting to indicate significant heritability for many different "mental abilities." The actual variances and the intraclass correlations of the twins are seldom reported, but the papers do provide, in addition to F ratios, such highly derived statistics as phi coefficients, varimax rotations, discriminant functions, canonical variances, and the roots and vectors of Gramian matrices. The entire mathematical apparatus hinges upon a critical assumption: that the environmentally produced within-family variance is equal for the MZ and DZ samples. Thus, if environmental within-family variance is in fact larger for DZs than for MZs, the F ratio will reflect this fact and will not be an indicator of heritability. This boils down to the simple proposition that, granted that MZs resemble one another more in I.Q. than do DZs, this may reflect nothing more than that MZs have had more similar environments.

There are in fact many nongenetic factors that might lead to different within-family environmental variances in samples of MZ and DZ families. The less obvious ones, which we consider first, involve problems of biased sampling. The F ratio cannot serve as an indicator of heritability in the population unless both the MZ and DZ samples are representative of the population. This is not always the case, as an analysis of the samples in Vandenberg's own Michigan Twin Study will make clear.[61] The samples consisted of 45 MZ pairs and 37 like-sexed DZ pairs between the ages of 12 and 20. The raw data make it possible to calculate that, for the pooled sample of 82 pairs, there was a significant correlation of $-.33$ between the twins' age and their mothers' education. There are many possible interpretations of this peculiar fact, but all of them indicate a biased sampling procedure. There is good reason to suppose that test scores vary both with child's age and with mother's education, and the confounding of these variables in Vandenberg's study presents extraordinary complexities for interpretation.

The situation, however, is much worse than so far indicated. For the MZ sample, the correlation between twins' age and mothers' education was a robust $-.51$. For the DZ sample, it was only $-.16$. Those two correlations differ significantly. The older MZ twins very much tended to come from poorly educated families, but that was not the case among DZ twins. There are many ways in which this fact might invalidate Vandenberg's use of the F ratio. For example, suppose that twins tend to become less alike as they grow older, and suppose as well that this tendency is less marked in poorly educated, "deprived" households. These plausible assumptions would produce a significant F ratio, misinterpreted as demonstrating "heritability." The taint of biased sampling will not be removed by varimax rotations of the data.

There is in fact evidence to suggest that random samples of MZ and DZ twins *cannot* each be representative of the population. For example, Smith, studying twins in 1965, found that his DZ families came from a significantly lower socioeconomic status than did his MZ families.[62] That, Smith indicated, is probably a consequence of the known fact that DZ twins are much more likely to be born to older mothers, who have had several pregnancies. The probability of having MZ twins, on the other hand, does not vary with maternal age. These facts mean that the relative frequencies of the two types of twins in different social classes is related to differential age-fertility characteristics of the classes. Thus, in the unlikely event that a mental tester secured truly random samples of all available MZs and DZs, the DZ sample *should* have a lower mean social status. This is a further complication for the interpretation of Vandenberg's F ratio.

The various sampling problems, however, pale into relative insignificance compared to a fundamental objection to be made to the use of the F test as an indicator of heritability. The essential assumption that relevant environmental differences impinging upon MZ pairs and DZ pairs are equal is, on its face, absurd. There is much evidence to demonstrate that in fact the environmental differences to which MZs and DZs are exposed are not equal. For example, Wilson in 1934, reported that 43% of 70 MZ pairs had never spent a day apart, compared to 26% of 69 like-sexed DZ pairs.[63] For the same two groups, 76% of MZs indicated that they had the same friends, compared to 52% of DZs. The Smith study, with slightly larger groups, also indicated that MZs are much more likely than DZs to have the same friends, 58 compared to 33%. Forty percent of Smith's MZs reported that they studied together, compared to only 15% of like-sexed DZs! There is some possibility that studying together might tend to produce similar test scores. The fact is clear that MZs experience much more similar environments than do DZs, and this fact alone could easily be responsible for the greater I.Q. similarity of MZs.

The same fact was demonstrated in a very large national like-sexed twin study by Nichols,[64] but an unnoted aspect of Nichols' data introduces a new variation with considerable theoretical import. The twins were asked to indicate, on a questionnaire, "all [lengthy] periods of separation and [major] differences in experiences and illnesses." Their answers led Nichols to classify 18% of MZs, and 25% of DZs, as differing appreciably in "similarity of experience" ($p < .01$). The more interesting fact, however, points toward a basic distinction to be made between male DZs and female DZs. The study involved 209 male and 273 female DZ pairs. Thirty-three percent of the male DZs, but only 20% of the female DZs, were classified as differing in experience ($p < .01$). This finding, ignored by Nichols, strongly indicates that male DZs have less similar environments than do female DZs. This is of course consistent with the fact that, at least until very recently, girls led more "protected" lives, more restricted to a relatively narrow range of environments.

The idea that male DZs have less similar environments than female DZs is further supported by a sampling bias evident in many twin studies that sample schools. The population of like-sexed twins must contain about half male and half female pairs. Further, within each sex, the proportion of twins who are DZs must be identical. The studies, however, tend to find a disproportionately small number of male DZs. This effect is very prominent in Schoenfeldt's national high school sample.[65] This supposedly representative sample found that only 26% of 203 like-sexed male pairs were DZ, compared to 36% of 290 female pairs ($p < .05$). The Vandenberg Louisville Twin Study found only 33% of 104 same-sexed male pairs to be DZ, compared to 49% of 132 female pairs ($p < .02$).[66] There is a tendency in the same direction, though not statistically significant, in each of the four remaining school samples for which I have found the requisite data — Vandenberg's Michigan study,[67] and studies by Snider,[68] Nichols,[69] and Stocks and Karn.[70] The studies tend to locate fewer DZ pairs in general (and fewer males in general) than would be expected on the basis of population statistics, but it is clearly male DZs who are most emphatically underrepresented. The usual explanation offered for the shortage of DZ twins *in general* is that, since they are genetically more different than MZs, they are more likely to be in different grades, or schools, less likely to be noticed and identified as twins, etc. This plausible explanation, however, does not in any obvious way suggest that male DZs should be more difficult to locate than female DZs. The male and female DZ pairs are equally similar genetically, so the suggestion is again strong that male DZs must experience more dissimilar environments. Further, if one accepts the traditional explanation for the shortage of DZ twins in general in school samples, it would follow that those male DZs who are located are more similar than male DZs in general, and that this source of bias is *less* strong for the sample of female DZs.

These observations suggest an obvious test of the environmental interpretation of I.Q. resemblances between twins. We have two different types of evidence which indicate that male DZs have more dissimilar environments than female DZs. The critical question is whether male DZs have more dissimilar I.Q.'s than female DZs. We should note that if they do, two consequences follow. First, our assumption that systematic within-family environmental differences in fact differentially affect the I.Q. resemblances of the various twin categories will be upheld. This is not a small matter since, second, it is precisely the unrealistic assumption that they do not which allows the hereditarian to interpret differences between MZs and DZs as indicating "heritability."

To answer our critical question, Vandenberg's F ratio provides the most appropriate test. We expect, under an environmentalist hypothesis, the within-pair I.Q. variances of male DZs to be significantly larger than that of female DZs. The hereditarian—since each type of twin pair has the same genetic similarity—must expect these two variances to be equal.[71] There are, unfortunately, few studies that present the actual within-pair variances for male and female DZ twins. The usual procedure is to pool the data for both sexes, and even when results are given separately for each sex the data are generally summarized in terms of intraclass correlations. The Vandenberg studies present only the F ratio for the two sexes pooled. Three studies, however, present raw data from which the critical within-pair variances can be calculated separately for each sex; I have found no others.

The raw data for three tests administered in the Michigan Twin Study have been published by Clark, Vandenberg, and Proctor.[72] There are data for 14 male and 23 female DZ pairs. For the Primary Mental Abilities Verbal test, which Vandenberg reported to be significantly heritable, male DZs had a significantly greater within-pair variance, $F = 3.25$. For the PMA Reasoning test and for Raven's Progressive Matrices, for which Vandenberg did not find a significant heritability, the male DZs had larger within-pair variances, but not significantly ($F = 2.27$, $F = 1.41$). The Snider study gave the Iowa Basic Skills Vocabulary Test to 80 male DZ pairs and 114 female DZ pairs. The male DZs had a significantly higher within-pair variance, $F = 1.41$. The Stocks and Karn study gave the Stanford-Binet test to 12 male and 15 female DZ pairs. The males again had a significantly higher within-pair variance, $F = 6.61$. For 28 opposite-sexed DZ pairs included in the Stocks and Karn study the within-pair variance was in turn significantly larger than that of even the male DZs, $F = 2.76$.

The quaint notion of a constant "within-family environmental variance" acting equally on all categories of twin pairs seems clearly untenable. Within each of the three studies where calculation was possible, male DZs had significantly larger within-pair I.Q. variance than did female DZs. This difference between the sexes, it should be noted, seems specific to DZs. Within the same three studies there is no indication at all that male and female MZs have different within-pair variances. The dissimilarity of male DZs is uniquely large, just as male DZs are uniquely underrepresented in twin samples. The likelihood seems high that the most dissimilar male DZs are precisely those who escape the sampling net, so existing samples probably underestimate the magnitude of this environmental effect. The evidence makes clear that the practice of presenting twin data based on the pooling of sexes will in some instances be extremely misleading. What is true for male MZ-DZ comparisons may be false for female MZ-DZ comparisons. The situation is exacerbated by the fact that in several studies of same-sexed twins the zygosity and sex classifications are far from orthogonal.

We have seen strong evidence that systematic differences in within-family environmental variance make male DZs more dissimilar in I.Q. than female DZs. This is clearly not a genetic effect. We know that, within each sex, MZs have more similar environments than do DZs. We thus expect MZs to be more alike in I.Q. than DZs, though it should be easier to demonstrate this difference for males than for females. There is no reason to conclude that MZ-DZ differences in I.Q. resemblance, when found, have a genetic basis. The genetic theorist is left in the untenable position of asserting that the male DZ within-pair variance is large relative to female DZs, because of environmental reasons — but large relative to male MZs because of genetic reasons! The parsimonious resolution of this absurdity is simply to reject the idea that MZ-DZ differences in I.Q. have any genetic component.

There is of course one sense in which all differences in I.Q. resemblance among twin categories have a genetic basis. The fact that MZ twins experience very similar environments is a consequence of their genetic identity. The parents and people who deal with MZs respond to their genetically determined physical resemblances, as do the twins themselves. Thus it is true, but misleading, to state that MZ twins have very similar I.Q.'s "because" they have identical genes. The identical genes led to similar environments, which in turn produced similar I.Q.'s. To proceed from this observation to the assertion that genes determine individual differences in I.Q. in the population is a fallacy. The genes in this view do not determine what level of I.Q. a pair of MZs will attain. They merely make it likely that the twins will have similar environments, and thus similar I.Q.'s.

The fallacy can be illustrated by an analogy. There was a sense in which black slavery had a clear genetic basis. The black man's skin color is determined by his genes, and there was a strong tendency for slavery to run in black families. The black man was a slave "because" of his genetically determined skin color. We do not conclude from these observations that the black man carries slavery genes. We recognize that his genetically determined physical appearance profoundly affected the way in which people in his environment reacted to him. The physical resemblance of MZs similarly "causes" their I.Q. resemblance. We cannot conclude from twin studies that there are "I.Q. genes," although we recognize that in an indirect sense genes are involved in determining twin I.Q. resemblance.

The preceding analysis of male and female DZs, it should be noted, was appropriately based on an examination of the F ratio between within-pair variances. The resemblance between twins can also be expressed in terms of the intraclass correlation, but comparing correlations will not provide a sensitive test of the hypothesis of different within-pair variances. That is because the correlation, unlike the F ratio, is sensitive to between-family as well as within-family variance. The same within-family variance will produce a high correlation if between-family variance happens to be high, and a low correlation if between-family variance happens to be low. The differences between families in social class, intellectual environment, etc., will obviously produce considerable sampling fluctuation in between-family variances for MZs and DZs. The comparison of intraclass correlations may thus sometimes lead to conclusions very different from those obtained by comparing within-family variances. For example, Vandenberg has published F ratios for quite large samples of MZ and same-sexed DZ twins.[73] For the Object Aperture test of spatial ability, given to 130 white MZ and 90 white DZ pairs, the F ratio was a trivial 1.11. There is thus no evidence for a heritable factor in this test. The intraclass correlations for the *same* twins on the same test were published by Osborne and Gregor.[74] The correlation for MZs was .57, and for DZs .27. These two correlations differ significantly ($p < .005$), suggesting a very strong "heritability." For 31 black MZ and 14 black DZ pairs given the Newcastle Spatial Test, Vandenberg reported an F ratio of .52. The MZs in fact had a larger within-pair variance, almost significantly so. For the same twin pairs on the same test, Osborne and Gregor reported correlations of .86 for MZs and .59 for DZs. These two correlations differ significantly ($p < .05$). The correlations suggest "heritability," but the within-pair variances clearly do not. The most sensitive procedure for testing the genetic model's critical postulate of equal within-family environmental variance for all twin categories is obviously one that removes as many irrelevant sources of variation as possible. That is what the F test does, and by all the available data the genetic model fails.

To most theorists, of course, the point of twin I.Q. studies is not to test the validity of a genetic model but rather — taking such a model for granted — to estimate the heritability (h^2) of I.Q. The heritability of a trait, it will be recalled, is defined as the proportion of the phenotypic variance attributable to genetic factors. To estimate the *degree* of heritability, which in theory can range from zero to 100%, it is necessary to move beyond the simple F test to procedures that simultaneously take account of between-family and within-family variances. There are several procedures that have been proposed for estimating heritability from twin data, most of which involve the comparison of intraclass correlations. The indices in common use, as Professor Jensen has pointed out, have the very melancholy property of not being monotonically related to each other.[75] The Jensen paper presents a fully explicated rationale for estimating heritability on the basis of MZ and DZ correlations, and we shall now follow him.

The procedure involves a number of assumptions. First, the MZ and DZ twins must each be representative samples, in terms of their genes and environments, of the population for which h^2 is to be estimated. Second, one must know what the genetic correlation is both for MZs and for DZs. For MZs it is clearly 1.00, but for DZs (as for sibs) it is affected by assortative mating and dominance. The preferred estimate suggested by Jensen is .55. Third, one must make the familiar and false assumption that within-family environmental variance is the same for MZs and DZs.

Once those assumptions are made, the mathematics boils down to a few very simple arithmetical operations. The total I.Q. variance in a study of MZ and same-sexed DZ twins can now in theory be divided into three components. The percentage of variance attributable to the genes (h^2) is calculated by subtracting the DZ correlation from the MZ correlation, and then dividing by ($1.00 - .55$). With h^2 thus calculated, the remaining variance is environmental, but it in turn can be divided into two components. The within-family environmental variance is derived by subtracting the MZ correlation from 1.00. This follows since the failure of MZs to be perfectly correlated in I.Q. can reflect nothing but the hypothesized within-family environmental variance (plus measurement error). Finally, subtracting the two already derived components from 1.00 is said to give the proportion of variance attributable to between-family environmental differences. This model assumes that the three estimated components, when summed, will not be larger than 1.00, but it is possible that, to the embarrassment of the model, this illogical outcome can occur. When it does occur, it will be attributed either to sampling fluctuation or to an overestimate of the true genetic correlation between DZs.

Professor Jensen, in the paper that presents this simple linear model, surveyed "all the major twin studies using intelligence tests" in order to provide ten specimen estimates of h^2 calculated in the manner just described. The heritability estimates presented by Jensen showed some—but not too much—variation from study to study. With the assumption of a DZ genetic correlation of .55, the heritability estimates in "all the major twin studies" ranged from 47 to 91%. This relatively modest variation is not embarrassing to a genetic theorist since, as Jensen indicated, "heritability estimates are specific both to the population from which the twin samples are drawn and to the particular test used for measuring intelligence." The apparently impressive fact is that all the major twin studies agree in yielding very substantial estimates of I.Q. heritability.

The apparent agreement, however, depends in part upon the fact that the ten estimates tabled by Jensen include several repetitions in which the estimates are based upon measurements of the very same twins. The Stanford-Binet I.Q.'s reported by Holzinger in 1929 are used to provide one estimate, and the Stanford-Binet I.Q.'s of the *same* twins reported by Newman, Freeman, and Holzinger in 1937 are used to provide another estimate. The Otis I.Q.'s of the very same twins are used to provide still a third estimate! The Burt twins also provide two estimates—one said to be based on Stanford-Binet I.Q.'s, the other on "adjusted scores." The Shields study also provided Jensen with an h^2 estimate, based upon comparing 36 nonseparated MZ pairs to 7 DZ pairs, 4 of which had been separated. The Jensen summary of "major twin studies," on the other hand, omits a good number of studies that compare MZ and same-sexed DZ twins. The omitted studies used sample sizes comparable to the included studies, and there is no reason to suppose that they are less sound methodologically.

Perusal of some of the omitted studies is instructive. The Blewett study,[76] employing the PMA battery in England, is included by Jensen, who uses only the "composite" score to estimate heritability. The Vandenberg Michigan Twin Study used the same test battery on larger twin samples. The raw data for two of the PMA subtests, Verbal and Reasoning, have been published by Vandenberg.[77] The intraclass correlations can thus be calculated and compared to those published by Blewett. The Vandenberg correlations were calculated with sexes pooled within zygosity classification, to make them comparable to Blewett's and those of the other studies cited by Jensen. For the Verbal test, Vandenberg's MZs had a correlation of .90, compared to .75 for his DZs. The corresponding correlations for Blewett's twins were .73 and .15. The Jensen procedure yields a heritability estimate of 33% for Vandenberg's twins, compared to a nonsensical estimate of 129% for Blewett's twins. For the Reasoning test, Vandenberg's correlations were .81 and .72; Blewett's were .71 and .19. The heritability of reasoning is thus estimated as a modest 20% for Vandenberg, compared to a nonsensical 116% for Blewett. The Blewett paper provides correlations (.76 and .44) for a general "intelligence factor" extracted from the PMA battery by factor analysis. This yields a heritability estimate of 71%, which can be reasonably compared to Vandenberg's data for Raven's Progressive Matrices, also published in raw form. The Raven test is said to be very highly loaded on "g," the theoretical general intelligence factor. The Vandenberg twin correlations on Raven's test were .58 and .53, yielding a heritability estimate of only 11%.[78]

The Jensen summary also omits the Stocks and Karn study, which reported Stanford-Binet correlations of .84 for MZs and .87 for same-sexed DZs. These data yield an extraordinary, and nonsensical, heritability estimate of *minus* 7%. The omitted study by Churchill[79] contains WISC correlations of .93 and .24, which provide an equally extraordinary and nonsensical heritability estimate of 153%. Thus, for what we might call a "roughly representative" set of twin studies, heritability estimates of I.Q. range from minus 7 to plus 153%.[80] We begin to suspect that there is considerable imprecision involved in the estimation of I.Q. heritability. We have already seen that the model that underlies the estimation procedure is itself based on false assumptions.

There is still another difficulty that besets all twin studies, one we have not yet noted. The fact is that errors occur in the determination of zygosity, that is, in classifying a given twin pair as either MZ or DZ. There is no single criterion, or set of criteria, that can sort out zygosity without error. The presence of a single chorion at birth, if clearly demonstrated, is often accepted as proof that a given pair is MZ, but many MZ pairs have separate choria. When several blood groups are tested, discordance between a twin pair in any single blood group establishes that the pair is DZ; but concordance of all blood groups tested only establishes a probability (in the order of .90 or .95) that a pair is MZ. Thus an exclusive dependence on blood testing to establish zygosity will result in misclassifying some true DZs as MZs. To counteract this, many studies use blood testing to establish positive DZs, but then reclassify some twins who are concordant for all blood groups as DZs. This is done when, despite full blood concordance, pronounced physical differences exist between pair members. For example, in Vandenberg's Michigan Twin Study blood testing definitely established that 30 pairs were DZ. There were 52 pairs concordant for all tested blood groups, but fully 7 of these were classified as DZ because of pronounced physical differences. [81] There may of course have been some physically similar DZs, with concordant blood groups, who were misclassified as MZs. When a study does not use blood testing, the tendency to classify on the basis of physical similarity and dissimilarity will be given even freer rein.

The question is whether the undoubted errors in classification make any real difference. The argument has often been made that errors in classification can only *reduce* the apparent effect of heredity in twin studies. Thus Burt, who relied heavily on "impressionistic judgement" to establish zygosity, thought it "highly unlikely that any misclassifications have been made; but, if they have, their effect would be to reduce the differences between the correlations for monozygotic and dizygotic pairs." [82] The argument here is wholly circular, since it assumes that physical similarities between twins—zygosity aside—have no relation to I.Q. similarities. We can grant that, on average, true MZs have higher I.Q. correlations than do true DZs, but we suppose that that is a consequence of the fact that the great physical similarity of most MZs exposes them to highly similar environments. We now ask which twins in any given study are most likely to be misclassified, and the answer is obvious. Those true MZs who do not resemble one another physically are likely to be misclassified as DZs, and those true DZs who do resemble one another physically will be misclassified as MZs. The basis of classification—physical resemblance—is, under an environmental hypothesis, itself the "cause" of the I.Q. resemblances which the classification is supposed to demonstrate to be of genetic origin. Thus the misclassified true DZs could conceivably increase the observed I.Q. correlation for MZs, while the misclassified true MZs could be decreasing the observed I.Q. correlation for DZs. There is, however, no independent evidence for this possibility. We can never know which particular twin pairs have been misclassified, nor can the "impressionistic judgement" of physical similarity be readily quantified. These considerations do at least indicate how easily an unthinking postulation of the very genetic influence that is supposed to be *proved* by data analysis can lead one into logical error when attempting to unravel the enormous confounding of genetic and environmental variables in the real world. Further, it is clear that twin studies vary considerably in the precision with which zygosity determination has been made, and that this must constitute a further source of the variability in estimates of I.Q. heritability.

To sum up, our study of kinship correlations has revealed no evidence sufficient to reject the hypothesis of zero I.Q. heritability. The available data are at many critical points almost wholly unreliable. The correlation between separated siblings might be of particular interest since (under the false assumption of uncorrelated environments) its divergence from genetic expectation could be used to estimate heritability. The widely circulated assertion that the "median correlation" found in studies of separated sibs is .47 is, however, false. The two studies other than Burt's found much lower correlations, figures wholly consistent with zero heritability. The comparison of DZ and sib correlations is also theoretically relevant, but we have no very good estimate of the "true" I.Q. correlation for DZs. The published "medians" involve systematic biases that minimize this difference. When comparisons are made within the same study, the DZ correlation is perceptibly higher than that for sibs, with the exception of Burt's study. There is suggestive evidence that the singleton sibs of twins may resemble them much less than, in a genetic view, they should. The data for more remote kinship categories are very sparse and largely attributable to Burt's "assessments." There is thus no firm data base against which to assess genetic models that purport to predict the full range of kinship correlations. There is substantial evidence to suggest that the correlations for sibs and for parent-child are somewhere in the neighborhood of .50, but even at these points there is considerable variation from study to study. The genetic models thus have no basis on which to conclude whether or not dominance is present and cannot distinguish "dominance" from systematic environmental effects. The sib and parent-child correlations are in any event as consistent with an environmental as a genetic interpretation. The facts that twin correlations are high, and that MZs resemble one another more than DZs, are wholly consistent with the expectations of an environmental view. The data strongly suggest that male DZs display more within-pair I.Q. variance than do female DZs, and male DZs also report more dissimilar experiences than do female DZs. These facts undercut the theoretical basis for estimating I.Q. heritability from MZ and DZ correlations. The heritability estimates calculated from such data fluctuate wildly from study to study, and they include a theoretically absurd negative estimate, as well as theoretically absurd estimates larger than 100 percent. The orderliness attributed to median kinship correlations, and the cross-validating consistency said to characterize different methods of estimating heritability, are in part the product of systematic bias and in part wholly imaginary.

NOTES TO CHAPTER FOUR

1. *The Family-History Book*, ed. C. B. Davenport, Eugenics Record Office Bulletin No. 7 (Cold Springs Harbor, N.Y., 1912), p. 62.
2. L. Erlenmeyer-Kimling and L. F. Jarvik, "Genetics and Intelligence: A Review," *Science*, 142, (1963), 1478.
3. *Intelligence: Genetic and Environmental Influences*, ed. R. Cancro, (New York, Grune and Stratton, 1971), p. 185.

4. C. Burt, "The Genetic Determination of Differences in Intelligence: A Study of Monozygotic Twins Reared Together and Apart," *British Journal of Psychology*, 57, (1966), 151.

5. A. R. Jensen, "How Much Can We Boost IQ and Scholastic Achievement?", *Harvard Educational Review*, 39, (1969), 48.

6. R. J. Herrnstein, *"I.Q. in the Meritocracy"*, (Boston, Atlantic Monthly Press, 1973).

7. Erlenmeyer-Kimling and Jarvik, *Genetics*, p. 1478.

8. *Psychopathology of Mental Development*, ed. J. Zubin and G. A. Jervis, (New York, Grune and Stratton, 1967), p. 450.

9. E. L. Thorndike, "The causation of fraternal resemblance," *Journal of Genetic Psychology*, 64, (1944), 249 – 264.

10. F. N. Freeman, K. J. Holzinger, and B. C. Mitchell, "The Influence of Environment on the Intelligence, School Achievement, and Conduct of Foster Children," *Twenty-Seventh Yearbook of the National Society for the Study of Education, Part I,* (Bloomington, Ill., Public School Publishing Co., 1928).

11. C. Burt, "The Evidence for the Concept of Intelligence," *British Journal of Educational Psychology*, 25, (1955), 167.

12. The intraclass correlation, with a large number of cases, will be numerically virtually identical to the double-entry correlation, and with a smaller number of cases will approximate it. That is not so with respect to "age entry."

13. M. P. Honzik, "Developmental Studies of Parent-Child Resemblance in Intelligence," *Child Development*, 28, (1957), 215 – 228.

14. G. H. Hildreth, *The Resemblance of Siblings in Intelligence and Achievement*, (New York, Teachers College, Columbia University, 1925).

15. Burt, *Genetic Determination*, p. 151.

16. A. R. Jensen, "Kinship Correlations Reported by Sir Cyril Burt," *Behavior Genetics*, 4, (1974), 20.

17. A. R. Jensen, *Genetics and Education*, (New York, Harper and Row, 1972), p. 124.

18. C. Jencks, *Inequality: A Reassessment of the Effect of Family and Schooling in America*, (New York, Basic Books, 1972), p. 319.

19. R. Pintner, "The Mental Indices of Siblings," *Psychological Review*, 25, (1918), 252 – 255.

20. R. Pintner, G. Folano, and H. Freedman, "Educational Research and Statistics (Sibling Resemblances on Personality Traits)," *School and Society*, 49, (1939), 190 – 192.

21. H. D. Carter, "Family Resemblances in Verbal and Numerical Abilities," *Genetic Psychology Monographs*, 12, (1932), 1 – 104.

22. V. M. Sims, "The Influence of Blood Relationship and Common Environment on Measured Intelligence," *Journal of Educational Psychology*, 22, (1931), 56 – 65.

23. Burt, *Genetic Determination*, pp. 146 – 150.

24. L. Herrman and L. Hogben, "The Intellectual Resemblance of Twins," *Proceedings of the Royal Society of Edinburgh,* 53, (1933), 105 – 129.

25. L. Tabah and J. Sutter, "Le Niveau Intellectuel des Enfants d'une Même Famille," *Annals of Human Genetics,* 19, (1954), 120 – 150.

26. M. V. Matthews, D. A. Newlyn, and L. S. Penrose, "A Survey of Mental Ability in a Rural Community," *Sociological Review,* 29, (1937), 20 – 40.

27. R. Byrns and J. Healy, "The Intelligence of Twins," *Journal of Genetic Psychology,* 49, (1936), 474 – 478.

28. D. B. Blewett, "An Experimental Study of the Inheritance of Intelligence," *Journal of Mental Science,* 100, (1954), 922 – 933.

29. Burt, *Genetic Determination,* p. 150.

30. Jensen, *How Much,* p. 49.

31. Herrnstein, *I.Q.,* p. 169.

32. Cancro, *Intelligence,* p. 187.

33. S. N. Mehrota and J. Maxwell, "The Intelligence of Twins. A Comparative Study of Eleven-Year-Old Twins," *Population Studies,* 3, (1950), 295–302.

34. T. Husen, *Psychological Twin Research. I. A Methodological Study.* (Stockholm, Almqvist and Wiksell, 1959).

35. Husen, *Twin Research,* p. 46.

36. *Methods and Goals in Human Behavior Genetics,* ed. S. G. Vandenberg, (New York, Academic Press, 1965), p. 240.

37. H. H. Newman, F. N. Freeman, and K. J. Holzinger, *Twins: A Study of Heredity and Environment,* (Chicago, University of Chicago Press, 1937), p. 97.

38. J. Shields, *Monozygotic Twins Brought Up Apart and Brought Up Together,* (London, Oxford University Press, 1962), p. 253.

39. B. Snider, *A Comparative Study of Achievement Test Scores of Fraternal and Identical Twins and Siblings,* Unpublished doctoral dissertation, State University of Iowa, 1955, pp. 150 – 153.

40. P. Stocks and M. N. Karn, "A Biometric Investigation of Twins and Their Brothers and Sisters," *Annals of Eugenics,* 5, (1933), 1 – 55.

41. J. Partanen, K. Bruun, and T. Markkanen, *Inheritance of Drinking Behavior. A Study of Intelligence, Personality, and Use of Alcohol of Adult Twins.* (Helsinki, The Finnish Foundation for Alcohol Studies, 1966), p. 91.

42. *Genetic and Environmental Factors in Human Ability,* eds. J. E. Meade and A. S. Parke, (New York, Plenum Press, 1966), pp. 206 – 208.

43. Jensen, *How Much,* pp. 48 – 49.

44. J. L. Gray and P. Moshinsky, "Studies in Genetic Psychology: The Intellectual Resemblance of Collateral Relatives," *Proceedings of the Royal Society of Edinburgh,* 53, (1933), 188 – 207.

45. Ibid, p. 190.

46. E. Dexter, "On Family Resemblance Beyond the First Degree of Relation," *School and Society,* 19, (1924), 502.

47. Herrnstein, *I.Q.,* p. 168.

48. C. Burt, "Quantitative Genetics in Psychology," *British Journal of Mathematical and Statistical Psychology,* 24, (1971), p. 17.

49. C. Burt and M. Howard, "The Multifactorial Theory of Inheritance and its Application to Intelligence," *British Journal of Statistical Psychology,* 9, (1956), 95–131.

50. Burt, *Quantitative Genetics,* p. 18.

51. Jensen, *How Much,* p. 35.

52. Burt, *Quantitative Genetics,* p. 15.

53. Herrnstein, *I.Q.,* p. 109.

54. R. A. Fisher, "The Correlation Between Relatives on the Supposition of Mendelian Inheritance," *Transactions of the Royal Society of Edinburgh,* 52, (1918), 399–433.

55. When $C_1 = 1$, the "broad heritability" of I.Q. is 1.00. When, e.g., $C_1 = .75$, the broad heritability of I.Q. is .75. Note that C_1 can express the effect of nonsystematic, random environmental influences only.

56. Herrnstein, *I.Q.,* pp. 169–170.

57. These empirical correlations are given in Burt, *Quantitative Genetics,* p. 15. This later paper does not calculate "theoretical values" for various kinships, but instead uses the C_1, C_2, and M parameters to apportion I.Q. variance in the population into four additive components. In this later paper, Burt adopted a new method for estimating C_1. He simply took the "empirical" correlation between MZ twins reared apart (.874) as the estimate of C_1. Then C_2 was estimated by plugging the C_1 value into the formula for the parent-child correlation. The new method of estimating C_1, plus the use of parent-as-adult rather than parent-as-child, resulted in theoretically permissible estimates of the four variance components. The widely reprinted "theoretical values" for kinship correlations, however, were published in 1966 in Burt, *Genetic Determination.* That paper indicated clearly (p. 150) that the theoretical values were calculated by the formulas given in Burt and Howard, *Multifactorial,* pp. 115–116. The method of estimating C_1 has relatively little effect on predicted kinship correlations, but it can drastically affect the proportions of population variance assigned to dominance, and to environment.

58. H. E. Sutton, S. G. Vandenberg, and P. J. Clark, "The Hereditary Abilities Study: Selection of Twins, Diagnosis of Zygosity and Program of Measurements," *American Journal of Human Genetics,* 14, (1962), 52–63.

59. *Progress in Human Behavior Genetics,* ed. S. G. Vandenberg, (Baltimore, Johns Hopkins Press, 1968), pp. 153–204.

60. The assumption must also be made that genetic-environmental covariance is negligible. There is no within-family genetic variance in an MZ family, and thus no covariance. That of course is not true in DZ families. This presents no problem to theorists who arbitrarily consider the covariance as genetic rather than environmental.

61. Sutton et al., *Hereditary Abilities*, pp. 53–57.
62. Vandenberg, *Methods and Goals*, pp. 51–53.
63. P. T. Wilson, "A Study of Twins with Special Reference to Heredity as a Factor in Determining Differences in Environment," *Human Biology*, 6, (1934), 324–354.
64. R. C. Nichols, "The Inheritance of General and Specific Ability," *National Merit Scholarship Research Reports*, 1, (1965), p. 8.
65. L. F. Schoenfeldt, "Hereditary-Environmental Components of the Project Talent Two-Day Test Battery," *Proceedings of the 16th International Congress of Applied Psychology*, (Amsterdam, Swets and Zeitlinger, 1969), p. 746.
66. S. G. Vandenberg, "A Twin Study of Spatial Ability," *Multivariate Behavioral Research*, 1969, 4, p. 276.
67. Sutton et al., *Hereditary Abilities*, pp. 53–57.
68. Snider, *Comparative Study*, pp. 150–151.
69. Nichols, *General and Specific*, p. 13.
70. Stocks and Karn, *Biometric Investigation*, pp. 46–50.
71. Differences between male and female within-pair I.Q. variances might *ex post facto* be attributed to some form of sex-linked inheritance. There is, however, no substantial evidence for sex linkage with respect to I.Q. There is no evidence for male-female differences in the within-pair variances of male and female MZs, or of same-sexed male and female sib pairs.
72. P. Clark, S. Vandenberg, and C. Proctor, "On the Relationship of Scores on Certain Psychological Tests with a Number of Anthropometric Characters and Birth Order in Twins," *Human Biology*, 33, (1961), 167–170.
73. S. G. Vandenberg, "A Comparison of Heritability Estimates of U.S. Negro and White High School Students," *Acta Geneticae Medicae et Gemellologiae*, 19, (1970), 280–284.
74. R. T. Osborne and A. J. Gregor, "Racial Differences in Heritability Estimates for Tests of Spatial Ability," *Perceptual and Motor Skills*, 27, (1968), 735–739.
75. A. R. Jensen, "Estimation of the Limits of Heritability of Traits by Comparison of Monozygotic and Dizygotic Twins," *Proceedings of the National Academy of Science*, 58, (1967), 149–156.
76. Blewett, *Experimental Study*, p. 931.
77. Clark, Vandenberg, and Proctor, *Relationship of Scores*, pp. 167–170.
78. These heritability estimates make no correction for the unknown test reliabilities. The Jensen procedure routinely corrects for an assumed test reliability of .95, which differentially increases the MZ and DZ correlations, thus increasing the heritability estimate. This makes no real difference for the present analysis. The reported correlations would be slightly decreased by partialing out age effects, but again no real difference ensues for present purposes.

79. J. A. Churchill, "The Relationship between Intelligence and Birth Weight in Twins," *Neurology*, 15, (1965), pp. 343 – 344.
80. The possibility of "negative heritability" of some traits has been foreseen by Professor Jensen in a footnote on p. 296 of his *Genetics and Education*, (New York, Harper and Row, 1972): "one reasonable interpretation is that for the particular trait in question MZ twins take on complementary (rather than similar) roles to a greater degree than do DZ twins." That is, to safeguard against embarrassing outcomes, the *ad hoc* assumption is made that the environments of MZs may differ *more* than those of DZs. The *F* ratios for intelligence, on the other hand, are asserted to demonstrate heritability in the face of clear statistical evidence that highly relevant environmental differences are, in fact, greater for DZs.
81. Sutton et al., *Hereditary Abilities,* p. 59.
82. Burt, *Genetic Determination,* p. 142.

5
STUDIES OF ADOPTED CHILDREN

The elder girl is a feebleminded Nam, has had an illegiti-
mate child, and has since married the father. The younger
girl, b. 1888 in N. H., is of special interest, for, when
young, she was adopted and reared by a good family in B.
She could not advance at school, and is lazy and shiftless,
though chaste. When away in Vermont where she now
lives, married though childless, she dresses neatly; but
when in N. H. she reverts to old slack and slovenly ways;
such is the influence of an improved environment.

—Dr. A. H. Estabrook, 1912[1]

The practice of adoption seems to provide unique opportunities for the study of heritability. The adopted child, of course, grows up in a familial environment provided by his adoptive parents. To the degree that familial environment determines I.Q., the I.Q.'s of adopted children should reflect the environments of the homes in which they have been reared. The child, however, carries the genes of his biological parents. Thus, if I.Q. is largely genetically determined, the child's I.Q. should correlate with that of his biological parents. That would be so even though the child had never lived with, or even known, his true parents.

The hereditarian view very clearly predicts a correlation between the adopted child's I.Q. and that of his biological parent. The I.Q. is in this view an essentially biological trait, rather like eye color, though somewhat more susceptible to environmental influence. The parent's I.Q., like his eye color, was determined by his genes. The child's I.Q. and eye color were in turn determined by the genes

111

passed on by his parents. The environmentalist view, however, does not necessarily predict a correlation between the adopted child's I.Q. and the *I.Q.* of the adoptive parent. What it *does* predict is an effect of the home environment on the adopted child's I.Q.

This is not a minor quibble. The environmentalist must account, in nongenetic terms, for the I.Q correlation found between parent and child in *normal* families. This is simply done by assuming that, in a normal family, parental I.Q. is itself related to a number of environmental variables that affect the child's I.Q. That is, high I.Q. parents normally provide environments favorable to the development of a child's I.Q. There is no *a priori* guarantee that the relations between parental I.Q. and relevant features of the familial environment are the same in adoptive as in natural families. For example, low I.Q. parents who choose (and are allowed) to adopt children might conceivably provide excellent environments. What is required in principle is careful measurement of the relevant environmental variables in both adoptive and natural families. The I.Q.'s of children in both types of family should, in the environmentalist's view, be correlated with such measures. The degree to which the I.Q.'s of parent and child are correlated would depend on the relations between parental I.Q. and the environment. The existing studies of adopted children, unfortunately, provide virtually no evidence on this theoretically critical point.

Probably the most widely cited single result of such studies is the "fact" that the I.Q.'s of adopted children are significantly correlated with those of their biological mothers. The standard reference is a 1949 study by Skodak and Skeels.[2] The study presented I.Q. data for 63 adopted children and their biological mothers. The correlation was a robust .44 when the children were tested at an average age of about 13. The children had been placed in adoptive homes before they were 6 months of age. The correlation had literally been .00 when the same children were tested at an average age of about two, but became statistically significant when tests were given at the age of about four. The general pattern, as Honzik[3] later pointed out, is characteristic of parent-child I.Q. correlations in natural families. The behavior geneticist Vandenberg has asserted that this study "provides the strongest evidence possible for hereditary factors in intelligence."[4] Professor Herrnstein has suggested that there appears to be no plausible environmental way to explain these findings.[5]

Though data on the I.Q. correlation between adopted children and their true mothers are very rare, the Skodak and Skeels study does not stand alone. There has been at least one other study, by Snygg, which reported such data.[6] The Snygg study was in fact cited by Skodak and Skeels, but it has *not* been cited by subsequent discussants of the adopted child literature. The correlation between the I.Q.'s of 312 foster children and those of their true mothers was reported by Snygg to be a very modest .13. To make the Snygg data more comparable to that of Skodak and Skeels, we can note that for 70 children tested at the age of "5 years or more" the correlation was a nonsignificant .12. The Snygg study, like that of

Skodak and Skeels, employed the Stanford-Binet test. There is no obvious reason to assume that one or the other reported correlation is a more valid estimate of the genetic determination of I.Q.

The Snygg discussion pointed explicitly to a complexity inherent in all studies of adopted children: "At the time of the last test many of these older children were living in adoptive homes in the selection of which their mothers' scores may have played some part." The possibility of *selective placement* must always be considered carefully, because it is freighted with consequence for the interpretation of correlations involving adopted children. The demonstration of a correlation between the I.Q.'s of adopted children and of their biological parents by no means necessarily implicates genetic factors. The adopted children have not been delivered to their foster homes by storks. They have typically been placed there by adoption agencies, and such agencies attempt to "fit the child to the home." The agencies are keenly aware of the mental testers' assertion that I.Q. is heritable. They often strive to place a child with "good heredity" in a similarly "good" home. The agencies may have knowledge of the true mother's I.Q., and they almost always have knowledge of her socioeconomic and educational status. They invariably have, by law, detailed knowledge of the characteristics of would-be adoptive parents. Thus, if children of high I.Q. biological mothers are systematically placed into homes conducive to the development of high I.Q., such selective placement would guarantee the development of a *nongenetic* correlation between adopted child and biological mother. The Skodak and Skeels study provides data from which the magnitude of selective placement can be estimated; as we shall see, such data provide the plausible environmental way to interpret the Skodak and Skeels results.

THE FREEMAN, HOLZINGER, AND MITCHELL STUDY

There have been four major studies of adopted children, which have attempted to answer rather different questions. We shall review them in sequence. The first such study was reported in 1928 by Freeman, Holzinger, and Mitchell.[7] The study contains a plethora of interesting findings, but, like the work of Snygg, it has virtually disappeared from contemporary reference lists. The Stanford-Binet test was administered to a main group of 401 children living in foster homes, and the Otis intelligence test was administered to many foster parents. The environments of the foster homes were rated on a numerical scale, with scores ranging from a possible low of 6 to a possible high of 30. The home rating was the composite of six subratings: "material environment, evidences of culture, occupation of foster father, education of foster father, education of foster mother, and social activity of foster parents."

The main findings included such facts as the following. The I.Q.'s of 401 foster children were significantly correlated (.48) with the ratings of the foster homes. For smaller samples, the children's I.Q.'s were also correlated significantly with the I.Q.'s of the foster parents; .37 in the case of fathers, .28 in the case of mothers. The child's I.Q. was significantly correlated (.42) with the foster parents' education.

These results on the surface suggest a powerful role for environment. The correlations reported for foster children approximate those characteristically reported for normal children. The data, however, came under immediate criticism from Burks[8] and from Terman. Burks indicated that "the presence (about 8 percent of the total group) of negro children, who, of course, were placed in negro homes" constituted a degree of selective placement which might be sufficient to invalidate the results. This criticism may be in large measure responsible for the contemporary neglect of this study. The study's authors, however, "indebted to Professor Terman for this suggestion,"[9] recalculated the major correlations reported in their study *excluding* all black children. The correlations were slightly increased when the black children were omitted.

The idea of selective placement, it can be seen, is double-edged. The hereditarians, when confronted by evidence of a significant correlation between adopted children's I.Q.'s and their home environments, are at once alerted to the possibility. The correlation is said to be an artifact of the tendency to place genetically superior children in high-quality homes. There is some amusement in the fact that, when displaying correlations between adopted children and their *biological* parents, a distinguished hereditarian can conceive of no plausible environmental way to explain the findings.

There are in fact clear indications within the Freeman et al. report that, black children aside, selective placement did occur in their sample. The selective placement was sufficient to account, *under a hereditarian hypothesis,* for some fraction if not all of the reported correlations. We shall soon see, however, that there is also very clear evidence for selective placement in the study purported to provide the "strongest evidence possible" for heredity. The selective placement is sufficient, *under an environmental hypothesis,* to account for the data. The selective appeal to selective placement as a means of interpreting data can only be viewed as a reflection of the preconceptions and biases of investigators.

The Freeman et al. study contains a host of subsidiary findings, some of them of considerable interest. For example, for 125 pairs of separated siblings, reared in different foster homes, the I.Q. correlation was only .25. That is very much lower than the .50 reported for siblings reared in their parents' homes. The effect of different environments in attenuating the correlation between biological siblings was presumably limited by the fact that there were "very few cases in which the foster homes of a pair differed in any marked degree." The authors nevertheless divided the separated sib pairs into two halves: those reared in the most, and in the least, similar homes. The two correlations were, respectively, .30 and .19. This is suggestive evidence that, if sibs were to be reared in very different homes, the correlation might be .00. The authors also reported on 72 pairs of unrelated foster children reared in the same homes. For these children, the I.Q. correlation was a substantial .37.

The detailed analysis of the data suffered from a complication with which we are already familiar. For 484 children, there was a significant correlation ($-.38$) between age and I.Q. Perplexed by this phenomenon, the authors calculated the age-I.Q. correlation for the 905 children on whom the Stanford-Binet test had originally been "standardized." The correlation for the standardization sample was a significant $-.24$, and the authors pointed to arithmetical errors made by Terman in computing the norms for his standardization sample.

STUDIES BY BURKS AND BY LEAHY

The next two studies will be considered together, since they involved an identical design. The first study, by Burks,[10] was published in the same year, and in the same volume, as the Freeman et al. study. The second was published by Leahy in 1935.[11]

These studies were designed to allow comparisons between foster families and "matched groups" of natural families. The basic argument is as follows. Whatever relation exists between an adopted child and his adoptive home (or parents) is exclusively environmental in origin. The relation between a natural child and his parents (or home environment) will include all these environmental elements; but more importantly, it will *also* include the effects of shared genes. Therefore, under an hereditarian hypothesis, I.Q. correlations involving natural children should be very much larger than those involving adopted children. The ideal finding would be correlations close to zero for adopted children; but it is always possible that selective placement might spuriously inflate the correlations for adopted children. To the degree that I.Q. is not entirely heritable, there is in any event room for significant correlations in the adopted case. The only requirement is that any such correlations be significantly lower than those found in "matched" control (natural) families.

This logic should be examined very closely. The logic holds only if, *with respect to relevant environmental variables, the adoptive and natural families have been matched both for means and for variances.* There is an immediate problem concerning the identification of "relevant" environmental variables. We have a fair "global" conception of what constitutes a favorable environment for the development of I.Q., but the critical aspects of environment are by no means understood in detail. We must be content with the "matching" of families on only a few very rough indices which may reasonably be regarded as indicative of a good environment, such indices as parents' occupation, education, income, or I.Q. We have, as already indicated, no certainty that these indices reflect the environment of the very special class of foster homes in the same way that they reflect the relevant environment of natural homes.

These considerations aside, it is essential that for whatever environmental indices are employed, the two types of families be matched both for means and for variances. The rigorous selection process through which adoptive parents are filtered tends to result in a relatively homogeneous class of adoptive homes. This means, as subsequent data analysis will show, that when adoptive and natural families have equal means for a particular trait, the adoptive families will often have a significantly smaller variance. That in turn means, as a purely statistical consequence, that correlations of adoptive I.Q.'s—or of anything else—will be lower with such traits than in the case of natural families. To correct statistically for such restriction of range within adopted families involves assumptions that may be wholly untenable. Those assumptions are also involved in the case where the two types of families have equal variances for an environmental characteristic but have different means.

The occurrence of equal variances for a trait in the two types of homes means that a comparison of correlations will not be invalidated by the statistical artifact of restricted range. When the home environments differ in mean values, however, the comparison of correlations implicitly involves an assumption that would be made by no sensible environmentalist theory. That assumption is that equal increments of environmental "goodness" are equally effective in elevating I.Q. at all points along a dimension running from the poorest to the best homes.

The problem here can be illustrated by imagining a research project aimed at deciding whether Disease X is more genetically or more environmentally determined. The environmentalists have argued that the disease is a consequence of poor nutrition. The hereditarians, pointing to the fact that the disease tends to run in families, have argued that it is produced by a heritable predisposition. Two investigators study two different samples of children, using family income as a rough index of family nutritional status. There is a robust correlation between occurrence of the disease and family income in Sample A, but a much weaker correlation in Sample B. This is true despite the fact that the variance of family income is identical in the two samples. The difficulty is that the range of incomes in Sample A was $1–$7,000, and the range in Sample B was $7,001–$14,000. That is, the variance in Sample B was almost entirely within a range where nutrition is likely to be adequate for the prevention of Disease X. Thus, in a similar way, it is possible that the elevated mean environmental status of adoptive families attenuates the correlation between environmental variables and the adopted child's I.Q.

To put it in still another way, we suppose that environmental variables are linearly related to I.Q. development only within a limited range of values. We know that, on the average, children of people who have completed college have higher I.Q.'s than the children of grade-school dropouts. This causes us to state, accurately enough, that there is a correlation between years of parental education and child's I.Q. That does not necessarily mean that there will be any difference in I.Q. between the children of parents who have completed five years of post-graduate education and of those who have completed only one.

These considerations are not an exercise in idle abstraction. We shall repeatedly encounter, in reviewing the adopted child studies, instances of the adoptive families being significantly more favored with respect to theoretically relevant environmental variables than are the "control" natural families to which they are compared. This vitiates the theoretical significance of the comparison of correlation coefficients. That is not to say that, within each type of family, the correlations themselves are without interest. We shall only have to beware of simplistic interpretations.

When we now examine the Burks and Leahy studies, the major results are at first glance impressive testimony to the potency of heredity. The two studies each compared correlations obtained in a group of adoptive families to those obtained in a matched control group of natural families. Burks gave the Stanford-Binet test to both children and parents; Leahy gave the same test to children, and the Otis test to parents. The two studies each rated various aspects of the children's home environments. The correlations between control child's I.Q. and the I.Q. of its biological mother and father were, in the Burks study, .46 and .45. The correlations in the Leahy study were .51 with each natural parent. These are much larger than the correlations reported between adopted children and foster parents. The latter were reported as a mere .19 and .07 by Burks, and as .20 and .15 by Leahy. The Burks study utilized the "Whittier index" of home environment. That index correlated .42 with child's I.Q. in natural families, but only .21 in adoptive families. The results for a "culture index" of the homes were very similar in pattern. The Leahy study gave each home an "environmental status score." The score correlated .53 with child's I.Q. in natural families, but only .19 in adoptive families. The conclusion from all this has been reprinted in countless psychology textbooks: The prepotency of heredity is demonstrated by the fact that biological children resemble their parents to a much greater degree than do adopted children.

We shall have to examine these studies in greater detail before accepting the textbook conclusion. Particularly, we should be concerned with the way in which adoptive and control families were matched and with the success of that matching. Professor Jensen has written that "part of Burks' study consisted of a perfectly matched control group of parents rearing their own children,"[12] but caution may nevertheless be in order.

We might suppose that a "perfect" matching with respect to one environmental variable would pretty much preclude perfect matching with respect to very many others. The matching procedures in fact employed by Burks and by Leahy were virtually identical. The investigator began by locating a group of adopted children whose parents would cooperate. The volunteer adoptive families were then matched to control families on the basis of a very limited number of variables. These variables were: age and sex of the child, occupational category of the father, and "type of neighborhood." Further, in each study, Jewish, black, and south-European family stocks were excluded. The Burks study was limited to adopted children placed before 12 months of age; the Leahy study used a 6 months criterion. This matching procedure, it may be observed, does not constitute an extraordinarily rigorous control of environmental variables. The only environmental variables directly controlled were parent's occupation and neighborhood.

With respect even to these variables, the matching in the Burks study was not exactly "perfect." The minor deviations in occupational classification between the two groups were reasonably explained by Burks as "due to insufficient coordination between the three field workers when carrying out the matching process." There were, however, a number of much more significant differences between the two groups of families. The Burks data clearly indicate a number of differences that would have been anticipated by the use of common sense. The adoptive parents were significantly older than the control parents, and there were significantly fewer siblings in the adoptive than in the control homes. These were not trivial differences. Fifty-four percent of the adoptive mothers were 41 years old or more, compared to only 17% of the control mothers. The number of only children in control families was not indicated; no fewer than 63% of the adopted children were only children.

These differences are presumably the consequence of the fact that, normally, married people attempt to have their own children before adopting. The adoptive parents in the Burks study had been married an average of 8.7 years before applying for children. To an environmentalist, it does not seem implausible that the parent-child I.Q. correlation, or correlations between child I.Q. and measures of home environment, may be affected by such variables as parental age and presence or absence of sibs. The Whittier Home Scale employed by Burks as a measure of home environment included as a major component the number of rooms in the house. What was the theoretical basis on which number of rooms was assumed to be possibly relevant to I.Q. development, but not number of sibs?

There were other statistically significant differences in the Burks study between the two types of families. The mean income of the (smaller) adoptive families was more than one and one-half times as large as that of the control families. This was true despite the fact that families had been matched for occupation. The adoptive fathers were 5 years older than the control fathers, but it seems doubtful whether incomes were increasing 10% a year during the 1920's; in any event, the adopted children had been reared in markedly wealthier homes. The value and the size of the homes owned by adoptive families was very much greater than that of the homes owned by controls, and the proportion of homes owned (rather than rented) was also significantly greater. This was true despite the fact that the families had been matched for "type of neighborhood."

The type of adoptive home involved in the Burks study is clearly illustrated by a detailed examination of the data she presented for "Whittier Ratings of Homes." The data were presented in two forms—for the "standard scale" and for an "extended scale." The five components of the Whittier Scale were each rated on a scale ranging from one (poor) to five (good). For Necessities, Parental Conditions, and Parental Supervision, however, the standard scale was extended to a six-point scale. This was done because "the Whittier standard of 5 did not seem adequate for a number of our cases."

The Whittier scale for Necessities assigned a score of one for "Old ragged dirty clothes. Little food, very plain . . . basement of cheap tenement house. Hardly bare necessities. . . ." The standard scale maximum of five points was assigned to "Architect, well-to-do. . . . Table ware indicates abundant food. . . . Fine carpets, rugs and pictures. Modern conveniences. . . ." The extended scale maximum of six was given to homes "Conspicuously superior to the level receiving 5 points. Seldom given to any home. Denotes unusually luxurious living conditions."

The mean Necessities score on the standard scale was 4.7 (out of a possible maximum of 5) for 206 adoptive homes. For 104 control homes, the mean score was 4.6. These two means were not significantly different. Very clearly, the majority of the homes in this study were reasonably well-to-do. The standard deviations of the Necessities scores were also given; they were 0.4 for the adoptive homes and 0.6 for the control homes. From these numbers it can be calculated that *the variance in adoptive homes was significantly lower than in control homes.* The adoptive homes were closely bunched near the top of the Necessities scale. This fact alone could account for the failure to find strong correlations between I.Q. of adopted children and measures of home environment. The matching of adoptive and control homes seems to have been something less than "perfect." Further, since the I.Q.'s of adoptive and natural parents were reported to be essentially equal, it seems likely that the correlation between parental I.Q. and home environment may have been different in the two types of families.

For the "extended" Necessities scale (with a six-point maximum) the means for adoptive and control families were 4.9 and 4.7. These were not significantly different. The standard deviations were 0.6 and 0.7. Thus the variances on the extended scale did *not* differ significantly. This equality of variance, however, was purchased by extending the scale values to a point beyond which any conceivable environmental theory would maintain that there might be a relation between "Necessities" score and I.Q. Fine carpets and rugs seem as likely to be associated with I.Q.-developing environments as do "unusually luxurious living conditions." Though Burks reported that a score of six was "seldom given to any home," the data in fact indicate that approximately 20% of the adoptive, and 10% of the control homes, were luxurious enough to require the six-point rating.

We might, as earlier indicated, profit from a knowledge of the correlation between *parental* I.Q. and various environmental factors in adoptive homes. We have suggested that these correlations might differ substantially from those obtaining in normal homes. That would in turn mean, under an environmental hypothesis, that parent-child I.Q. correlations *should* differ in the two types of homes. Though Burks gives, in her Table 35, the requisite data for parental I.Q.'s in control homes, she unfortunately provides no analogous data for adoptive homes. That is the only time, in a paper containing 45 tables, when available comparative data for the two types of homes are not provided.

The Leahy report does not include so detailed a presentation of data as does Burks'. There are no data at all on such variables as parental age, number of sibs, and family finances, but it seems reasonable to assume that the same significant differences existed in this highly similar study. Further, in the Leahy study, the "environmental status score" did differ significantly for the two types of families. The Leahy environmental rating was a composite of "occupational status, education of parents, economic status, degree of social participation, cultural materials, and child training facilities in the home." The families had been precisely matched for parental occupation and education, so the superiority of the adoptive families obviously lay in the other variables. Within each of her five occupational categories, the environmental status score of adoptive homes exceeded that of controls. The effect can be computed to be statistically significant in four of the five cases. For the lowest occupational category, the t value, with 45 degrees of freedom, is 4.27. The adoptive environments provided by "slightly skilled workers and day laborers" were very clearly different from those provided by their "matched" counterparts in natural families. The environments of economically poor adoptive homes did not of course obtain so high a score as those provided by "professional" adoptive parents. But, insofar as the composite environmental status score constitutes a scale of measurement of *relevant* variables, it seems plausible to suppose that the working-class adoptive families were quite high on the scale, thus reducing the relevant variance within the adoptive families. The status score variance was in fact less for the 194 adoptive homes than for the equal number of control homes, but the difference fell short of statistical significance. The scores of each group, however, contain a large and equal component of variance attributable to occupation and education of parents. Were this component to be removed, it seems very probable that the F ratio between the remaining variances would be statistically significant. We can thus conclude that in the Leahy study the environments of adoptive homes were both better and less variable than those of control homes.

There were still other differences between the families in the Leahy study. From her own paper it can be calculated that the Stanford-Binet vocabulary score of adoptive parents was significantly higher than that of control parents. From data she later made available to Wallis,[13] it can be calculated that adoptive mothers had a significantly *lower* Otis intelligence score than did control mothers. This seems paradoxical, but it may be related to the very high probability that the adoptive mothers were older, and to the fact that vocabulary scores hold up better with age than do other components of I.Q. tests. This line of reasoning suggests that the very equality in Stanford-Binet I.Q.'s reported by Burks for her two types of parents may mask real differences in favor of the adoptive parents.

The relative lack of variance in the environments of adoptive homes might suggest to an environmentalist that the I.Q.'s of adoptive children should be less variable than the I.Q.'s of control children. That is precisely what was observed in the Leahy study. The mean I.Q. of the adopted children was only trivially higher—110.5 compared to 109.7. The standard deviations, however, were 12.5

and 15.4, a statistically significant difference in variance. This fact was noted by Leahy, who described it as "innate positive skewness in intelligence" among the adopted children. The I.Q. variances of adopted and control children did not differ significantly in the Burks study. Within the Burks study, however, the I.Q. variance for adopted children was inflated by the presence of a relatively large number of adopted children with *very* low I.Q.'s—some as low as 40 and 50, entirely outside the range of the control children in her or in Leahy's study. There are reasons to imagine that the Burks study, unlike Leahy's, may have included a number of organically damaged adopted children. The Burks study, but not Leahy's, included legitimate children who had been surrendered by, or taken away from, their natural parents. These children had also lived with their true parents for a longer period than had Leahy's children.

Perhaps the most interesting differences reported by Leahy involve comparisons not described by Burks. For Leahy's adoptive families, the correlation in Otis score (I.Q.) between father and mother was .57; within the natural families, the same correlation was only .41. Though Leahy did not comment on the fact, the difference between these two correlations is statistically significant. With respect to education, however, the correlation between father and mother in adoptive families was only .59; in natural families it was .71! This difference is again statistically significant. Within this study at least, the whole nexus of environmental variables theoretically related to child's I.Q. seems to differ systematically between the two types of families. To regard the two types of families as "matched" for relevant environmental variables seems at the least an unwarranted hyperbole. The suggestion is very strong that the selective processes that work to establish adoptive families result in environmental constellations atypical in a large number of ways. There is a distinct possibility that adoptive and natural families can *never* be appropriately matched. That would mean that the genetic hypothesis is in this instance untestable.

Though Leahy had information about the education of 96 *true* mothers of adopted children, she used these data only to demonstrate that selective placement in her study, though significant, was in her view modest. There was no report of the correlation between true mother's education and adopted child's I.Q. That is unfortunate, since much theoretical stress has been placed on the .32 correlation between these variables reported by Skodak and Skeels.

There are other problems with the Burks and Leahy data, which can be briefly summarized. The age-I.Q. confound clearly appears in the Leahy data, since she reported that "in these data, age and IQ for adopted correlated from −.17 to −.19, for controls from −.13 to −.18." These unspecified correlations were at least in some instances statistically significant. The wording of Leahy's sentence clearly implies that a negative age-I.Q. correlation was also present among parents, since the children had been given only a single I.Q. test. The only correlations published by Leahy had in fact been "partialled" for age, though there is no evidence that the age-I.Q. correlations were linear.

The Burks study is almost unique among studies of the period in failing to report a significant I.Q.-age correlation among children. For foster fathers, however, the age-I.Q. correlation was a significant −.23; for control fathers, it was a trivial −.03. The foster fathers, it will be recalled, were significantly older than the control fathers. For many I.Q. tests, as Burks noted, "there is a negative correlation between performance and chronological age after an age of approximately thirty," and any such correlation would obviously affect the foster more than the control group. But, since "partial correlation technique . . . did not affect the correlations beyond one point in the second decimal place . . . the factor of age was not considered in the subsequent correlations involving intelligence." The use of partial correlation technique when the data strongly imply nonlinearity seems especially ill-advised. The I.Q.'s of older parents appear to have been systematically underestimated, and this distortion was especially pronounced in the adoptive group.[14] That in turn distorts the cross-comparison of correlations.

The Burks study is further complicated by her use of the Stanford-Binet test with adults. The standardization of the test for adults by Terman in 1916 was performed on a sample consisting of "30 business men . . . 150 'migrating' unemployed men . . . 150 adolescent delinquents . . . and 50 high-school students. . . ."[15] The original scoring procedure allowed a maximum "mental age" of only 19.5 years, equivalent to an I.Q. of 122. The scoring procedure employed by Burks awarded "bonus points" to testees who successfully answered the most difficult test items. That made possible a maximum mental age of 21.5 years, equivalent to an I.Q. of 134. The procedure was necessary for "a few of the brightest adults." The amended scoring procedure still left the test too easy for some subjects. The maximum score of 21.5 years—possible only by answering every question correctly—was attained by 9% of the control fathers, but by less than 3% of the adoptive fathers. Those proportions differed significantly, still further distorting the comparison of correlations across adoptive and control groups.

The studies of adopted children seem also to share common sampling problems. Unskilled laborers made up only 2% of the adoptive fathers in both the Burks and Leahy studies, which is not difficult to understand. The sex bias in the sampling is not so simply interpreted. Females made up 59% of Burks' 214 adopted children, and 61% of Leahy's 194. The preponderance of female children was statistically significant in each case. This seems to approximate a Law of Adopted Child Studies. Though Freeman et al. provided no information about child's sex, precisely 60% of Skodak and Skeels' 100 adopted children were also females.

The conclusions arrived at by Burks and by Leahy may not be shared by all readers who are aware of the complexities of their data. With a quantitative bent of mind, Burks was able to conclude that "about 17 percent of the variability in intelligence is due to differences in home environment." The data led Leahy to a somewhat more extreme position: "Variation in IQ is accounted for by variation in home environment to the extent of not more than 4 per cent."

The design of the Burks study, and the conclusions to be drawn from it, have recently been considerably improved by Professor Herrnstein. He has reported that "the foster children's I.Q.'s correlated with their natural parents' I.Q.'s more than with their foster parents'. . . . The control-group correlations, for parents raising their natural children, were only slightly higher than the true parent-child correlations in the experimental group, comprising adopted children. The study clearly and unequivocally showed that the home environment, when disentangled from the genetic connection between ordinary parents and their children, accounts for relatively little of the variation in children's I.Q.'s."[16]

The difficulty with this description of a particularly clear and unequivocal demonstration is that it is wholly false. The fact is that Burks did not have, and did not report, I.Q.'s for the true parents of the adopted children. The correlations involving the true parents of Burks' adopted children exist only in Professor Herrnstein's reading or recollection. There, indeed, matters do seem to be clear and unequivocal. This misreading of experimental data in favor of an hereditarian interpretation is, as a subsequent chapter will demonstrate, common in influential reviews of the heritability literature. Those reviews in many instances do not correspond with simple facts.

There are real data within the adoption studies, however, which are entirely inconsistent with an hereditarian position. The relevant data were provided casually both by Freeman et al. and by Leahy. Their theoretical significance seems not to have been grasped. There are some adoptive parents who have, in addition to an adopted child, a biological child of their own. These biological children were often tested by the investigators in the course of their home visitations. The correlations in I.Q. between such biological children and their parents is of unique interest. These children constitute the best imaginable "matched control group" for the adopted children. They have been reared in "adoptive families" and thus exposed to precisely the same atypical environmental constellations as their step-sibs. The truly interesting comparison is that obtained when the *same* parent is correlated with (*a*) his natural child and (*b*) his adopted child.

The only published I.Q. correlations involving natural children of adoptive parents employed the *midparent* I.Q. score. That is simply the averaged I.Q. of mother and father. Typically, the correlation of child's I.Q. and midparent I.Q. is considerably larger than that obtained when a single parent's I.Q. is employed. Table 9 presents the correlations reported for natural children of adoptive parents, together with other relevant correlations from the same adoption studies.

The first point to be made about Table 9 is that, within each column, there is no significant heterogeneity among the various reported correlations. Thus the data from the separate studies may reasonably be pooled, and that has been done in the bottom row of the table. The pooled data indicate, as has long been recognized, that parent-child I.Q. correlations in adoptive families are lower than those obtained in natural families. That is the case, to a statistically significant degree, whether the child in the adoptive family is biological, or in fact adopted. The interesting finding is that, *within* adoptive families, the correlations of biological and adopted children with their parents do *not* differ significantly. The lack of a

TABLE 9

I.Q. Correlations from Studies of Adopted Children

Study	Adopted child × Adoptive midparent	Own child × Adoptive midparent	Control child × True midparent
Freeman et al. (1928)	.39 ($N = 169$)	.35 ($N = 28$)	—
Burks (1928)	.20 ($N = 174$)	—	.52 ($N = 100$)
Leahy (1935)	.18 ($N = 177$)	.36 ($N = 20$)	.60 ($N = 173$)
Pooling all studies	.26 ($N = 520$)	.35 ($N = 48$)	.57 ($N = 273$)

significant difference occurs within each of the two studies in which this comparison can be made. Within the Freeman et al. study the correlation for adopted children is a trifle higher, while in the Leahy study it is a little lower.

These data are not definitive, but they are all we have. They suggest that the failure to obtain "normal" parent-child correlations in adoptive families is a consequence of peculiar environmental circumstances that seem to characterize adoptive families. They offer no support for the idea that I.Q. is heritable; if it were, then within families containing both biological and adopted children, the I.Q. resemblance of the biological child to the parents should greatly exceed that of the adopted child. Further, if I.Q. were highly heritable, the correlation between biological child and parent should approximate that obtained in normal families. The data instead indicate that, within adoptive families, it *makes no difference* whether or not the child shares the parent's genes. There seems to be no plausible hereditarian way to explain this finding.

THE SKODAK AND SKEELS STUDY

The final adoption study to be reviewed is that of Skodak and Skeels.[17] Their work is probably more widely cited in textbooks than is any other adoption study. Two of their findings have commanded very wide attention. The first has already been cited. They reported a significant correlation (.44) between the I.Q.'s of adopted children and the I.Q.'s of biological mothers with whom they had not lived. The second major finding was that the I.Q.'s of adopted children correlated .32 with the educational levels of their biological mothers, but only .02 with the educations of their foster mothers.

The design of the Skodak and Skeels study differed from that of Burks and Leahy. Skodak and Skeels studied *a single group* of 100 adopted children. They had, however, some information about the biological parents of the children, as well as about their foster parents. The I.Q.'s of 63 biological mothers were available, as were the educational levels of 92. For the adoptive mothers, educational levels of all 100 were known. There were not, however, any I.Q. tests given to the adoptive parents. That is why comparisons involving biological and adoptive parents had to be based on educational levels, rather than on I.Q.'s. The Skodak and Skeels 1949 paper was the last in a series of reports which had followed the children over time. The children had been given Stanford-Binet tests on four separate occasions. The *average* ages of the children at the times of testing were about 2, 4, 7, and 13 years, but with considerable variability. The 100 children reported on in the 1949 paper were the survivors of an original group of 180. There had been, for various reasons, dropouts in the course of this long-term study. The final report included a splendidly detailed appendix with considerable raw data. That appendix made possible many of the calculations reported on below.

We shall first consider the comparison stressed by so many commentators on the study. The fact that child's I.Q. correlated .32 with biological mother's education and .02 with adopted mother's has been interpreted as powerful evidence for the dominance of heredity. The results described, however, were obtained during the fourth I.Q. testing, when the children averaged about 13 years of age. Professor Herrnstein has indicated that "At no age did the children's I.Q.'s show a significant correlation with their foster parents' educational level."[18] That is quite true—as applied to the 100 children in the final report. The preceding 1945 report, however, had included 139 children, tested at about the age of seven.[19] For that larger sample, the children's I.Q.'s had correlated .24 with biological mothers' education and .20 with foster mothers'. These correlations were each statistically significant and did not differ significantly. Which inference about heritability are we to accept? That flowing from the larger, or from the smaller, sample?

The hereditarian can and will argue that the genetic resemblance between child's I.Q. and biological parent's I.Q. (as indexed by education) "matures" over time. Facial hair in males, for example, is genetically determined, but it does not appear until a particular stage of development has been reached. This maturational argument, however, contradicts another observation frequently made by hereditarians. The characteristic I.Q. differences between occupational classes are observed in the children of members of the various classes by the age of five and one-half.[20] That has been said to indicate the genetic determination of social class differences in I.Q.

There are other possible interpretations for the "emergence" of a stronger correlation with biological mothers' education, coupled with the disappearance of the correlation with foster mothers' education. Though psychologists rarely speak of them, studies of this sort are plagued by *sampling problems*. Perhaps the changing correlations in Skodak and Skeels' longitudinal study are due to changes in the composition of their sample over time. This could easily occur if the dropouts were not random, but instead were selected with respect to the variables being correlated.

There is clear evidence that exactly this occurred in the course of the Skodak and Skeels study. For example, their final report indicates that 51% of the 100 foster mothers who remained in the study until its conclusion had attended college. The 1945 paper contains data that enable us to calculate that, of 38 adoptive mothers who dropped out of the study between 1945 and 1949, only 29% had attended college. Those two proportions differ significantly. Thus, over time, the sample became progressively restricted to a more homogeneous group of very highly educated adoptive parents. That increasing homogenization of adoptive mothers paralleled the decline—in fact, disappearance—of a significant correlation between child's I.Q. and adoptive mothers' education. That scarcely seems surprising. With respect to *biological* mothers' education, the "dropouts" included a slight excess of college-educated mothers, but the effect was not statistically significant. There were in any event very few college-educated biological mothers, only about 8% in the final sample.

To compare, in the final sample, correlations of child's I.Q. with number of years of education of biological and adoptive mothers seems absurd. There was an *enormous* difference in the mean educational level of the two groups. We have seen that the proportions attending college were 8 and 51%, respectively. There are also problems with the variances of the educational levels of the two groups of mothers. Professor Herrnstein in his analysis of the Skodak and Skeels data has called attention to a significant difference between the two variances.[21] The numerical variance was larger for the adoptive mothers. Thus, Herrnstein indicates, it should have been easier on statistical grounds to demonstrate a correlation between child's I.Q. and adoptive mother's years of education. This concern for the logic of comparing correlations is highly to be commended. We have earlier in this chapter seen how it affects the interpretation of other adoption studies. This particular instance, however, saddles environmentalists with a nonsensical view, and it nicely illustrates why, in comparisons of this sort, samples must be matched *both* for means and for variances.

The use of number of years of parent's education as a scale implies, for example, that the difference between completing one and five years of grade school is exactly equal to the difference between completing high school and college—four years of education in each case. The assumption is thus made that the I.Q. difference between college and high school graduates is identical to that between grade one and grade five dropouts, and that the difference in intellect-fostering environments provided by parents is also identical in these cases. These assumptions seem ridiculous and are not supported by any data. The problem remains whether or not the variances around the two different means are equal. The variables of theoretical interest are parental I.Q. and the quality of the environments provided by adoptive parents. The relations between the scale "years of parental education" and each of these variables are such that the numerical variances around different means on the scale simply do not have the same psychological significance. This is a complicated way of saying something very simple. There are probably not many things in the world that are correlated with the number of years a person has attended college, and that is all that is involved in the educational differences among the bulk of the adoptive mothers. With the passage of time, the Skodak and Skeels sample came to consist even more exclusively of highly educated foster mothers. The originally observed correlation of child's I.Q. with foster-mother education thus disappeared. There is no mystery in the ultimate lack of correlation between child I.Q. and adoptive parent education, and there is no point in comparing that correlation with one between child I.Q. and biological parent education. The very high educational levels of the foster parents, incidentally, would lead an environmentalist to expect that the children would develop high I.Q.'s. The mean I.Q. of the 100 Skodak and Skeels adopted children was in fact 117; the mean I.Q. of 63 biological mothers was 86.[22]

The comparison with foster mothers aside, the fact remains that the children's I.Q.'s *did* correlate significantly with biological mothers' education (and I.Q.'s). This was true although the children had been separated from their biological mothers before the age of 6 months. This seems to provide strong presumptive evidence for the importance of the genes in determining I.Q. The genes, however, seem to have worked in a peculiar fashion. For the 92 cases in which biological mother's education was known, the correlation with child's I.Q. was .32. The Skodak and Skeels appendix provides raw data for all 40 boys and 60 girls in the final sample. The correlation of girls' I.Q.'s with biological mothers' education was a significant .44. The same correlation for boys was −.01. These two correlations differ significantly—an effect not exactly predicted by genetic theory. The mean I.Q. of boys and of girls was an identical 117. The two sexes, however, differed significantly in I.Q. variance. The standard deviations were 17.3 for girls and 12.1 for boys. The regression between parent and child I.Q. is assumed by geneticists to be linear, so it is appropriate to "correct" the boys' correlation for restriction of range. The correction does not change the correlation to the second decimal.

There are still further complications in these data. The girls' I.Q. was significantly correlated with their age (−.31), and, in the case of girls, biological *mother's* education was significantly correlated with *child's* age (−.52). For boys, these correlations were −.09 and .10, not remotely approaching significance. The girls appear to have been drawn from a radically different population than the boys. The poor standardization of the Stanford-Binet test might account for some of the negative correlation between child's age and I.Q., but why is it that, to such a striking degree, the biological mothers of the younger girls are relatively better educated? The sampling problem is evidently not to be brushed aside lightly in the consideration of these studies.

The Skodak and Skeels children did *in fact* come from two entirely different sources. The first was a state-supported public agency, compelled by law to accept all children placed by unmarried mothers. The second was a private agency, which could and did select its clientele. The final sample contained 76 children from the public agency, 21 from the private agency, and 3 who had been independently placed in adoptive homes. The appendix does not indicate which child came from which source, nor does it provide any indication of the sex distribution within either source.

We can obtain a pretty clear idea of the difference between these two sources by comparing data in the first two papers of this series, published by Skeels in 1936[23] and in 1938.[24] The first paper reports on 73 children, all of whom came from the public agency. The second paper presents pooled data for 147 children. To the original sample there had subsequently been added 40 children from the public agency and 34 from the private agency. The data presented in the two papers are sufficient to establish that, for the original 73 cases, only 54% of the biological mothers had even entered high school. For the 74 subsequently added cases, 74% of the biological mothers had entered high school. These proportions differ significantly, but they vastly understate the difference between mothers using the public and private agencies. That is so since the cases added in 1938 themselves mostly came from the public agency. Fewer than half of the new cases came from the private agency, but this was sufficient to make the pooled new sample significantly different from the old. The data in fact establish that virtually every mother using the private agency had at least entered high school. The data also clearly indicate that the I.Q.'s of mothers using the private agency were higher. Presumably the bulk of the older children in the final Skodak and Skeels sample came from the source tapped earliest, the public agency. That would account for the negative correlation between biological mother's education and child's age, though not, without more information, for the sex difference in this correlation.

There are also clear indications that the children from the private agency were placed into "better" adoptive homes than the children from the public agency. For the original 73 public agency children, only 76% of the adoptive mothers had attended high school. For the 74 added children, 91% of the foster mothers had attended high school. The difference is statistically significant, and of course again understates the difference between the public and private samples. These data document the existence of selective placement. They indicate that the children from the private agency were placed into "better" adoptive homes. Their *biological* mothers in turn had higher educations and higher I.Q.'s. The observed correlation between child and biological parent is as reasonably attributable to selective placement as to genetic factors. We assume that the children from the private agency had a higher mean I.Q. as a result of this selective placement, but the data with which to test this hypothesis are not available.

There may, of course, have been selective placement *within* the two separate samples that constitute the Skodak and Skeels group. The appendix provides data that make it easy to demonstrate such placement for the final group of 100 children as a whole. There were eight *biological* mothers who had attended college, and 12 who had failed to complete grade school. The educations of the adoptive mothers to whom the children of these biological mothers were given differed significantly: 13.9 years for the foster mothers given the children of college-educated biological mothers, compared to 11.8 for the adoptive mothers given the children of grade-school biological mothers. The same selective placement can be demonstrated in mirror image. There were 12 foster homes in which both parents had *completed* college, and 22 foster homes in which neither parent had completed high school. The educations of biological mothers of the children assigned to these two classes of adoptive homes differed significantly: 11.3 compared to 9.1 years. These data reflect a simple social fact. The children of unmarried mothers who have gone to college are much more likely to be assigned to college-educated adoptive parents than are the children of grade-school dropouts. The simple social facts, however, often elude the grasp of genetic theorists.

The evidence is overwhelming that the Skodak and Skeels children were placed into foster homes on the basis of biological mother's education, or of variables correlated with it. We can assume that the children of highly-educated biological mothers were placed into "good" foster homes, homes conducive to the development of a high I.Q. The correlation between child's I.Q. and biological mother's education follows directly from this fact. When assessing the suitability of a foster home, however, the agencies may be guided by many more factors than the foster parents' I.Q. and occupation. They have examined the foster home and the foster parents, and their reputation in the community is known. The goodness of the foster home may be only very moderately correlated with such blunt variables as years of education and occupational status. That is especially likely to be the case in a farming state such as Iowa, where the Skodak and Skeels study was performed. They in fact indicated that many of the farm homes—about 25% of the total sample—were rich in environmental and cultural opportunities. The farm adoptive parents had had less formal education than the city parents. There is no particular reason to suppose that a prosperous Iowa farmer in the 1930's had more formal education than an impoverished farmer. It is not obvious that the environment he provided for his foster child was more deprived than that provided by a highly educated city dweller during the Great Depression. The selective placement interpretation of the biological mother-child correlation clearly implies that child's I.Q. must be related to some aspects of the foster home environment; but it emphatically does not imply that those aspects must be highly correlated with foster parents' education or occupation. There is no reason to suppose that those blunt indices of foster home environment should correlate with child's I.Q.—particularly when, as in this case, there is such a restriction of meaningful range.

There is a considerable light cast on these matters by an observation fully recorded by Skodak and Skeels. They isolated for separate study the 11 children whose biological mothers had I.Q.'s below 70, and the 8 children whose biological mothers had I.Q.'s of 105 or above. The variable selected for study here, it should be noted, was biological mother's I.Q.—not, as in our own analysis, her education. The children of these two extreme groups of biological mothers themselves differed significantly in I.Q., but Skodak and Skeels raised the question of whether this difference might be the result of selective placement. Their first approach was to examine the parental education and occupation of the foster homes into which the two groups of children had been placed. There were, for these blunt measures, no significant differences between Group (a)—children of low-I.Q. biological mothers—and Group (b).

The authors reported that

> If reliance were to be placed on these data alone, the inference would be fairly clear. However, comparison of the actual situation in the homes leads to a different conclusion. As a group, the homes of Group (b) are superior to the homes of Group (a) on every count on which the homes can be evaluated. The average income of Group (b) is easily double the average income of Group (a) families. Five of the eight had sent their children to private schools, nursery schools, or camps for more than one year. . . . None of the families in Group (a) had been either interested or able to afford similar opportunities. . . . In the number of books, the extent of participation in . . . organizations . . . the number of toys, school equipment, typewriters, personal radios . . . the homes in Group (b) were definitely superior to the homes in Group (a). . . . The present measures of education and occupation do not evaluate the crucial differences between outstanding, average, or less effective homes. [25]

This paragraph, with its vivid documentation of selective placement, had been noted by Professor Herrnstein. He wrote that "Skeels and Skodak [sic] felt that intangible factors in the foster homes—not reflected in gross indices of education and occupation—were crucial, but they were not able to anchor their impression to testable hypotheses." [26] The professor's partiality towards the gross indices favored by behavior geneticists is understandable, but it is not clear why such variables as average income, private school attendance, number of books, typewriters, radios, etc., are regarded as "intangibles."

The Skodak and Skeels study that we have just reviewed has been held up by leading hereditarian theorists as providing "the strongest evidence possible for hereditary factors in intelligence." The data are said to be such that there seems to be no plausible environmental way to account for them.

We have not commented on the observation that in the Skodak and Skeels study—as in other studies of adopted children—the mean I.Q. of the adopted children is much higher than that of their biological mothers. That is not necessarily inconsistent with genetic theory, as both Professors Jensen and Herrnstein have been at pains to point out. First, the mean I.Q. of the 63 biological mothers for whom data were available was only 86; unless they had mated with men of even lower I.Q., some regression toward the mean from this value would be expected. Second, it is not asserted by genetic theorists that environment has *no* effect on I.Q. The assumption can be made—and it corresponds to fact—that adoptive homes are much superior to average homes. The elevated I.Q.'s of the adopted children have been interpreted by both Jensen and Herrnstein as a composite of two effects: one component attributed to regression, and another to unusually favorable environment. The question is whether the amount of I.Q. elevation attributed to environment by this sort of analysis is reasonable in light of the hereditarian assumption that only about 20% of I.Q. variance is caused by nongenetic factors.

Professor Jensen, "using the simplest model," calculates that genetic theory alone would predict a mean children's I.Q. of 96, *if* the children had been reared in average homes.[27] The average I.Q. of the children, he reported, was actually 107, or 11 points higher than that predicted by genetic theory. That suggested the possibility—not at all implausible—that the children had been reared in homes about 1.6 standard deviations better than normal. That follows since a normal distribution of environmental effects on I.Q. would have a standard deviation of 6.71 under the assumption of 80% heritability.

The details of the simple genetic model employed by Jensen were not spelled out, but they could not have varied much from that employed by Herrnstein, which is spelled out.[28] The Herrnstein model predicted an average I.Q. of 94.4 for the children, and he reported their actual I.Q. to be 106. That is 11.6 points higher than predicted by theory. This discrepancy is again reasonably attributable to the superior adoptive home environments, even assuming that environment can account for only 20% of I.Q. variance in the population.

The model assumes, however, as Herrnstein pointed out, that the fathers averaged 100 in I.Q. If the fathers' mean I.Q. was less than 100, the model underestimates the contribution of environment. Conversely, if the fathers' mean I.Q. was more than 100, the model overestimates the environmental contribution. The idea that the mates of women with an average I.Q. of 86 might have an average I.Q. higher than 100 seems implausible. There seems to be a considerable likelihood that the fathers' I.Q. averaged much less than 100, and thus that the effect of environment on the children's I.Q. has been seriously underestimated by Jensen and Herrnstein.

There is no need to remain in total ignorance of the true fathers' probable I.Q. The analyses of the Skodak and Skeels study—purported to demonstrate the importance of heredity—have always and necessarily employed parental education as an index of parental I.Q. The biological fathers, like the biological mothers, had averaged ten years of school. The best estimate we can make, therefore, is that their average I.Q. was also 86. Further, the occupational levels of the true fathers were extraordinarily low. Half were day laborers, and another quarter were semi- or slightly-skilled workers. The mean I.Q. in such low-status occupations, as the hereditarians have often reminded us, is low. The case cannot be proved, but it seems likely that, despite the apparent precision of the numerical quantities produced by Jensen and Herrnstein, the contribution of environment estimated by a not-so-simple genetic model would be embarrassing to a genetic theorist.

This review of the adopted child studies has produced no unambiguous evidence that supports the idea that I.Q. is to any degree inherited. The comparison of correlations across adoptive and natural families has no theoretical point unless relevant aspects of familial environment have been matched for both means and variances. This condition is not even approximated in the existing studies. The correlation between adopted child's and biological mother's I.Q., in the one study that detected it, was as easily attributable to selective placement as to the genes. The data documenting selective placement were no less real than those documenting genetic relatedness. There is surely no comfort for a genetic interpretation in the fact that adopted girls' I.Q., but not adopted boys', correlated with biological mothers' education. That outcome—together with other anomalous results—can reasonably be regarded as the joint product of selective placement and sampling irregularities. The correlations between adoptive parent and child, when observed, are ambiguous; it might reasonably be argued that genetically bright children have been selectively placed. The fact that, in the available data, adoptive parents' natural children are no more highly correlated with them than are their adopted children is simply inconsistent with a genetic interpretation. The fact that adopted children's I.Q.'s are very much higher than those of their biological parents forces hereditarians to concede some role to environment. There do not appear to be any equivalent data that compel a similar concession by environmentalists. The hypothesis of zero heritability stands unscathed.

The review does suggest some possible studies that could produce less ambiguous data. The existence of adoptive families that contain both natural and adopted children provides an obvious opportunity, and a large-scale, well-controlled study of such families might be revealing. The idea that there is any genetic determination of I.Q. necessarily implies that, in such families, the natural child will resemble the parents more closely than will the adopted child—unless, of course, selective placement has perfectly assigned children with good genes to adoptive homes in which the parents have identically good genes. The failure of adopted children to resemble the parents as much as do the natural children would tend to imply some role for heredity—unless, of course, very early experience with the biological mother, or variables such as prenatal nutrition, have a lasting effect. There is also the possibility that the mere fact of being the adopted child in such a family might tend to estrange some children from the parents, thereby reducing the correlation.

The prevalence of divorce suggests other research opportunities. From a genetic standpoint there is no reason why, on a general I.Q. test, a child should resemble one parent more than the other. There are obvious environmental reasons to suppose that, if parents separate when a child is very young, the child might resemble the parent who rears it more than the other. The fact that parents resemble one another in I.Q. may place a limit on the discrepancy that could be obtained between the child's correlations with the two parents, but the results of a large-scale study could be suggestive. The greater the discrepancy, the more embarrassing the result would be for a genetic theory of I.Q.

NOTES TO CHAPTER FIVE

1. *The Family History Book,* ed. C. B. Davenport, Eugenics Record Office Bulletin No. 7, (Cold Springs Harbor, N.Y., 1912), p. 62.
2. M. Skodak and H. M. Skeels, "A Final Follow-Up Study of One Hundred Adopted Children," *Journal of Genetic Psychology,* 75, (1949), 85 – 125.
3. M. P. Honzik, "Developmental Studies of Parent-Child Resemblance in Intelligence," *Child Development,* 28, (1957), 215 – 228.
4. *Intelligence: Genetic and Environmental Influences,* ed. R. Cancro, (New York, Grune and Stratton, 1971), p. 189.
5. R. J. Herrnstein, *I.Q. in the Meritocracy,* (Boston, Atlantic Monthly Press, 1973), p. 148.
6. D. Snygg, "The Relation Between the Intelligence of Mothers and of their Children Living in Foster Homes," *Journal of Genetic Psychology,* 52, (1938), 401 – 406.
7. F. N. Freeman, K. J. Holzinger, and B. C. Mitchell, "The Influence of Environment on the Intelligence, School Achievement, and Conduct of Foster Children," *Twenty-Seventh Yearbook of the National Society for the Study of Education, Part I,* (Bloomington, Ill., Public School Publishing Co., 1928), 103 – 217.
8. B. S. Burks, "Comments on the Chicago and Stanford Studies of Foster Children," *Twenty-Seventh Yearbook of the National Society for the Study of Education, Part I,* (Bloomington, Ill., Public School Publishing Co., 1928), 320.
9. Freeman, Holzinger, and Mitchell, *Influence,* p. 183.
10. B. S. Burks, "The Relative Influence of Nature and Nurture upon Mental Development: A Comparative Study of Foster Parent-Foster Child Resemblance and True Parent-True Child Resemblance," *Twenty-Seventh Yearbook of the National Society for the Study of Education, Part I,* (Bloomington, Ill., Public School Publishing Co., 1928), 219 – 316.
11. A. M. Leahy, "Nature-Nurture and Intelligence," *Genetic Psychology Monographs,* 17, (1935), 235 – 308.
12. A. R. Jensen, "How Much Can We Boost IQ and Scholastic Achievement?", *Harvard Educational Review,* 39, (1969), 54.
13. W. D. Wallis, "Observations on Dr. Alice M. Leahy's 'Nature-Nurture and Intelligence'," *Journal of Genetic Psychology,* 49, (1936), 315 – 324.
14. Burks did not in fact calculate I.Q.'s for the parents in her study, but simply assigned to them "mental ages." Since the chronological age of all parents was greater than 16, the "I.Q." would have been derived in each case by dividing the years of mental age by 16. Thus, for correlational purposes, there is no difference between an adult's mental age and his I.Q.

15. L. M. Terman, *The Measurement of Intelligence*, (Boston, Houghton Mifflin, 1916), p. 54.
16. Herrnstein, *I.Q.*, pp. 182 – 183.
17. Skodak and Skeels, *Final Follow-Up*, pp. 82 – 125.
18. Herrnstein, *I.Q.*, p. 148.
19. M. Skodak and H. Skeels, ''A Follow-Up Study of Children in Adoptive Homes,'' *Journal of Genetic Psychology*, 66, (1945), 21 – 58.
20. L. M. Terman and M. A. Merrill, *Measuring Intelligence*, (Boston, Houghton Mifflin, 1937), p. 48.
21. Herrnstein, *I.Q.*, p. 148.
22. The mean I.Q. of 117 for adopted children applies to their last testing, at an average age of about 13, with the revised 1937 Stanford-Binet. Their true mothers had been tested with the 1916 Stanford-Binet. The children, on that test, had a mean I.Q. of 107.
23. H. M. Skeels, ''The Mental Development of Children in Foster Homes,'' *Journal of Genetic Psychology*, 49, (1936), 91 – 106.
24. H. M. Skeels, ''Mental Development of Children in Foster Homes,'' *Journal of Consulting Psychology*, 2, (1938), 33 – 43.
25. Skodak and Skeels, *Final Follow-Up*, p. 114.
26. Herrnstein, *I.Q.*, pp. 152 – 153.
27. A. R. Jensen, *Genetics and Education*, (New York, Harper & Row, 1972), p. 16.
28. Herrnstein, *I.Q.*, p. 151.

6
THE ACCURACY OF SECONDARY SOURCES

He does not point to a single example of an "overstatement" or a "misstatement" in my paper.

—Professor Arthur Jensen, 1969[1]

Most people, even academics, do not have the time, training, or occasion to work through the technical literature on a controversial subject. Instead, they must rely on professionals for a disinterested evaluation. . . . With improvements in the statistical techniques of quantitative genetics and in the quality and quantity of intelligence testing, the heritability of I.Q. has doubtless become psychology's best proved, socially significant empirical finding.

—Professor Richard Herrnstein, 1973[2]

We depend, for the most part, on a relatively few writers to summarize for us the massive research literature on the heritability of I.Q. The number of relevant studies is enormous, and few who are not intimately concerned with the topic can have the time or inclination to read the original studies. The gist of the data is supposedly available in reviews written by authorities and in textbooks. What most of us "know" about I.Q. research comes from these sources. The question that we now raise is whether these secondary sources can be relied upon to present accurate accounts of the actual research. This chapter will document only a few examples of influential authorities inaccurately reporting the results of I.Q. studies. The errors tend to become common currency, as one writer tends to copy another.

We shall begin with a couple of examples from a major document, Professor Jensen's 1969 article in the *Harvard Educational Review*.[3] There Jensen attempted to distinguish between two different forms of mental deficiency. The two different forms have been variously named: imbeciles vs. feebleminded, or clinical vs. "cultural-familial" retardation, for example. The point of the distinction is simple. The *very* severely retarded are said to be produced by aberrant "major gene" defects, or perhaps prenatal trauma, or postnatal neurological damage. The higher grade defectives are said to represent the lower extreme of a normal distribution of I.Q.'s. *Their* lack of intelligence presumably reflects the normal polygenic determination of I.Q. This distinction thus leads to different predictions about the I.Q.'s of relatives of the two classes of retardates.

Professor Jensen wrote that "the strongest evidence we have that IQ's below 50 are a group apart from the mildly retarded, who represent the lower end of normal variation, comes from comparisons of the siblings of the severely retarded with siblings of the mildly retarded. In England, where this has been studied intensively, these two retardate groups are called imbecile (IQs below 50) and feebleminded (IQs 50 to 75). Figure 3 shows the IQ distributions of the *siblings* of imbecile and feebleminded children (Roberts, 1952). Note that the siblings of imbeciles have a much higher average level of intelligence than the siblings of the feebleminded." We have reproduced Jensen's Fig. 3, and its caption, as our Fig. 3.

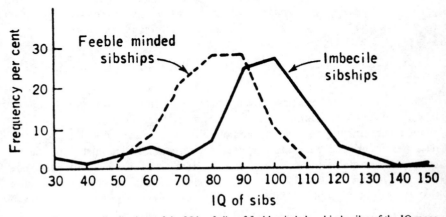

FIG. 3. Frequency distributions of the IQ's of sibs of feebleminded and imbeciles of the IQ range 30–68. (Roberts, 1952.) Reproduced with permission of the publisher from Arthur R. Jensen, "How Much Can We Boost IQ and Scholastic Achievement?", *Harvard Educational Review*, 39, Winter 1969. Copyright © 1969 by President and Fellows of Harvard College.

What Professor Jensen has told us is that Roberts, in England, studied the sibs of people whose I.Q.'s ranged between 30 and 68. Those with I.Q.'s in the 30–50 range are called imbeciles, and those with I.Q.'s in the 50–68 range are called feebleminded. The sibs of imbeciles can be seen to have *higher* I.Q.'s than the sibs of the feebleminded. The difficulty here is that Jensen's description of Roberts' procedure is inaccurate. We shall examine the Roberts paper in some detail.

The Roberts data were reported in his Galton Lecture to the Eugenics Society in 1952. There Roberts had reported that he had attempted to find all children in a particular area whose I.Q.'s were between 35 and 60. There were 271 such children, and 562 of their schoolage sibs were I.Q. tested. When the 271 subject children were separated according to their I.Q.'s, and the sibs' I.Q.'s then examined,

> that added little to what we knew before and it was difficult to get any further. My colleagues and I were distinctly shaken. Was the hypothesis only very partially true after all? We felt that this might indeed be so. No doubt it is interesting and stimulating to find that one has been wrong for twenty years, but it takes a little effort to square the shoulders.
>
> We then tried an experiment. Looking at a two-way table showing the 271 subjects arranged in order of I.Q., with the I.Q.'s of their sibs alongside them, I divided the families by brute force into two groups, doing the job quickly and ruthlessly, with as little juggling as possible.[4]

The two distributions of sibs' I.Q.'s plotted by Roberts were based on this "brute force" division of the 271 subject children. They were *not* based on dividing the subject children into higher and lower I.Q. categories. The figure originally published by Roberts employed in its body the terms "feeble-minded families" and "imbecile families." The version of the figure published by Jensen has changed "families" to "sibships."

The procedure employed by Roberts may seem confusing, so it is best to spell it out explicitly. For 20 years Roberts and his colleagues had entertained the theory that there were two distinct types of mental deficiency, controlled by different genetic mechanisms. To test this theory, they assembled a group of subject children with I.Q.'s ranging from 35 to 60. They expected to find that the sibs of subjects whose I.Q.'s were near 35 would have much higher I.Q.'s than the sibs of subjects whose I.Q.'s were near 60. *They did not find this.* They then squared their shoulders and arbitrarily divided the subject children into two groups on a new basis. The new basis was simply this: If the subject child's sibs had high I.Q.'s, the child was called an imbecile, but if his sibs had low I.Q.'s he was called feebleminded. Then it was reported that the sibs of imbeciles had higher I.Q.'s than the sibs of feebleminded children, and the two distributions were plotted graphically. The assignment of a subject to one class or the other was not based upon *his* I.Q., but upon his *sibs'* I.Q. Professor Jensen's assertion that "feeble-minded" refers here to children with "IQs 50 to 75," and that "imbecile" refers to "IQs below 50," is false. The word "feebleminded" in the Roberts study refers to any subject child, *regardless* of his I.Q., whose sibs were judged to have "low" I.Q.'s.

This study, Professor Jensen has informed us, is "the strongest evidence we have" for the theory. The cited quotation from Jensen, together with the caption he provided for the figure, must lead to one of three conclusions. Perhaps Jensen has not read the Roberts paper carefully; or he has read it and misunderstood it; or he has chosen his words with disingenuousness. The same Roberts figure, it may be noted, has been reproduced by Vandenberg.[5] The two distributions of I.Q.'s were described by Vandenberg as belonging to the sibs "of high-grade and low-grade mental defectives." The Vandenberg version of the figure, like Jensen's, replaces Roberts' word "families" with the word "sibships" within the body of the figure.

The reader may be perplexed by the fact that, although Roberts began by collecting all children with I.Q.'s between 35 and 60, he then described the same children as having I.Q.'s between 30 and 68. The explanation is simple. The I.Q.'s of all children—sibs as well as subjects—were changed after the fact, "to secure comparability at different ages at test." The "adjustment" raised I.Q.'s "by about 6 points on the average," but it clearly lowered some by at least 5 points. The adjustment was carried out because I.Q. correlated negatively with age. Whatever one thinks of the adjustment, it can in no way remedy a severe sampling bias that contaminates this "strongest evidence." The adjustment was performed after the selection of children to be included in the study had been made. This must mean that defective *younger* children escaped inclusion in the original pool of subjects, since their I.Q.'s were "spuriously" high. This was not a trivial effect, as Roberts and Mellone indicate in another publication that "Subjects of I.Q. 35–60 were considerably more numerous at 12 than at 8."[6] They presented a table that pooled the I.Q.'s of the sibs and *cousins* of the subject children. The cousins were not mentioned in the Galton Lecture cited by Jensen and Vandenberg. There is no way of knowing whether the cousins of the two "groups" of subject children had different I.Q. distributions. From the table, it can be calculated that among sibs and cousins aged 5 through 9, only 4% had unadjusted I.Q.'s in the 35–60 range; among sibs and cousins aged 10–14, 10% had such I.Q.'s. The difference is significant.

The difficulties confronted by Roberts in his forcible separation of subject children into two groups should not be underestimated. Forty percent of his subjects had only one sib. For these cases, the *only* way of determining whether the subject belonged in the "imbecile" or "feeble-minded" group was examining the I.Q. of his single sib. The more skeptical might assume that, though the division was performed with "as little juggling as possible," 20 years of commitment to a theory might subtly have influenced the outcome.

The Roberts paper presents data on maternal fertility. This makes it possible to calculate that the 122 "imbecile" subjects had a mean of 3.61 living sibs, while the 149 "feeble-minded" subjects had a mean of 4.31 living sibs. We know that "all the sibs of school age were tested," so presumably more sibs of "feeble-minded" subjects were tested. The total number of tested sibs was 562, so we can deduce that 521 living sibs were not of school age, and thus not tested. There is no way in which we can know how many scores entered the two distributions plotted in Roberts' figure. There would be 333 sibs of "feeble-minded" subjects, and 229 sibs of "imbeciles" *if* the proportions of sibs *of school age* were the same in each group. We know, however, that subject's age biased the selection of the original sample, and that could have many possible implications for the proportions of school-age sibs. The numbers in each plotted distribution are simply not reported, nor are the means, nor the standard deviations. Thus, even overlooking the arbitrary nature in which the two groups were constituted we have no way of knowing whether any apparent differences in the I.Q. distributions are significant.

The same paper by Roberts was again cited by Jensen in 1970, as follows. "The well-known excess or bulge at the lower end of the IQ distribution is attributable to major gene defects and brain damage which override normal polygenic determinants of intelligence. A study in England based on a complete sample of 3361 children showed actual frequencies not in excess of the frequencies expected from the normal or Gaussian distribution *above* IQs of 45. But the frequency of IQs *below* 45 was almost 18 times greater than would be expected (Roberts, 1952)."[7] Professor Jensen's citation is accurate here, but it does not convey the full flavor of Roberts' finding. The Roberts paper indicates that, in a sample size of 3,361, the normal curve predicts an expected number of 0.7 children with I.Q.'s "below 44.97." The "observed number" of such children is given as 12.5. We are not told how I.Q.'s were measured to within one-hundredth of a point, nor how Roberts managed to "observe" the extra .5 child. The two very small frequencies do differ by a factor of about 18, but one suspects that some form of "adjustment" was used in order to make possible the "observation" of fractions of children. There were 58.4 children "observed" with I.Q.'s between 44.97 and 67.57. There are no data provided by Roberts about the *upper* extremes of the I.Q. distribution in his sample.

To return to Jensen's 1969 paper, however, in the paragraph following his citation of Roberts, Jensen observes: "Another interesting point of contrast between severe mental deficiency and mild retardation is the fact noted by Kushlick (1966, p. 130), in surveying numerous studies, that 'The parents of severely subnormal children are evenly distributed among all the social strata of industrial society, while those of mildly subnormal subjects come predominantly from the lower social classes. . . .'"

We interrupt at this point to comment. The sentence actually written by Kushlick was: "*It has long been known that* parents of severely subnormal children are evenly distributed among all the social strata of industrial society. . ." (italics added).[8] The Kushlick paper reviews a number of reports about "subnormality," but *cites none to document this assertion*. There are enormously complex sampling problems in determining the numbers of "severely subnormal," since not all are reported to public authorities, and whether and where they are institutionalized — to say nothing of how they are diagnosed — is severely confounded with social class. These difficulties are circumvented by Kushlick's phrase "It has long been known." The probative force of Kushlick's assertion is approximately equal to that of a scholarly report of 1491 indicating that "It has long been known that the world is flat."*

The Jensen article, in any event, continued to quote Kushlick as follows: "There is now evidence which suggests that mild subnormality in the absence of abnormal neurological signs (epilepsy, electroencephalographic abnormalities, biochemical abnormalities, chromosomal abnormalities or sensory defects) is virtually confined to the lower social classes. Indeed, there is evidence that almost no children of higher social class parents have IQ scores of less than 80, unless they have one of the pathological processes mentioned above." The implication by Jensen is entirely clear. The well-to-do are assumed to be genetically gifted. When upper-class parents have a subnormal child, it is the result of a rare and unfortunate biological accident, "a pathological process." The occurrence of subnormal children of lower class parents, representing "the lower end of normal variation," is only to be expected.

To support his assertion that almost all subnormal children of upper-class parents had "pathological processes," Kushlick cited only a single study which in fact examined such children for pathology. That study was reported by Stein and Susser in 1963.[9] They investigated primary school children in an English city who had been referred to the health service as educationally subnormal, and whose I.Q.'s were under 80. They divided *schools*—not parents—into those of high and low "social standing." They found that only 11.9% of referred children from low-standing schools had "neurological lesions or marked sensory defects." That was true of fully 50% of referred children from high-standing schools. This difference, however, is not so impressive as may first appear. There were 118 referred children from the low-standing schools, and a grand total of 2 children from the high-standing schools. The difference was thus due to a clinical defect in a *single* child from a high-standing school. That child, incidentally, did *not* have a "lesion"; he was a diabetic, who had been "excluded from the category 'clinically normal.'" To increase their number of cases from high-standing schools, the authors moved on to another city. There they found another nine children referred from such schools. Two of the nine were said to have central nervous system lesions, and another three had "chronic diseases," including asthma.

---

*The same paper by Kushlick later refers (p. 144) to "the excess of severely subnormal subjects among children of lower social class families." The *parents* of such children had earlier been said to be "evenly distributed among all the social strata. . . ." These two assertions, if correct, imply that there are no class differences in the proportion of families containing a severely subnormal child, but that in at least the lower classes *severe subnormality tends to be shared by sibs*. The definition of severe subnormality used by Kushlick was I.Q. below 50, the "imbeciles" referred to by Jensen. The Kushlick assertions thus seem difficult to square with the I.Q. distribution of "imbecile families" plotted by Roberts, but, as is often the case, precise quantitative data are lacking.

The Stein and Susser data, although probably affected by different referral policies in the two types of school, do indicate that the absolute number of "upper class" children with I.Q.'s below 80 is low. That fact — that children from poor families have I.Q.'s roughly in the range of Italian immigrants during the 1920's — has long been known. There is no indication in their data, however, that — granted an I.Q. below 80 — an upper-class child is any more likely to have "neurological signs," etc., than is a lower-class child. The upper-class child evidently stands a better chance of having his stupidity attributed to his asthma or his diabetes, rather than to his genes.

The development of Professor Jensen's argument bears careful analysis. First, we are told that the *very* severely retarded — "IQ's below 50" — result from genetic effects different from those of the polygenes that determine the normal distribution of I.Q. This is demonstrated by appealing to "the strongest evidence we have," which is represented as having found precisely what it *failed* to find. We are then told that another authority, "in surveying numerous studies," has indicated that the very severely retarded are equally probable in all social strata. That authority, it develops, cites no sources for that assertion, but indicates that "it has long been known." There now remain the mildly subnormal, with I.Q.'s in the 50–79 range. Their I.Q.'s are presumably normally determined by polygenes, but here Professor Jensen cannot leave well-enough alone. The very rare upper-class child with so low an I.Q. might theoretically be allowed to have poor polygenes. But instead, authority is cited to show that such rare children have neurological signs, biochemical and chromosomal abnormalities, etc. The cited evidence for this assertion is pathetically weak. The polygenes with which Professor Jensen has endowed the upper classes are splendid indeed.

The 1969 Jensen paper included the graph reproduced here as our Figure 4.[10] Professor Jensen admonished his readers to "Note that the condition of being reared together or reared apart has the same effect on the difference in magnitudes of the correlations for the various kinships. (The slightly greater difference for unrelated children is probably due to the fact of selective placement. . .)." The reader will observe that the very moderate effect of "separation" is about the same for siblings and for DZ twins; since sibs and DZ twins are genetically similarly alike, this makes good genetic sense. We have earlier noted, however, that the median of about .40 reported for separated sibs by EKJ was based on only two studies, and that their own reference list included a third study with separated sibs, which changes the median to .25. The additional study would change the appearance of Jensen's figure considerably. The figure itself appears on the page after a table of medians, of which "Most of the values are taken from the survey by Erlenmeyer-Kimling and Jarvik." That table gives a median value of .47 for 33 studies of separated sibs, and that value would also change the appearance of the figure. Perhaps Jensen was fortunate in not using that value; he later indicated that Burt informed him in conversation that 30 of those 33 studies were the result of a misprint.

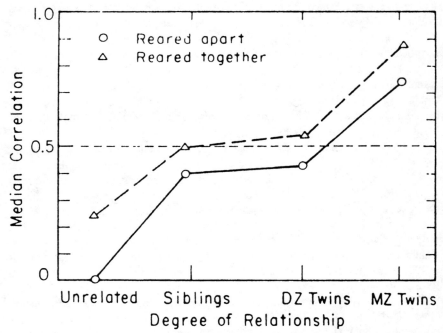

Fig. 4. Median values of all correlations reported in the literature up to 1963 for the indicated kinships. Reproduced with permission of the publishers from Arthur R. Jensen, "How Much Can We Boost IQ and Scholastic Achievement?", *Harvard Educational Review*, 39, Winter 1969. Copyright © 1969 by President and Fellows of Harvard College.

These difficulties are entirely understandable, compared to the point plotted as the median of an unspecified number of studies of DZ twins reared apart. That point is assuredly not "After Erlenmeyer-Kimling & Jarvik, 1963." They provided *no* data for DZ twins reared apart, nor did Burt. The only data I have found for DZ twins reared apart were given by Shields in 1962;[11] following his scoring procedure, the correlation can be calculated as .05. *That* value would wreak havoc with Professor Jensen's figure, but I would hesitate to employ it, since it was based on only four twin pairs. Perhaps the sample sizes of the unnamed studies on which Jensen's median is based were larger; or perhaps smaller.

The following year Jensen published a review of the four major studies of separated identical twins.[12] The four studies together provide a total of 122 twin pairs, and Jensen asked: "Are the main parameters of these samples sufficiently alike to permit the data from the several studies to be analyzed as a total composite that would allow new and stronger inferences than would be possible for any one of the studies viewed by itself?" To this end, Jensen published raw I.Q. scores for all 122 pairs, and then proceeded to a statistical analysis.

There are a number of errors in Jensen's description of the four studies. The I.Q.'s of the Burt twins had been personally provided by Burt, who had never published them. They were described by Jensen as "obtained from an individual test, the English adaptation of the Stanford-Binet." That is not the case. The scores are in fact some form of "adjusted assessments." Jensen wrote that "All of Shields' twins were separated before 6 months of age and 21 of the pairs were separated at birth." That is not the case. There were in fact 19 pairs said to be separated at or near birth, but only 28 of the 44 pairs were separated before, or at, 6 months; others were separated at 7, 8, and 9 years. The Juel-Nielsen study was described by Jensen as having used "a Danish adaptation of the Wechsler-Bellevue Intelligence Scale (Form I), which in the general population has a mean = 100 and SD = 15." The wording used by Jensen here is ambiguous, as Juel-Nielsen's is not. What is the "general population" in which the Wechsler, like the Stanford-Binet, is said to have a mean of 100 and standard deviation of 15? The mean I.Q. of Juel-Nielsen's twins was 107, with a standard deviation of 9. The author warned explicitly that "There is no Danish standardization of the test . . . a fact that must be taken into account in the evaluation of the results."[13]

The "I.Q.'s" given by Jensen for Shields' twins were calculated by Jensen, since Shields provided only raw scores for his two separate tests. The transformation to I.Q.'s was accomplished as follows: "A raw score of 19 on the Vocabulary scale and of 28 on the Dominoes Test correspond to IQ 100 in the general population. The raw score means were transformed in accord with these population values and the standard deviation was transformed to accord with the population value of SD = 15. The IQ's thus obtained were then averaged to yield a single IQ measure for each subject." To perform this transformation, Jensen had to know the "population" means and SD's of Shields' two tests. For the Dominoes, Shields reported that "A score of 28 corresponds to I.Q. 100," and for the Vocabulary scale, "A score of 19 would be about I.Q. 100."[14] There was *no* indication, however, of population SD's. Thus Jensen had to estimate the "population" SD from the *sample SD*'s given by Shields. There is a problem here. For the Vocabulary scale, the separated twins had an SD of 5.7, and the control twins an SD of 4.0. These two "estimates" *differ* significantly. The estimate used by Jensen, it can be deduced, was the larger estimate provided by the separated twin sample itself. This was done despite the fact that the separated twins had a significantly lower mean Vocabulary score than the control twins. The control twin mean, 19, corresponded exactly to Shields' description of the population mean; the mean for separated twins was only 16.1. The effect of Jensen's choice of the larger estimate of population SD is simple: It *reduces by 30 percent* the co-twin difference in "I.Q." which would have been obtained had the smaller estimate been used. That is, it makes members of a twin pair look more alike. The same problem exists, and the same choice was made by Jensen, in estimating a population SD for the Dominoes test; but in this case, the difference between the two sample SD's was not statistically significant.

The entire procedure of estimating "I.Q.'s" from Shields' raw scores is very questionable. The Dominoes test standardization data, such as they are, come from a British army sample, size unspecified. The mean raw score was 27.5, but raw scores were *not* normally distributed, as I.Q.'s are alleged to be. Thus, no matter what raw score *SD* is set equal to 15, the resulting transformation will not produce I.Q. scores. The Vocabulary scale used by Shields was only *part* of a larger test, which had been standardized on "2300 men." The score on the part must be used to estimate an "expected score" on the whole. The raw score means *and* the raw score *SD*'s vary considerably with age; again, the raw scores are emphatically not normally distributed. The Shields sample contained mostly women; certainly the Dominoes, and evidently the Vocabulary scale, were "standardized" on men. These facts are all ignored in Professor Jensen's report that the raw scores were "transformed in accord with these population values."

There is also a problem with the I.Q.'s given by Jensen for Juel-Nielsen's twins. The twins (or at least most of them) had been tested on two separate occasions by Juel-Nielsen, who thus published two separate I.Q. scores for each twin. Though Jensen does not indicate this, the numbers he publishes are the *means* of the two test administrations. This again makes co-twins look more alike than they would if scores on the first test alone had been used. That might be because random errors of measurement are being smoothed out by averaging two tests. There is also the possibility, however, that a convergence of scores on the second testing is the result of the twins' having discussed the test with each other. To guard against this likelihood, Juel-Nielsen had tried to administer the first test simultaneously to co-twins.

Whatever doubts we have about the validity of the 244 "I.Q.'s" presented by Professor Jensen, we are at least reassured by the precision of his statistical analysis of the numbers: "All the present analyses were calculated by computer, with figures carried to five decimals and not rounded till the final product." The difficulty here is that Professor Jensen appears to have used a faulty computer. For example, his paper is very much concerned with the use of the mean absolute difference between co-twins as a measure of their resemblance. For Shields' sample — using Jensen's own "I.Q.'s" — the mean difference is given as 6.72, with a standard deviation of 5.80. The actual values, as calculated by me from Jensen's own numbers, are 6.82 and 5.90. For Juel-Nielsen, he gives a mean of 6.46 and standard deviation of 3.22; the actual values are 6.42 and 3.29. For Newman, Freeman, and Holzinger, Jensen gives values of 8.21 and 6.65; the actual values are 8.21 and 6.84. The incorrect standard deviation of 6.65, given by Jensen, corresponds exactly to that published by Newman, Freeman, and Holzinger. Their value would have been regarded as correct when they published it; at that time the error of not subtracting a degree of freedom when calculating the variance of a sample was common. Thus it might appear that Jensen simply copied Newman et al.'s values. The fact is that he also reproduces exactly their calculation of the standard deviation of raw I.Q. scores, similarly incorrect. This reproduction of error subtracts some force from Jensen's observation that "The few instances of slight discrepancies between these statistics and the corresponding figures of the original authors are all within the range of rounding error." The calculational errors involved here, unlike the errors made in the "transformation,'' are all small—but we have a right to expect more from quantitative genetic theorists who take pains to tell us that they carry calculations to five decimals.

We shall from this point on suspend the facts, and assume that Jensen's numbers represent valid I.Q. scores and are arithmetically correct. Professor Jensen now wishes to demonstrate that the distributions of the co-twin differences in the four studies do not differ significantly. This must be done if he is to use the pooled data to estimate heritability. He reports that ''Bartlett's test was performed on the standard deviations of the absolute differences (SD_d) and revealed that on this parameter the differences among the studies are nonsignificant at the .01 level.'' The wording here seems strange, and the kindest characterization that we can make of it is that it is disingenuous. The fact is—though Jensen does not report it —that applied to his own numbers, Bartlett's test produces a value of chi square that *is significant at the .02 level.* The wording will not be explained by assuming that Professor Jensen is committed to the .01 level of significance. There is one other occasion in the same paper when Jensen uses the chi-square statistic. There, quite unlike the example we have cited, he reports the actual value of chi square ''is only 3.08, $p = 0.80$. (Chi square with 7 degrees of freedom must exceed 14.07 for *significance at the .05 level*)'' (italics added). This passion for communicating unnecessary numerical detail is abandoned by Professor Jensen when chi square hovers between the .02 and .01 levels of significance.

Professor Jensen now goes on to use the pooled twin data to estimate the heritability of I.Q. To do this he uses a correlation statistic based on the co-twin differences which have been systematically deflated by his ''I.Q. transformation.'' The assumption is made that the numbers come from some ''population'' in which the standard deviation is 15. There is also — charged as a debit against environment—a correction for ''errors of measurement.'' That correction is made despite the fact that the Juel-Nielsen data, based on two test administrations, have already reduced measurement error; despite the fact that the ''measurement error'' in Burt's ''assessments'' is incalculable, and doubtless bias rather than random error; and despite the fact that the reliabilities of Shields' tests are unknown. We assume that in making his quantitative heritability estimate Jensen carried his figures to five decimals, but final results were rounded. The analysis indicated that 85% of I.Q. variance is due to heredity, 10% to environment, and 5% to test error.

There are other errors in the Jensen paper, but we pass over them. We must comment, however, on how Jensen disposes of the 10% of I.Q. variance that his quantitative analysis has left to environment. We again observe his apparent compulsion not to leave well enough alone:

A substantial and perhaps even a major proportion of the nongenetic variance is attributable to prenatal and other biological influences rather than to differences in the social-psychological environment. . . . Differences in the favorableness of intrauterine environment are reflected in differences in birth weight between twins . . . and the differences in birth weight are known to be related to IQ disparities in twins. . . . The mean difference of 6.9 IQ points between the heavier and lighter MZ twins (52 pairs) in the studies summarized by Scarr is not far from the mean IQ difference of 6.6 between all the twins in the present study.

Thus, in Professor Jensen's view, what little effect environment has is in "major proportion" not a social or educational effect, but the result of "prenatal" influences. This possibility has also captured the imagination of Professor Herrnstein, who wrote that "the twin studies that Jensen surveyed showed that the single most important environmental influence on I.Q. was not education or social environment, but something prenatal, as shown by the fact that the twin heavier at birth usually grew up with the higher I.Q."[15] This conclusion from "the twin studies that Jensen surveyed" led Professor Herrnstein, in his next sentence, to speculate that "an environmental handle on I.Q." might be "the gestating mother's diet." This speculation seems logical enough, granted that education and social environment have been proved to have so little effect.

There is no obvious reason for Professor Jensen to call attention to the close correspondence between the figures 6.9 and 6.6. The 6.9 I.Q. point difference based on 52 twin pairs surveyed by Scarr refers to an average amount by which the I.Q. of the twin heavier at birth *exceeded* that of the lighter twin. The average difference of 6.6 "I.Q. points" based on the 122 twin pairs surveyed by Jensen refers to the absolute difference between co-twins, *regardless* of whether it favors the heavier or lighter twin.[16] There is no reason not to suppose that, among the 122 twin pairs surveyed by Jensen, the heavier and lighter twins had, on average, identical I.Q.'s.

There is, in fact, considerable reason to suppose that this was the case. There are no birth weight data given by Burt or by Newman et al. The birth weights of 27 pairs of separated twins and 34 pairs of nonseparated twins were known to Shields, who reported that "Birth weight was not associated with test score differences."[17] This total sample size, it might be noted, is larger than Scarr's. The birth weights of 7 twin pairs were known to Juel-Nielsen, but failed to have "any significance for the intelligence test scores."[18] With social environment threatening to claim a full 10% of I.Q. variance, Professor Jensen was evidently compelled to cite data from Scarr, who had not studied separated twins. Those data were used to deflate theoretically an estimate of postnatal environmental influence derived, after Professor Jensen's fashion, from the study of separated twins. The contradictory data from the twin studies that the Jensen paper purported to survey — based on a larger sample than Scarr's — were simply ignored. This in turn enabled Professor Herrnstein to report to the readers of *Atlantic Monthly* that "the twin studies that Jensen surveyed showed that the single most important environmental influence on I.Q. was . . . something prenatal." Professor Herrnstein, of course, has added his own embellishment. The data, in his hands, "showed" something prenatal to be "the single most important environmental influence." Professor Jensen more modestly suggested that the research "indicates that a substantial and perhaps even a major proportion of the nongenetic variance is attributable to prenatal and other biological influences." We shall review in the final chapter the actual evidence for prenatal determinism.

There is evidence to suggest that still others among quantitative hereditarian theorists are not immune to error. Professor Vandenberg,[19] in a distinguished

1968 volume published by Rockefeller University Press, reproduced a table based upon one that had been published by Halperin[20] in 1945. The Vandenberg table is given here as our Table 10. The table purports to indicate both the percentages and absolute numbers of children of different types born to parents of different types. The mental typology labels children with I.Q.'s in the 50–70 range "defective," and those with I.Q.'s in the 70–85 range "inferior." The I.Q. values, however, have been entirely invented. The entries in the body of the table refer to the sibs of children committed to a state institution for the feebleminded. The sibs were assessed by Halperin as defective, inferior, or average on the basis of information obtained from families and schools "in the form of test scores, Binet findings, educational achievement scores, and scholastic reports." There is no indication by Halperin of what "I.Q.," or I.Q. equivalent, corresponded to the borderline between categories. The parents had been classified on the basis of a test (given to less than one-quarter of them), and information obtained from "social welfare agencies, schools, hospitals, local physicians, and ministers and priests." The ministers and priests, of course, may have followed Burt's practice of administering "camouflaged intelligence tests" in the course of their pastoral duties, but it is doubtful whether anyone has communicated with them to determine where on the scale of I.Q. values they established their cutting points. The point here is both serious and familiar: The quantitative aura surrounding heritability data is in large measure specious. The very rough classification of parents' mental status was based on information that, according to Halperin, was "reliable" for 45% of families, "less reliable" for 51%, and "unreliable" for 4%.

TABLE 10

Vandenberg's Table[a]

The percentage of average, inferior, and mentally defective children born to various combinations of parents. The number of cases are shown in brackets

Parents	N	% Average or above	% Inferior IQ 70–85	% Defective IQ 50–70
Average × average	18	73 (13)	5 (1)	22 (4)
Average × inferior	59	64 (38)	33 (19)	3 (2)
Inferior × inferior	252	28 (70)	57 (144)	15 (38)
Inferior × defective	89	10 (9)	55 (49)	35 (31)
Defective × defective	141	4 (6)	39 (55)	57 (80)

[a]Reproduced with the permission of the publisher from S. G. Vandenberg, "The Nature and Nurture of Intelligence," in D. C. Glass, ed., *Genetics*, (New York, Rockefeller University Press, 1968).

We shall again suspend our doubts and, for the sake of argument, assume that the numbers are based upon valid measurements. The question we now raise concerns the accuracy of the arithmetical operations that produced Table 10. The actual table published by Halperin, on which Vandenberg's is based, is presented as our Table 11.

Professor Vandenberg, it will be noted, has spared his readers some irrelevant details. The Halperin table, for example, treats as two separate categories the cases when average father is married to inferior mother, and when inferior father is married to average mother. To simplify matters, Vandenberg establishes a single category: one parent average, and one parent inferior. Thus one must add together the numbers in two separate rows of Halperin's table. The reader is invited to perform the relevant operation. The raw numbers that *should* be entered in the second row of Vandenberg's table are, consecutively, 29, 12, and 18. The numbers actually entered by Vandenberg are 38, 19, and 2. That, of course, produces a gross error in computing the percentages of children of each type born to marriages of this type. The numbers entered by Vandenberg in the fourth row of his table, like those in the second, are grossly in error. The first, third, and fifth rows of his table present a different kind of problem: Since both parents are of the same type, it is only necessary to copy faithfully the numbers set out in a single row of Halperin's table. This has been successfully accomplished in the first Vandenberg row, though the accomplishment is marred by a very minor error in calculating percentages. The third and fifth rows of Vandenberg's table, involving only copying, are unfortunately grossly in error.[21]

TABLE 11

Halperin's Table[a]

An Analysis of the Mental Status of Parents and Offspring in 142 Families						
			(Following Penrose)			
			Observed Number of Sibs in Each Grade			
Number of Families	Parental Ratings		Defective	Inferior	Average	Above Average
	Father	Mother				
4	Average x Average		4	1	12	1
11	Average x Inferior		12	7	24	0
0	Average x Defective		—	—	—	—
5	Inferior x Average		6	5	5	0
66	Inferior x Inferior		91	114	45	2
20	Inferior x Defective		37	24	4	0
0	Defective x Average		—	—	—	—
3	Defective x Inferior		10	12	2	0
34	Defective x Defective		95	41	5	0
			255	204	97	3

[a]Reproduced with permission of the publisher from S. L. Halperin, "A Clinico-Genetical Study of Mental Defect," *American Journal of Mental Deficiency*, 50, (1945), 8-26.

The errors here have real theoretical consequence. The Halperin data were given by Vandenberg immediately after his reprinting of Roberts' two I.Q. distributions for the sibs of low-I.Q. children. The two Roberts distributions were incorrectly represented by Vandenberg as having been derived from "high-grade and low-grade mental defectives." The reader of Vandenberg's paper would conclude that only 7.8% of children born to parents at least one of whom is average, compared to 15.1% of the children of two "inferior" parents, have I.Q.'s between 50 and 70. That I.Q. range covers precisely the values described by Jensen as "the lower end of normal variation," the consequence of normal polygenic mechanisms. The data as presented could thus be taken as strong support for the polygenic determination of I.Q.'s in the 50–70 range. The I.Q. values, however, have been invented. Further, according to Halperin's table, the percentages assigned to this fictitious I.Q. range should be, for the two types of matings, 29% and 36%.

The 1972 edition of Wechsler's "Measurement and Appraisal of Adult Intelligence" incorporated Vandenberg's errors.[22] The volume republished Roberts' two I.Q. distributions, with Vandenberg's caption. The text clearly implied that one curve was for the sibs of individuals with I.Q.'s in the 50–70 range, and the other for the sibs of those with lower I.Q.'s. The Roberts data were buttressed by Halperin's data, described as indicating that "the mating of a person of average or above intelligence with one whose IQ was between 70 and 85 yielded a number of offspring of whom 3 per cent earned IQ's between 50 and 70." The I.Q. ranges 50–70 and 70–85 had been added on to Halperin's work by Vandenberg and, in his version of Halperin's table, assigned to *children*. This addition has now been embellished. The children are now said to have "earned" these I.Q.'s, and fictitious I.Q. numbers are now assigned to parents as well. The "3 per cent" is a simple copying of Vandenberg's error; the "true" number, from Halperin, is 31 percent. The very influential Wechsler compendium is clearly to some extent based on copying still other secondary sources and preserves their errors intact. Those errors will make their way from Wechsler to still other "reviews of research."

Professor Vandenberg has been a major contributor to the "quantitative" literature on I.Q. heritability. The data collected by Vandenberg in a host of twin studies have been published by him in a highly digested form. The data as actually presented take the form of F ratios and factor loadings, the products of a long chain of complicated arithmetical and mathematical operations. These data are said to demonstrate the heritability of such innate traits as Numerical Ability and Clerical Speed and Accuracy. The reader, under the circumstances, is entitled to wonder whether numerical or clerical errors may intervene between the raw data and the published summaries.

The most mathematically sophisticated model for estimating heritability is doubtless that of Jinks and Fulker, published in 1970.[23] Professor Herrnstein refers glancingly to their "highly technical discussion" and "variety of analytic techniques" before reprinting the close match that they obtained between "obtained" and "theoretical" kinship correlations.[24] The theoretical correlations had been estimated by a model making use of observed correlations. The match was sufficiently close for Professor Herrnstein to reprint the theoretical correlations complete to four decimal places. Professor Herrnstein did not bother to inform his readers of the assumptions made by the model, or of the source of the data to which the model had been fitted.

The Jinks and Fulker analytic techniques are mathematically elegant, but they are applied to I.Q. data that are, at the least, of questionable validity. The major application of the model — which produced the closely matching obtained and theoretical correlations reprinted by Herrnstein — was to the kinship correlations reported by Burt in 1966. The Burt data were selected "because they are not only based on large numbers and many groups, but also result, largely, from the application of a single, highly reliable test." The correlations employed by Jinks and Fulker were in fact based upon Burt's "final assessments." These, it will be recalled, deliberately removed the "disturbing effects of environment" from scores on unspecified group and individual tests administered to unknown subjects an unspecified number of times. The Burt data are marvelously consistent with a genetic interpretation; and a genetic model that failed to fit them closely would be poor indeed.

The Jinks and Fulker model assumes, in many applications, that there is no (statistical) interaction between genotype and environment. Their procedure includes tests for the detection of any such interaction. To test for "GE interaction" in the Newman et al. separated twin data, they applied Cochran's test to co-twin I.Q differences: "Just as heterogeneity of variance within inbred lines denotes GE, so does heterogeneity of variance within twins. . . $C = 0.2714$. The .05 level of significance for C is 0.3894, so we conclude there is, again, no evidence for GE."

That conclusion, however, can easily be reversed. The Cochran test is extremely sensitive to the maximum difference observed between a pair of twins. For the Newman et al. sample, the largest observed I.Q. difference between a pair of twins was 24. I.Q. points. That was the celebrated case of Gladys and Helen, separated twins with I.Q.'s of 92 and 116. These I.Q.'s were based on the 1916 Stanford-Binet and had been calculated in a manner Terman himself had demonstrated to be inappropriate. The test had been designed primarily for children. When applied to well-educated adults, it produced scores that were far too low. The items on the adult scale were, in short, too easy. This led to an anomalous result. When a 14-year-old successfully answered every item on the test, his I.Q. was scored as 139. When he became 16 years old, the same performance produced an I.Q. of 122, although he had answered exactly the same questions in exactly the same way. This absurdity led Terman as early as 1925 to suggest a corrected scoring procedure, which gave "bonus" months of "mental age" to high-scoring adults.[25] From Helen's reported mental age, it can be deduced with precision that, properly scored, her "real" I.Q. was in fact 125. Thus the real difference between Gladys and Helen was 33 points, not 24. We now apply Cochran's test to the real I.Q.'s of the 19 twin pairs and we find $C = .4132827324$. That is statistically significant at the .05 level. We have now demonstrated, with the aid of an elegant mathematical-genetical model, that a significant genotype-environment interaction exists. To be fair, however, we should note that the scores of a few others of the adult twins in the sample should have been adjusted. The exact adjustments, unlike Helen's, cannot be easily deduced, but none would much affect a between-twin difference, so our result seems likely to stand.

The Jinks and Fulker procedure provides another test for GE interaction, which is said to be indicated by a correlation between the means and the within-pair differences of a set of twins. This follows since the mean score of a pair of identical twins is said to estimate their genotype, while the score difference between them estimates the effect of environment. This test was applied by Jinks and Fulker to Shields' vocabulary data for separated and control identical twins. The vocabulary test was assumed by Jinks and Fulker to measure "verbal intelligence potential" and "I.Q.". For both separated and control twins, Jinks and Fulker found negative correlations between pair means and pair differences, at a level of "borderline significance." That suggested to them that for *this* form of "I.Q.," a GE interaction might exist. "The negative sign of the correlation indicates that environmental deviations are larger for the individuals with the lower I.Q.'s. These individuals seem, therefore, to be more at the mercy of the environment than those with higher I.Q.'s and, perhaps, reach their potential with less certainty. This fact would, of course, have important implications for educational practice suggesting that individuals at the lower end of the distribution need more careful nurturing than those at the higher end, if they are to develop fully their verbal intelligence potential."[26]

The tools of mathematical-genetical analysis, evidently, enable us to provide helpful hints to educators about the care and feeding of different genotypes. The vocabulary test is assumed to measure a "potential" which is in turn assumed to be encoded in "the genes." The test score is regarded as a kind of X-ray device, enabling us to see the otherwise invisible genotypes. We might, however, reach different conclusions if we examine the actual properties of the test. The instruction manual for the Mill Hill Vocabulary Test (kindly provided by Shields) gives some data about the distribution of test scores in "the population." From that manual we can perform the following calculation.

We consider only two twin pairs, between 30 and 45 years old. For one pair the raw scores on the test are 26 and 47. For the other pair the raw scores are 66 and 76. We follow Jinks and Fulker and correlate, for raw scores, pair means with pair differences. For the first set of twins, the values are 36.5 and 21; for the second set, 71 and 10. We observe a clear negative correlation and conclude that a genotype-environment interaction exists.

We now read the manual carefully and observe that a raw score of 26 falls at the 5th percentile of the population. The percentile values for the raw scores 47, 66, and 76 are 25th, 75th, and 95th. We follow Jinks and Fulker in assuming that vocabulary score measures "I.Q." or "verbal intelligence potential." The I.Q. is normally distributed in the population, with a mean of 100 and a standard deviation of 15. We must now transform the raw scores into I.Q.'s; but we respect the fact that the distribution of raw scores is severely skewed. The I.Q. equivalents of the percentiles at which our four hypothetical individuals fall indicate that the I.Q.'s of our first twin pair are 75 and 90. The I.Q.'s of the second twin pair are 110 and 125. That is, a pair mean of 82.5 is now associated with a pair difference of 15, as is a pair mean of 117.5. The correlation is obviously zero, so we now conclude that there is *no* genotype-environment interaction. Whether or not we observe an interaction depends upon our choice of scale. The choice of scale is arbitrary—as is the advice provided to educators by Jinks and Fulker. We are in fact dealing with test scores, not with potentials and genotypes.

There is an obvious reason why raw scores on the Mill Hill Vocabulary Test *should* produce a skewed distribution. The test is a multiple-choice test. Those who have taken such tests will recall that, if one does not know the answer, one guesses. The fewer answers one knows, the more guessing there will be. The more one guesses, the more one's score will be determined by chance. There must therefore be more "measurement error" associated with low scores than with high scores. Two twins brought up in similarly deprived environments will have low scores, and a relatively large between-twin score difference. This fact is now taken by the Jinks and Fulker model to be telling us something about the invisible genotypes of the twins, and about the educability of low scorers. The propensity of the unseen genotype to interact with environment can be eliminated by simply transforming the vocabulary scores. The model will still assert that the resemblance between twins in vocabulary score is due to their identical genotypes. The environmentalist will still conclude that the resemblance is produced by the highly similar environments of both control and so-called "separated" twins.

The Jinks and Fulker model also assumes that within-family environmental effects are the same in each category of family being examined. That boils down to the familiar — and untenable — assumption that identical and fraternal twins experience equally different environments. The model also assumes no correlation between genotype and environment. These assumptions can in principle be tested by comparing the total I.Q. variances for different types of families included in a particular model-fitting. When the variances are in fact heterogeneous, however, this can be attributed, as Jinks and Fulker in some instances do, to inadequate sampling of some family types.

The conceptual elegance of the Jinks and Fulker model will not compensate for the deficiencies of the data to which it is applied. We concur fully with Jinks and Fulker's admonition to other model-makers: "To fit a complex model to inadequate data may well lead to completely unfounded conclusions."

BURT'S ASSESSMENTS AGAIN

The inaccuracies of secondary sources are nicely illustrated by the uses that have been made of a table published by Burt in 1961.[27] The Burt table is reproduced as our Table 12. The table purports to show the distribution of "intelligence," for both adults and children, as a function of the occupational class to which the adult belongs. From the table Burt — and others who have followed him — draws conclusions about the distribution of I.Q. genes in various social classes, and about the amount of social mobility that may be expected in the course of a generation. There are some children of unskilled workers, it may be seen, who have good genes (high intelligence scores). These children may be expected, in an open society, to rise in social class, because of their genetic endowment. The table also indicates the number of upper-class children who may be expected to fall.

The source of the data was described by Burt as follows: "For the children the bulk of the data was obtained from the surveys carried out from time to time in a London borough selected as typical of the whole county. The methods by which the assessments for intelligence were made have been described in earlier papers and L.C.C. Reports. For the boys who belong to the highest occupational classes, drawn for example from families who would not ordinarily send their children to Council schools, much of the data was collected in the course of work on vocational guidance at the National Institute of Industrial Psychology. The data for the adults was obtained from the parents of the children themselves. . . . For obvious reasons the assessments of adult intelligence were less thorough and less reliable."[28]

That is to say, the numbers in Burt's table do not refer to I.Q. test scores. For adults, they are unadulterated "assessments" — that is, guesses. For children, a score on a group test had been adjusted on the basis of teachers' judgments. Those teachers who felt that well-bred children were brighter than their test scores indicated were free to influence the "adjusted assessments" appropriately. The common schools did not provide enough upper-class children, so Burt supplemented the school data with data derived from those upper-class families whose children were given vocational guidance at the National Institute of Industrial Psychology. That is not a normal sampling procedure in social surveys, but then again Burt's "intelligence" scores are not normal I.Q. test scores.

We should like to know how many adults and children were assessed by Burt. We should not be misled by the fact that the numbers inside the tables add up to 1,000: "the frequencies inserted in the various rows and columns were proportional frequencies and in no way represent the number actually examined: from Class I the number examined was nearer a hundred and twenty than three. To obtain the figures to be inserted (numbers per mille) we weighted the actual numbers so that the proportions in each class should be equal to the estimated proportions for the total population. Finally, for purposes of the present analysis

TABLE 12
Burt's Table[a]

I. Distribution of Intelligence According to Occupational Class: Adults

	50–60	60–70	70–80	80–90	90–100	100–110	110–120	120–130	130–140	140+	Total	Mean I.Q.
I. Higher Professional									2	1	3	139.7
II. Lower Professional							2	13	15	1	31	130.6
III. Clerical				1	8	16	56	38	3		122	115.9
IV. Skilled			2	11	51	101	78	14	1		258	108.2
V. Semiskilled		5	15	31	135	120	17	2			325	97.8
VI. Unskilled	1	18	52	117	53	11	9				261	84.9
Total	1	23	69	160	247	248	162	67	21	2	1000	100.0

II. Distribution of Intelligence According to Occupational Class: Children

	50–60	60–70	70–80	80–90	90–100	100–110	110–120	120–130	130–140	140+	Total	Mean I.Q.
I. Higher Professional						1		1	1		3	120.8
II. Lower Professional				1	2	6	12	8	2		31	114.7
III. Clerical			3	8	21	31	35	18	6		122	107.8
IV. Skilled		1	12	33	53	70	59	22	7	1	258	104.6
V. Semiskilled	1	6	23	55	99	85	38	13	5		325	98.9
VI. Unskilled	1	15	32	62	75	54	16	6			261	92.6
Total	2	22	70	159	250	247	160	68	21	1	1000	100.0

[a] Reproduced with permission of the publisher from C. Burt, "Intelligence and Social Mobility," *British Journal of Statistical Psychology*, 14, (1961), 3–24.

we have rescaled our assessments of intelligence so that the mean of the whole group is 100 and the standard deviation 15.'' That is the total information provided by Burt about how many assessments were made, and how. We know nothing about the sex distribution of subjects, either among adults or children.

We may now observe how these data have been cited in secondary sources. Professor Gottesman, writing in 1968 on *Biogenetics of Race and Class,* reprinted Burt's table, in support of the thesis that "the structure of modern societies is at least in part dependent on biological phenomena . . . that stratification is based on ability and, further, that individual differences in ability are partially genetically conditioned."[29] The tone here is much more moderate, but the resemblance to Henry Goddard's Princeton lectures of 1919 (see Chapter 1) is real.

Professor Gottesman reports that Burt had collected data on "intelligence in some 40,000 adults and their children . . . the N of 3 (per 1000) for Higher Professionals represents 120 fathers." The picture of Professor Burt collecting and analyzing I.Q. data of 40,000 adults and at *least* some 40,000 of their children will doubtless impress the readers of *Biogenetics of Race and Class.* Professor Burt has here accomplished single handedly more than the entire World War I test analysis program of the United States Army. The picture, however, exists only in the realm of fiction. There is no claim by Burt that he had assessed 40,000 adults, nor is there any claim that those assessed were "fathers." The statement by Burt was merely that the number of adults in Class I was "nearer a hundred and twenty than three." Professor Gottesman evidently chose to assume that that number *was* 120, rather than 62. Whatever he assumed the actual number of Class I adults to be, there is absolutely no warrant for dividing that number by 3, multiplying by 1,000, and asserting that the final product represents the number of adults assessed by Burt. That is what Gottesman has done. We can easily believe, from Burt's description of his procedure, that for some occupational classes the numbers actually assessed were *smaller* than the weighted proportions inserted into his table. With Burt, there is no way of knowing. The readers of Professor Gottesman also have no way of knowing that the numbers refer to "assessments" of intelligence, made in full knowledge of the occupational class of the people being assessed.

Professor Herrnstein, who appears also to have read his Goddard, also reprints Burt's table. The claim made by Herrnstein about the number of people studied is more modest, if not more accurate. The claims about the sampling procedure, and about what is being measured, are on the other hand inflated: "Table 7A shows the I.Q.'s of a representative sample of 1,000 men from all occupational levels."[30] There are three certain misstatements, and one probable one, in this brief sentence. The sentence describes the only *data* used by Herrnstein in an entire chapter written in support of his assertion that social standing is "based to some extent on inherited differences among people."

The reviews of the I.Q. literature tend sometimes to be selective in their choice of cited sources. This often leads one writer to assert as a broad generalization a proposition that is contradicted by some other authority. For example, Jensen, in

1969, pointed to the finding that twins tend to have slightly lower I.Q.'s than singletons and in support of this cited Swedish data reported by Husen. The effect was attributed by Jensen to "prenatal environment." Jensen wrote: "Monozygotic twins are slightly lower in IQ than dizygotic twins (Stott, 1960, p. 98) . . . suggesting that MZ twins enjoy less equal and less optimal intrauterine conditions than DZ twins or singletons."[31] The Husen study, however, had reported that "There is throughout a tendency among the identical twins to be slightly superior to the fraternals."[32] The Husen data had been used to assert that twins in general had lower I.Q.'s. The Stott data had been used to assert that MZ twins were inferior, and the contradictory Husen data had been ignored.

Professor Jensen also reported in 1969 that "first-born children are superior in almost every way, mentally and physically. This is the consistent finding of many studies. . . ."[33] The finding, however, seems not to be entirely consistent, since Burt and Howard—also sensitive to prenatal factors—had reported, in 1957, that "the first child . . . is . . . prone to suffer from pre-natal handicaps. . . . Some indication of the effects that follow may be gleaned by classifying test-results according to the order of the child's birth: with the majority of tests, as one of us has pointed out in earlier papers, the averages for first born and last born are decidedly lower than those for the intervening children."[34] The literature reviewing mental testing seems to be replete with references to "decided" differences, more or less "consistently" reported, from which insights into the genetic and prenatal determination of I.Q. can be gleaned by the analytically minded.

The introductory textbooks of psychology repeat what have now become classical errors. For example, of the ten most widely used texts in 1972, six printed the numerical value of the correlation between separated MZ twins found by Newman et al. The value was given in each case as .77, rather than the .67 actually published by Newman. There was no reference to the fact that the .77 value represents an "adjustment" made by McNemar on the basis of untenable assumptions (see Chapter 3). The correlations of Burt for uncles, grandparents, etc., were reprinted by another set of six texts; in no case was any reference made to the fact that the correlations were based on "assessments" rather than I.Q. test scores.

The textbooks perpetuate the notion that studies of adopted children have demonstrated that "differences in intelligence are set principally, but not entirely, by inheritance."[35] The final Skodak and Skeels study was cited by five texts, the Leahy study by two, and the Burks study by two. There was no reference to the earlier Skodak and Skeels study, on a larger sample, which had shown the adopted child's I.Q. to be equally related to the educational levels of adoptive and biological parents. There was not a single citation of the Freeman et al. study, which had shown large I.Q. correlations between adoptive child and adoptive parent. There was not a single citation of the Snygg study, which had shown no significant relation between the I.Q.'s of adoptive children and their biological parents.

The textbooks, like the authorities, tend to present a simple and clear picture. There is not one of the ten most widely used texts that does not conclude that heredity plays a significant role in the determination of I.Q. scores. The majority assign the major role to heredity. They do so on the basis of the data that have been reviewed in the preceding chapters.

NOTES TO CHAPTER SIX

1. A. R. Jensen, "Reducing the Heredity-Environment Uncertainty: A Reply," *Harvard Educational Review,* 39, (1969), p. 455.
2. R. J. Herrnstein, *I.Q. in the Meritocracy,* (Boston, Atlantic Monthly Press, 1973), p. 52.
3. A. R. Jensen, "How Much Can We Boost IQ and Scholastic Achievement?", *Harvard Educational Review,* 39, (1969), 1 – 123.
4. J. A. F. Roberts, "The Genetics of Mental Deficiency," *Eugenics Review,* 44, (1952), p. 74.
5. *Genetics,* ed. D. C. Glass, (New York, Rockefeller University Press, 1968), p. 24.
6. J. A. F. Roberts and M. A. Mellone, "On the Adjustment of Terman-Merrill I.Q.'s to Secure Comparability at Different Ages," *British Journal of Statistical Psychology,* 5, (1952), 66.
7. *International Review of Research in Mental Retardation, Vol. 4,* Ed. N. R. Ellis, (New York, Academic Press, 1970), p. 34.
8. *Genetic and Environmental Factors in Human Ability,* Eds. J. E. Meade and A. S. Parke, (New York, Plenum Press, 1966), p. 130.
9. Z. Stein and M. W. Susser, "The Social Distribution of Mental Retardation," *American Journal of Mental Deficiency,* 67, (1963), 811 – 821.
10. Though the 1969 Jensen paper does not indicate this fact, Professor Jensen has pointed out in personal correspondence that the figure he reproduced had been taken with permission from R. Heber, R. Dever, and J. Conry, The Influence of Environmental and Genetic Variables on Intellectual Development, in H. J. Prehm, L. A. Hamerlynck, and J. E. Crosson (Eds.), *Behavioral Research in Mental Retardation,* (Eugene, Oregon, University of Oregon Press, 1968), p. 4. The Heber et al. paper indicates that the figure was "Adapted from Erlenmeyer-Kimling, L., and Jarvik, L. F. Genetics and intelligence; a review. *Science,* 1963, *142,* 1477 – 1499."
11. J. Shields, *Monozygotic Twins Brought Up Apart and Brought Up Together,* (London, Oxford University Press, 1962), p. 253.
12. A. R. Jensen, "IQs of Identical Twins Reared Apart," *Behavior Genetics,* 1, (1970), 135. This paper has been published in slightly revised form in Jensen's *Genetics and Education,* (New York, Harper & Row, 1972). The revised version corrects some, but not all, of the errors cited in the text.

13. N. Juel-Nielsen, "Individual and Environment: A Psychiatric-Psychological Investigation of Monozygous Twins Reared Apart," *Acta Psychiatrica et Neurologica Scandinavaca,* Monograph Supplement 183, (1965), p. 54.
14. Shields, *Monozygotic Twins,* p. 59.
15. R. J. Herrnstein, "I.Q.," *Atlantic Monthly,* September, 1971, p. 58.
16. The reprinted version of the Jensen paper in his *"Genetics and Education"* (p. 324) adds a new and mystifying footnote. The text of Jensen's paper indicates that the Scarr figures refer to an I.Q. difference "in favor of the heavier twin." The footnote inexplicably and incorrectly says of the same differences, "These are all absolute (unsigned) differences."
17. Shields, *Monozygotic Twins,* p. 113.
18. Juel-Nielsen, *Individual and Environment,* p. 109.
19. Glass, *Genetics,* p. 25.
20. S. L. Halperin, "A Clinico-Genetical Study of Mental Defect," *American Journal of Mental Deficiency,* 50, (1945), 8 – 26.
21. The discrepancies between Vandenberg's table and that published by Halperin may have been caused by Vandenberg's copying the Halperin data from still other secondary sources. The essential features of Vandenberg's version of the table, including the same errors, are contained in a table published earlier by Gottesman in *Handbook of Mental Deficiency,* ed. N. R. Ellis, (New York, McGraw-Hill, 1963), p. 277. The situation would not be much improved, however, had the secondary sources copied Halperin's original table accurately. There is still another version of the table, published by Halperin himself one year after the original table appeared. That version is in S. L. Halperin, "Human Heredity and Mental Deficiency," *American Journal of Mental Deficiency,* 51, (1946), 160. There are substantial disagreements between Halperin's two versions of his own data, as well as between each version and the secondary sources.
22. J. D. Matarazzo, *Wechsler's Measurement and Appraisal of Adult Intelligence,* 5th Ed., (Baltimore, Williams and Wilkins, 1972), p. 311.
23. J. L. Jinks and D. W. Fulker, "Comparison of the Biometrical Genetical, MAVA, and Classical Approaches to the Analysis of Human Behavior," *Psychological Bulletin,* 73, (1970), 311 – 349.
24. Herrnstein, *I.Q.,* pp. 171 – 172.
25. L. M. Terman, *Genetic Studies of Genius, Volume 1, Mental and Physical Traits of a Thousand Gifted Children,* (Stanford, Stanford University Press, 1925), pp. 42 – 43.
26. Jinks and Fulker, *Comparison,* p. 336.
27. C. Burt, "Intelligence and Social Mobility," *British Journal of Statistical Psychology,* 14, (1961), 11.
28. Ibid, pp. 9 – 10.
29. *Social Class, Race, and Psychological Development,* Eds. M. Deutsch, J. Katz, and A. R. Jensen, (New York, Holt, Rinehart, and Winston, 1968), p. 35.

30. Herrnstein, *I.Q.*, p. 203.
31. Jensen, *How Much*, p. 67.
32. T. Husen, "Abilities of Twins," *Scandinavian Journal of Psychology*, 1, (1960), 130.
33. Jensen, *How Much*, p. 74.
34. C. Burt and M. Howard, "Heredity and Intelligence: a Reply to Criticisms," *British Journal of Statistical Psychology*, 10, (1957), 60.
35. C. T. Morgan and R. A. King, *Introduction to Psychology*, 4th Ed., (New York, McGraw Hill, 1971), p. 343.

7
I.Q. IN THE UTERUS

*And it came to pass, whensoever the stronger cattle did
conceive, that Jacob laid the rods before the eyes of the
cattle in the gutters, that they might conceive among the
rods.
But when the cattle were feeble, he put them not in: so
the feebler were Laban's, and the stronger Jacob's.*
—Genesis 30. 41–42

The subject matter of this chapter is not strictly relevant to the question of
whether I.Q. is determined by the genes. We shall be concerned here with the
degree to which intrauterine experience has been shown to be related to I.Q. There
is a curious but understandable tendency for theorists who stress the idea of I.Q.
heritability to suggest the womb as the locus for whatever meager effect environment is said to have on intellectual development. We have seen in the previous
chapter how Professors Jensen and Herrnstein concluded that "something prenatal" was a "major" or "single most important" environmental influence on
I.Q. This association of the hereditarian view with the idea of prenatal determinism is ideologically consistent. To stress that most I.Q. variance in the
population is genetic is to assert that education and social processes have very
little effect. From such an assertion it is an easy step to conclude that the trivial
effect of society on I.Q. is likely to be outweighed by unobserved events taking
place in the womb. The practical implication of the stress on prenatal factors, like
that of the hereditarian view, is that an effort to improve educational and social
environment will have almost no effect on I.Q. The prenatal stress, however, does

161

have one clearly humanitarian consequence. The gestating mother's diet, in this view, may play some role in determining her infant's I.Q. Those who are concerned with elevating I.Q. would thus do well to feed welfare mothers — at least while they are pregnant. The nutritional status of the father, however, would seem irrelevant.

The evidence said to support the notion that I.Q. is affected by intrauterine experience comes from a small number of studies. Those studies take the birth weight of an infant as an index of how well he has fared in the womb. Those infants who are born robust are assumed to have had good intrauterine experience and are thus expected to display relatively high I.Q.'s. There are a number of studies that purport to demonstrate a small positive correlation between birth weight and I.Q. They are not, however, central to the argument. The birth weight of infants is related to parents' social class and race, among other variables. These variables in turn are related to I.Q. scores and would account for an I.Q.–birth-weight relation with no need of invoking prenatal factors. The critical evidence is said to come from studies of the birth weights and I.Q.'s of identical twins.

There are, in the present instance, some very obvious theoretical advantages in the use of identical twins as subjects. The twins are of course genetically identical, which should make possible the detection of even very small prenatal effects. The more important advantage is that, for a given twin pair, social class and race are bound to be identical. Thus, if we look at birth weight difference in a pair of twins, and relate it to I.Q. difference between them, we are controlling absolutely for class and race. The detection of a birth-weight–I.Q. association would now be free from at least those confounding variables. The observation that the heavier twin had the higher I.Q. could now suggest a role for prenatal factors. The basic assumption is that the heavier twin received, in the womb, more than his share of the maternal blood supply and nutrients. There would still remain the possibility that the higher I.Q. of the heavier twin was a result of differential *postnatal* treatment accorded to him. The review of the evidence, however, will make it unnecessary for us to consider this possibility. There is in fact no credible evidence that, within a very wide range of nonpathological birth weights, the I.Q.'s of twins are related to their weights.

There can be no doubt that an occasional intrauterine disaster may organically damage a fetus. That in turn will sometimes result in a grossly undersized infant. For such a case it is entirely plausible to suppose that the damaged twin will display a lower I.Q. than his mate. We are concerned, however, with the birth-weight–I.Q. relation within the very wide limits of "normal" variation of birth weight. Thus it will be necessary, when considering the empirical evidence, to concern ourselves with the absolute birth weights of the twins, as well as with the weight differences between them.

The first relevant study is that by Babson et al. in 1964.[1] Their study was restricted in the following way. The smaller twin, or "runt," had to have weighed at least 25 percent less than his twin, as well as less than 2,000 grams. They located nine pairs of apparently MZ twins who met this criterion, as well as seven pairs of apparently DZ twins. For the MZ twins, in 6 cases the heavier twin had the higher Stanford-Binet I.Q. There was 1 case in which the lighter twin had the higher I.Q., and in 2 cases the I.Q.'s were identical. These frequencies did not differ significantly. The mean I.Q. advantage in favor of the heavier MZ twin (6.6 points) was, however, significant. For the DZ twins, the heavier had the higher I.Q. in only 4 of 7 cases, not remotely approaching significance.

This rather slender result was obtained in a sample of MZ twins in which the "runts" had *very* low birth weights. The mean weight of the runts was only 1,510 grams, compared to 2,350 grams for their twins. The two smallest runts weighed a mere *950* and *1,130* grams. They also had the two lowest I.Q.'s in the sample, 68 and 76. Without their inclusion, the study would have no significant results. The majority of American infants, singletons or twins, born at such very low weights do not survive the first month of life.[2] The occurrence of low I.Q.'s in a couple of survivors cannot be taken as in any way relevant to I.Q. determinants in a surviving adult population.

The Babson et al. study indicates that, in connection with I.Q. testing, "Information on the order of births and birth size was withheld from the examiners." The intent of this precaution is admirable, for it guards against the possibility that the I.Q. tester might unconsciously administer or score his test to accord with the theory being tested. The precaution in this case, however, may have been more noble in intent than effective in practice. For all nine MZ twin pairs, the heavier twin at birth was also by far the heavier at the time of the I.Q. testing. The next study to be reviewed suggests that the possibility of unconscious bias is by no means far-fetched.

The paper by Churchill, in 1965, investigated birth weight and I.Q. differences in twins who had been referred to a school clinic because of learning difficulties.[3] The test used was the Wechsler Intelligence Scale for Children, and again "The psychologist had no information about the birth weight." The twins were classified into four sets. There were 13 pairs who were monochorionic, and thus certainly identical. There were 9 pairs described as "clinically identical," 14 pairs described as "same-sex fraternal," and 14 pairs who were clearly opposite-sex fraternals. The author did not compute the I.Q. *correlation* between twins, since he was concerned only with the point differences within twin pairs. The raw data presented, however, make it possible to calculate correlations. For the 13 monochorionic pairs, the intraclass correlation is .991. That is very perceptibly larger than any reliability coefficient that has ever been claimed for the Wechsler test. That is to say, the monochorionic twins resembled each other more than the same individual, tested twice, resembles himself! The correlation for "clinically identical" twins, on the other hand, is only .756. That is significantly lower than for monochorionics ($p < .0002$), despite the smallish sample sizes. The mean I.Q. difference for the 13 monochorionic pairs was only 2.2 points. Four pairs had identical I.Q.'s, and 2 pairs differed by only 1 point. There is at least a reasonable doubt that, if the same individuals were to be tested on two consecutive occasions, such a close agreement in scores would be obtained. The Churchill procedure, like that of the great majority of twin studies, involved a single psychologist testing each set of twins on the same day. That is not the procedure of choice if one wishes to eliminate the possibility that the expectations of the examiner might unconsciously influence the administration and/or scoring of the test. Though the data are not given, it is possible that the twin heavier at birth was also heavier at test.

Taking the Churchill I.Q.'s as they stand, there was no effect of birth weight in either fraternal sample. There was, however, an apparent birth-weight effect among identical twins. For the 13 monochorionic pairs, the heavier twin had an average advantage of only 1.7 I.Q. points but the data were so regular that the effect was significant ($p < .05$). For the 9 "clinically identical" pairs, the heavier twin had an advantage of 8.0 points ($p < .001$). That is to say, peculiarly, that birth weight had a significantly greater effect ($p < .02$) for the "clinically identical" twins than for the indubitably identical monochorionics. That was true despite the fact that the mean difference in birth weight — 270 grams — was the same in each sample. For the two pooled samples of MZ twins, there were 14 cases in which the heavier twin had the higher I.Q., 3 cases in which the reverse was true, and 5 cases of tied I.Q.'s. The Churchill paper indicated that, where a significant birth-weight effect was observed, it was invariably on the performance scale of the Wechsler. There was no indication of a significant effect on the verbal I.Q. The mean birth weight of the lighter members of Churchill's 22 identical pairs was 2,270 grams, compared to the 1,510 grams for Babson et al.'s "runts." The range of weight among the 44 MZ twins was from 1270 to 3710 grams. The lightest twin in this study was heavier than the two true "runts" to whom the significant effect in the Babson et al. study may be attributed. Thus if the Churchill data are taken at face value, they would indicate an effect of birth weight within a reasonably normal range of weights. There are, as we have seen, several grounds for viewing the Churchill I.Q.'s with some misgiving, and a replication of this finding seems clearly called for.

The finding was soon replicated by Willerman and Churchill in 1967.[4] They indicated that a reexamination of the earlier Churchill data had suggested that "when all sets which contained at least one breech birth were excluded the birth weight and I.Q. relation was clearer." They now wished to establish whether, when breech births were excluded, there might be a birth-weight effect upon verbal I.Q. as well as upon performance I.Q. Toward that end, the new study reexamined "the data of the previous study" and added for the first time "data obtained from a new sample of identical twins of average intelligence." The earlier sample, it will be recalled, consisted of children referred because of learning problems.

The new paper was said to contain data for 13 sets of problem twins, which "had been included in the previous study." The raw data in the two papers, however, establish that only 8 of these identical twin pairs had in fact been among the 22 reported on in 1965; it is unclear when the remaining 5 pairs were obtained. The 14 "normal" pairs were of course all newly added since 1965. The new paper does not contain full scale I.Q.'s but does contain verbal and performance I.Q.'s for each subject. Within the normal sample, the heavier twins had significantly higher verbal and performance I.Q.'s, exceeding their mates by 5.6 and 6.8 points, respectively, Within the problem child sample — reduced by exclusion of breech births, and supplemented by new cases since 1965 — the heavier twins had significantly higher performance I.Q.'s (3.9 points) but their 2.8 point advantage in verbal I.Q. was not significant. For the pooled samples, the birth-weight effect was significant on each I.Q. measure. Pooling both samples, there were 18 cases in which the heavier twin had the higher verbal I.Q., 6 reversed cases, and 3 ties. For performance I.Q. there were 21 cases in which the heavier twin was higher, 3 reversed cases, and 3 ties. These data, granted the published I.Q. values, do suggest a possible birth-weight effect. The effect, however, is not quite so strong as was indicated by Kaplan in her 1972 review of work on malnutrition and mental deficiency, published in *Psychological Bulletin.*[5] Kaplan wrote of the Willerman and Churchill paper that "In all cases the twin member who was the smaller of the pair at birth achieved lower scores in verbal and performance I.Q. . . . the results were consistent across all pairs studied." That is not the the case; in fact, only 14 of the 27 pairs met the criterion described by Kaplan.

The Willerman and Churchill data were later supplemented in a 1969 paper by Scarr,[6] who called attention to the fact that the apparent effect in their data occurred within a range of reasonably normal birth weights. The Scarr study added the birth-weight and I.Q. data for 25 pairs of twins, which she herself had studied, to the data for Willerman and Churchill's 27 twin pairs. The I.Q. test employed by Scarr had been the Goodenough Draw-a-Person Test, which was said to correlate "moderately well" with the WISC verbal and performance scales. The Goodenough I.Q. scores of Scarr's twins were pooled with the performance I.Q.'s of the Willerman and Churchill subjects.

The pooled data indicated that the heavier twin in a pair tended to have the higher I.Q. The data also suggested to Scarr that the amount of difference between co-twins in I.Q. was a function of the amount of difference between them in birth weight. This was indicated by a table that divided all twin pairs into three classes: those in which each twin had a birth weight less than 2,500 grams, those in which each twin weighed more than 2,500 grams, and those in which one twin weighed more (and the other less) than 2,500 grams. For the pooled samples, the mean I.Q. advantage of the heavier twin was 5.2 points in cases where both twins weighed more than 2,500 grams, and 6.4 points when both twins weighed less than 2,500 grams. For 8 critical pairs in which only one twin weighed more than 2,500 grams, the I.Q. advantage of the heavier twin was a full 13.3 points. These Scarr data, it will be recalled, were cited by Jensen in 1970,[7] which in turn led Herrnstein[8] to report that the twin studies surveyed by Jensen had shown "something prenatal" was "the single most important environmental influence on I.Q."

The interpretation offered by Scarr hinges upon the assumption that large birth-weight differences produce large I.Q. differences. The point is made that six of the eight pairs in which one twin weighed less than 2,500 grams displayed birth-weight differences of 500 grams or more. That magnitude of birth-weight difference was said to indicate a possible "transfusion syndrome," involving the bleeding of one twin into the other through an intraplacental connection. This would result in "a very poor intrauterine experience" for the lighter twin, which in turn would produce a lowered I.Q. That is, the data were said to indicate a birth-weight effect at all levels of birth weight, but a particularly pronounced effect when twins differed by 500 grams or more. That large a weight difference was assumed to indicate a possible transfusion syndrome, a particularly lurid example of poor intrauterine experience. With a biological mechanism thus implicated, Scarr went on to extend her interpretation to singleton births, as well as to twins. The conclusion drawn was that, within the full range of normal singleton birth weights, "The bigger the better." That is, high birth weight is said to be associated with high I.Q. The use of identical twins as subjects has presumably controlled for race and class as confounding variables.

The parents of fat babies would do well, before celebrating, to examine the data more closely. First, we note that the mean within-pair I.Q. difference in the Willerman and Churchill sample, using the Wechsler, was 6.3 points. For Scarr's sample, using Goodenough's test, it was an incredible (for identical twins) 14.4 points. The t test applied to the two sets of difference scores gives a value greater than 4. When attention is shifted to the I.Q. advantage of the heavier twin, the variance of this measure is very significantly larger in Scarr than in Willerman and Churchill. The evidence is clear that these two "I.Q. tests" are by no means equivalent, and the pooling of I.Q. scores across the studies is unjustified.

With regard to Scarr's table, in any event, the apparent "differences" in birth-weight discrepancies across the three weight categories of twins do not remotely approach significance for the pooled samples. For Scarr's data, the F ratio is less than unity; for Willerman and Churchill's data, it is not significant. Thus, the appeal to "transfusion syndrome" is based upon nothing; there is no statistically significant difference among twin pairs assigned to different weight categories.

We can examine in detail the critical eight twin pairs in which only one twin weighed more than 2,500 grams. Two of those twin pairs had relatively trivial birth-weight differences, averaging 210 grams. For those two pairs, the mean I.Q. advantage of the heavier twin was 20 points. The remaining six pairs in this category each showed birth-weight differences greater than 500 grams, averaging 760 grams. The mean I.Q. advantage of the heavier twin was in this case only 11 points. That is, within the category, the larger birth-weight differences ("transfusion syndrome'') obviously did not produce larger I.Q. discrepancies. There are, in Scarr's other two weight categories, 4 twin pairs with weight differences larger than 500 grams. The heavier twin's I.Q. advantage in these four cases is less than 2 points. Further, since Scarr's sample does *not* exclude breech births, there is no reason not to include in her pooling *all* the identical twin pairs from Churchill's 1965 paper. The 3 discarded Churchill pairs where each was greater than 2,500 grams had a mean heavier twin advantage of 3 I.Q. points. The 3 pairs where one twin weighed less than 2,500 grams had a mean difference of 4 points, and the 7 pairs in which each twin weighed less than 2,500 grams had a difference of 9 I.Q. points in favor of the heavier twins. The addition of these excluded pairs—which can only serve to make the Scarr and Willerman and Churchill samples more comparable — would largely do away with even the appearance of a significant difference in Scarr's table. For a final observation, we note that Scarr's pooling produced 7 twin pairs with weight discrepancies of *40 grams or less*. The mean I.Q. advantage of the ''heavier'' twin was 11 points, compared to 8 points in the 7 twin pairs whose weight differed by *600 grams or more*.

Though Scarr stated that a ''transfusion syndrome'' had been ''shown to account for large I.Q. differences'' by Babson et al., that was not the case. Those authors had specifically described their ''runts'' as ''without specification of etiological mechanism(s).'' The most directly relevant data to a transfusion syndrome are probably contained in Churchill's 1965 paper. The fact is that the transfusion syndrome occurs only in monochorionic twins, and only about two-thirds of MZ twins are monochorionic.[9] The Churchill paper gives data for 13 pairs of specifically monochorionic twins. The mean performance I.Q. advantage of the heavier twin is 4 points, only about half that he observed in ''clinically identical'' twins who were not monochorionic.

The three weight categories in Scarr's table are essentially arbitrary and do not correspond in any meaningful way to the amount of weight difference between members of a twin pair. The ''critical'' category in her table in fact includes twin pairs with very minor weight discrepancies. Thus, her interpretation that the I.Q. discrepancy varied with the amount of birth-weight difference is wholly incorrect. The correlation (linear) between amount of birth-weight difference and amount of I.Q. difference for the 52 twin pairs in her pooled samples is − .02, and there is no hint of a correlation, linear or otherwise, in the pooled samples, or subsamples or subcategories. The effect of birth weight in these data is remarkably ungraded. For the pooled samples, the heavier twin had the higher I.Q. in 37 cases. The effect was reversed in 8 cases, and the I.Q.'s were equal in 7 cases. That is a statistically significant effect, but it is strangely unrelated to the magnitude of the birth-weight difference. The extrapolation to singleton children of ''The bigger the better,'' and the invocation of an unseen ''transfusion syndrome,'' like the appeal to ''poor intrauterine experience,'' represent a hollow pseudobiologizing which, as we have seen, is not uncommon in the I.Q. literature.

There are further problems with Scarr's data, but we shall indicate them only in passing. The birth weights of Scarr's twins were not obtained from hospital records but were recollected by the mothers when the twins were between 6 and 11 years old. There are no data to show that mothers can recall without confusion the birth weights of twins. There are suggestive indications within Scarr's data that the mothers of older twins reported relatively large weight discrepancies, and that mothers who "rounded" to half and full pounds also reported larger discrepancies.[10]

The Churchill, Willerman and Churchill, and Scarr data, taken together, do not constitute very impressive evidence. They are surely, *in toto,* no more impressive than a contradictory report by Shields, cited in an earlier chapter. For 34 pairs of nonseparated, and 27 pairs of separated, identical twins, Shields reported that "Birth weight was not associated with test score differences."[11] The context makes plain that Shields had asked the blunt question, without regard to magnitudes, is the heavier twin the one with the higher I.Q.?

The largest study of I.Q. and birth weight in twins was reported by Kaelber and Pugh in 1969.[12] They examined hospital records and were able to locate 374 twin pairs to whom I.Q. tests had been administered in the school system. The tests had not been given as part of a research project, but in the normal course of schooling. The children were between 6 and 16 years of age at the time of the study but were never seen by Kaelber and Pugh. The investigators merely examined hospital records and received I.Q. records from cooperating school officials. The "I.Q. tests" given to the children were thus very varied. There was no obvious way to determine the zygosity of the twins. The mean birth-weight difference was reported as 316.1 grams, with no indication of variability. The lighter twins averaged 2,375 grams, very close to the values in the Willerman and Churchill and Scarr studies.

For the entire sample of 374 twin pairs the mean I.Q. of the heavier twin was 106.40, compared to 105.13 for the lighter twin. This was not quite a statistically significant difference. There was, however, a tendency for this very small difference to occur with each of the various I.Q. tests that had been administered to different twin pairs. The authors next examined, pooling all tests, the mean I.Q. advantage of the heavier twin for various categories of twins. For like-sexed twins, the mean advantage was 1.13 points; for opposite-sexed twins (obviously all DZs), it was 1.62 points. Neither difference was significant. The authors then further subdivided the twin pairs according to whether the weight discrepancy was less than or more than 300 grams. This breaking point did not produce two equal-sized groups. There were 213 pairs with weight discrepancies less than 300 grams, and 161 pairs with larger discrepancies.

There were now four subgroups of twins, and in *one* the I.Q. advantage of the heavier twin was a statistically significant 2.23 points. That group consisted of 109 pairs of like-sexed twins, each with a weight discrepancy of 300 grams or more. The standard errors provided by the authors, however, make it possible to calculate that the I.Q. advantage of the heavier twin in this subgroup *did not differ significantly* from that in any other subgroup—including the 0.37 point advantage observed in like-sexed twins with weight discrepancies less than 300 grams. The I.Q. advantage of the heavier twin in the subgroup of opposite-sexed twins with weight discrepancies less than 300 grams was virtually as great—2.16 I.Q. points — as that observed in the "key" group, with characteristics diametrically opposed. This latter advantage was not significant, but it was based on a sample only half the size of the "key" group. There is thus no evidence in the Kaelber and Pugh study either for a significant overall effect or for significant differences in the magnitude of the "effect" in theoretically very distinct subgroups of twins.

The authors then went on to select very small like-sexed subgroups who, on the basis of information in hospital records, might shrewdly be guessed to be MZ or DZ pairs. They again found a significant heavier twin advantage only for "MZs" with weight discrepancies greater than 300 grams; but again, the advantage did not differ significantly from that observed in any other subgroup.

To buttress their arbitrary division of twins at the 300-gram weight difference line, Kaelber and Pugh reanalyzed Churchill's 1965 data, using the same 300-gram cutoff point. They did this in a curious way, separating Churchill's twins into like-sexed and opposite-sexed pairs. For the four subgroups, the I.Q. advantage of the heavier twin was significant only among like-sexed twins with a weight discrepancy greater than 300 grams. This result closely paralleled their own pattern for putatively MZ and DZ pairs; and again, the I.Q. advantage in the "key" group did not differ significantly from that in any other group. The fact is, however, that Churchill had examined his twins and had divided them into MZ and DZ groups. The MZ group is, of course, the most relevant; with identical genes, the birth-weight effect, produced by intrauterine environment, should be most clearly visible among them. The Churchill data indicate that, for 14 pairs of MZs with weight discrepancies less than 300 grams, the mean I.Q. advantage was 4.6 points. For 8 MZ pairs with discrepancies greater than 300 grams, the I.Q. advantage was only 3.6 points. This nonsignificant pattern "contradicts" the nonsignificant pattern reported by Kaelber and Pugh among their own MZ twins. Within the Churchill data, for like-sexed fraternal twins, anomalously, there was a nonsignificant tendency for the I.Q. advantage to be larger in twins with weight discrepancies larger than 300 grams. That tendency was responsible for the pattern reported by Kaelber and Pugh for Churchill's "like-sexed" twins—a pooling of MZs and DZs. Within Scarr's MZ data, it might be pointed out, there is no difference in I.Q. advantages between twin pairs above and below the 300-gram cutting point. The use of that cutting point by Kaelber and Pugh, like Scarr's use of three categories, seems entirely arbitrary. With Kaelber and Pugh's data, as with Scarr's, the arbitrary cutting point did not in fact produce any statistically significant difference. For the very large Kaelber and Pugh sample, moreover, there was no significant overall effect in favor of the heavier twin.

To be fair, however, it should be pointed out that in Kaelber and Pugh's large sample the birth-weight effect was *almost* significant ($.10 > p > .05$). The advantage of the heavier twin was very slight (1.27 I.Q. points), but the fact that such a slight apparent advantage occurred with each different I.Q. test is suggestive. There are several possible interpretations. The inclusion of a very few grossly underweight twins in the sample (like Babson et al.'s "runts") could produce such an effect. There is also the fact that, unlike in the other studies reviewed, the Kaelber and Pugh twins were not tested simultaneously. The twin pairs qualified for inclusion in the sample if each twin had been tested within a 1-year period. The very light-weight twins may well have been in poor physical health during childhood. Thus it is entirely conceivable that some small number may have begun school a year after their sturdier twins, and thus been tested at a later age. We have seen repeatedly that I.Q. tests are not well-standardized for age. Presuming that the I.Q. tests produced at this age level I.Q.'s negatively correlated with age, a slight and artifactual "birth-weight effect" could thus be observed in a sample of this sort. The same would be true if, as seems reasonable, starting school a year later — or simply missing some school because of ill health — slightly depresses I.Q. score. There is obvious reason to suppose that the lighter twins enjoyed poorer physical health and missed more school. The tiny and nonsignificant effect observed by Kaelber and Pugh is thus consistent with any of a large number of artifacts, as are the occasional "effects" reported by others. To some I.Q. theorists, evidently, ideas such as transfusion syndrome and intrauterine experience have a more romantic appeal than the homely notion that sickly runts miss more school and as a consequence do not do quite so well on I.Q. tests. The homely notion, however, has one clear advantage over the appeal to pseudobiology. It could be directly tested.

The review of these studies has indicated that there is no substantial evidence to support the notion that, within a very large range of birth weights, there is a positive relation between twins' weight and I.Q. The snippets of evidence depend upon arbitrary, and sometimes incorrect, statistical analyses of the data. They are contradicted by other evidence. There is thus no reason to suppose that "poor intrauterine experience," by producing unseen brain damage, accounts for any I.Q. variability in the vast normal population—and less reason to suppose that it is a major source of "nongenetic" I.Q. variation. The evidence is not one whit better than that supporting the idea that I.Q. is heritable. The fact that so far-fetched an idea as prenatal determination of I.Q. should enter psychological theory in the absence of strong evidence might seem perplexing. The uterus, however, here serves the same function as the genes: It rationalizes our failure to devise more effective educational and cultural institutions. The policy toward which the Jensen and Herrnstein interpretations of these studies point is obvious. To elevate the intellectual level of the citizenry, do not bother with attempts to reform educational or social practices. Pass out free food stamps.

A NOTE ON INBREEDING DEPRESSION

We conclude with a brief examination of another implausible effect which, according to hereditarians, demonstrates the heritability of I.Q. The claim has been made that I.Q. exhibits "inbreeding depression." This phenomenon is sometimes observed in the offspring of related individuals. The children of such matings are likely to receive some of the same genes twice from the same ancestor. Thus such children will on average be homozygous for more genes than is usual. That means that "harmful" genes inherited by such children will not be counteracted by "helpful" allelomorphs. The children of inbred matings might thus not be as vigorous or as tall as normal children. We would expect to observe lowered I.Q. in inbred children *if* I.Q. were heritable, and *if* genes favoring high I.Q. tended to be dominant.

There has been one large-scale study, by Schull and Neel,[13] which purports to demonstrate inbreeding depression for I.Q. Professor Vandenberg, who at one point has indicated that adoptive child studies provide "the strongest evidence possible for hereditary factors in intelligence,"[14] has elsewhere asserted that the Schull and Neel study offers "the most unassailable evidence we have for hereditary control over intelligence."[15] Professor Herrnstein indicates that this study provides evidence for inbreeding depression of I.Q. in the absence of any plausible environmental cause.[16] We shall briefly examine this unassailable evidence, with one eye cocked toward a familiar environmental variable.

The study was conducted in Japan, where marriage between first cousins, though unusual, is not so rare as among us. The Japanese version of the WISC was administered to 865 inbred children and to 989 control children in the city of Hiroshima. The inbred children, it should be noted, varied considerably in the degree of inbreeding. There were some children of first cousins, some of first cousins once removed, and some of second cousins. The "coefficient of inbreeding" thus varied by a factor of four within the inbred group. The control children, with unrelated parents, were assumed to have a zero coefficient of inbreeding.

The Schull and Neel study involves a number of statistical complexities. The WISC I.Q.'s varied systematically with child's age and with a rough measure of social class, as well as with degree of inbreeding. To "correct" for these confoundings, Schull and Neel employed multivariate regression analyses. These were supposed to "remove" the biasing effects of age and social class, and thus permit an assessment of the possible effect of inbreeding. When the multivariate statistical dust had cleared away, Schull and Neel concluded that they had demonstrated a slight, but statistically significant, inbreeding depression. They noted that the inbreeding effect was significant only within the female sample, but the effect remained significant when male and female data were pooled.

Their volume contains in its appendix a computer printout from which a number of calculations can be made. The control female children, for example, have a higher mean social status than the inbred females ($p < .001$). The control males, however, do not have a significantly higher social status than the inbred males. This observation, of course, nicely parallels the fact that "inbreeding" had a significant effect only within the female sample. We can also correlate degree of inbreeding with social class. For 890 females, the correlation was $-.12$; for 964 males, it was $-.08$. These significant correlations, observed although more than half of the children had zero inbreeding scores, amply confirm that inbreeding is more common in the lower social classes.

This confounding of social class with inbreeding poses extraordinarily severe problems. The regression analyses employed by Schull and Neel are intended to adjust for the effect of social class on I.Q., thereby permitting an evaluation of the "pure" effect of inbreeding. The difficulty, however, is that their measure of social class is very blunt. Within the Schull and Neel study, the correlations found between social class and the various WISC scales are significant, but low. Thus it seems very likely that social class effects beyond the reach of their blunt measure of class remain in the data. With a more sensitive measure of social class, it seems certain that a stronger correlation between inbreeding and class would have been detected. The more sensitive measure, if it were available, could easily eliminate the entire "inbreeding" effect. This is entirely feasible since, as Schull and Neel indicated, the apparent inbreeding effect was very small. They concluded, on the basis of their involved statistical analysis, that a child of first cousins would have on average an I.Q. only about 5 points lower than that of a child of unrelated parents.

That small effect emerged from a multivariate regression analysis which attempted to cope with a number of confoundings. The effect of social class was omnipresent. The data indicate, in addition to the confounding of social class with inbreeding, significant correlations between the *ages* of the children and their social class. For female children, the correlation was $-.11$; for males, it was $-.07$. These correlations were each statistically significant. The sampling procedure was clearly such that a tendency existed for the older children to come from a lower social class level.

The correlations are of course small, and significant only because of the large sample sizes. The reported inbreeding effect, however, was also small. For example, the raw correlations between degree of inbreeding and WISC Vocabulary scale score were only $-.14$ for females and $-.09$ for males. These were the highest correlations with inbreeding observed for any of the WISC scales. The effects of age, on the other hand, were considerably larger. The raw correlations between age and Vocabulary score were $.22$ for females and $.25$ for males. With multiple confounds of this magnitude, interpretation of the Schull and Neel data requires a considerable faith in the sensitivity of their statistical technique. Though multiple regression doubtless has many virtues, it can be no more sensitive than the measures to which it is applied. The measurement of age and of inbreeding coefficient is relatively straightforward, but the same cannot be said of Schull and Neel's attempt to measure social class in Japan.

The confounding of inbreeding with social class means that there is no strong reason for regarding the Schull and Neel data as demonstrating anything other than the familiar social-class – I.Q. correlation (and the poor standardization of the Japanese WISC). The realities of social class will not disappear for the convenience of biologically oriented theorists. The inbreeding depression effect on I.Q. is no more solidly supported than is the effect of intrauterine experience.

NOTES TO CHAPTER SEVEN

1. S. G. Babson, J. Kangas, N. Young, and J. L. Bramhall, "Growth and Development of Twins of Dissimilar Size at Birth," *Pediatrics,* 33, (1964), 327 – 333.
2. M. G. Bulmer, *The Biology of Twinning in Man,* (Oxford, Clarendon Press, 1970), p. 55.
3. J. A. Churchill, "The Relation Between Intelligence and Birth Weight in Twins," *Neurology,* 15, (1965), 341 – 347.
4. L. Willerman and J. A. Churchill, "Intelligence and Birth Weight in Identical Twins," *Child Development,* 38, (1967), 623 – 629.
5. B. J. Kaplan, "Malnutrition and Mental Deficiency," *Psychological Bulletin,* 78, (1972), 327.
6. S. Scarr, "Effects of Birth Weight on Later Intelligence," *Social Biology,* 16, (1969), 249 – 256.
7. A. R. Jensen, "IQ's of Identical Twins Reared Apart," *Behavior Genetics,* 1, (1970), 144 – 145.
8. R. J. Herrnstein, "I.Q.", *Atlantic Monthly,* September, 1971, p. 58.
9. Bulmer, *Twinning,* p. 56.
10. Though Scarr asserts that mothers recall the birth weights of their infants accurately, the only study she cites in support of that assertion involved a group of 19 Danish mothers — of *singleton* children. There appears to be no evidence on how well mothers of twins avoid confusion in recalling birth weights of their children. The Scarr data suggest, but not conclusively, that mothers may exaggerate the difference in birth weights of twins with the passage of time. There can be no argument on the point that, in such research, it is better to consult hospital records than to depend on mothers' recollections.
11. J. Shields, *Monozygotic Twins Brought Up Apart and Brought Up Together,* (London, Oxford University Press, 1962), pp. 112 – 113.
12. C. T. Kaelber and T. F. Pugh, "Influence of Intrauterine Relations on the Intelligence of Twins," *New England Journal of Medicine,* 280, (1969), 1030–1034.
13. W. J. Schull and J. V. Neel, *The Effects of Inbreeding on Japanese Children,* (New York, Harper and Row, 1965).
14. *Intelligence: Genetic and Environmental Influences,* ed. R. Cancro, (New York, Grune and Stratton, 1971), p. 189.

15. *Genetics,* ed. D. C. Glass, (New York, Rockefeller University Press, 1968), p. 44.
16. R. J. Herrnstein, *I.Q. in the Meritocracy,* (Boston, Atlantic Monthly Press, 1973), p. 157.

CONCLUSION

This book has attempted—with one exception soon to be noted—to review the major sources of evidence that have been asserted to support the view that I.Q. is heritable. The data have repeatedly demonstrated profound environmental effects on I.Q. scores in circumstances where the genes cannot be implicated. The apparent genetic effects, upon analysis, have invariably been confounded with environmental factors that have been slighted or ignored. The studies of separated MZ twins have ignored the correlated environments of the twins, as well as artifacts produced by the confounding of age with I.Q. and by unconscious experimenter bias. The apparent genetic orderliness of summaries of kinship correlations reflects systematic bias and arbitrary selection of data. There is in fact much that is not known, and what is known is no more consistent with a genetic than an environmental interpretation. The kinship data seem not to have been examined for relations inconsistent with an hereditarian position, and suggestive evidence for several such relations has been indicated. The hereditarian interpretation of studies of adopted children ignores the complex problems posed by the unique characteristics of adoptive families. To consider these problems is to reverse the apparent meaning of these studies. Those studies that do not support a genetic interpretation have disappeared from contemporary reference lists. The purported demonstrations of intrauterine effects and of inbreeding depression are, to say the least, unconvincing.

To assert that there is *no* genetic determination of I.Q. would be a strong, and scientifically meaningless, statement. We cannot prove the null hypothesis, nor should we be asked to do so. The question is whether there exist data of merit and validity that require us to reject the null hypothesis. There should be no mistake here. The burden of proof falls upon those who wish to assert the implausible proposition that the way in which a child answers questions devised by a mental tester is determined by an unseen genotype. That burden is not lessened by the repeated assertions of the testers over the past 70 years. Where the data are at best ambiguous, and where environment is clearly shown to have effect, the assumption of genetic determination of I.Q. variation in any degree is unwarranted. The prudent conclusion seems clear. There are no data sufficient for us to reject the hypothesis that differences in the way in which people answer the questions asked by testers are determined by their palpably different life experiences.

That conclusion is silent with respect to another possible question. There may well be genetically determined differences among people in their cognitive and intellectual "capacities." To demonstrate this, psychologists would have to develop test instruments that provide adequate measures of such capacities. They have not as yet done this; they have only developed I.Q. tests. This book has been about—and only about—the heritability of I.Q. test scores.

There is, to say the least, no guarantee that adequate measurements of "cognitive capacities" would produce a rank-ordering of people similar to that produced by existing I.Q. tests. The experience of most teachers is sufficient to suggest otherwise. The existing I.Q. tests, as they were designed to do, predict on a better than chance basis who will do well in the kinds of school training programs we now employ. They also predict, to some extent, who will "do well" in our economy, and in our job structure. That tells us nothing about the heritability of I.Q., or of success. The simpler interpretation is that those who have been trained to answer the kinds of questions asked by I.Q. tests have been trained to succeed in our society. To be so trained requires both the opportunity and the willingness to accept the training regimen. To assert that those without opportunity or willingness have defective genes is not a conclusion of science. The social function of such an assertion is transparently obvious. The successful are very likely to believe it, including successful professors.

The notion that I.Q. is heritable has been with us for so long that it is difficult for us to step back and appreciate fully the assumptions involved in that conclusion. The World War I Army Alpha test contained such multiple choice items as "The Brooklyn Nationals are called the Giants . . . Orioles . . . Superbas . . . Indians," and "Revolvers are made by Swift and Co. . . . Smith and Wesson . . . W. L. Douglas . . . B. T. Babbitt."[1] The Italian or Hebrew immigrant who could not answer such questions was thereby shown to have defective genes. The Stanford-Binet asked 14-year-olds to explain the following: "My neighbor has been having queer visitors. First a doctor came to his house, then a lawyer, then a minister. What do you think happened there?" Professor Terman explained that a satisfactory answer must normally involve a death: "The doctor came to attend a sick person, the lawyer to make his will, and the minister to preach the funeral." There were, however, "other ingenious interpretations which pass as satisfactory." For example, "A man got hurt in an accident; the doctor came to make him well, the lawyer to see about damages, and then he died and the preacher came for the funeral.'' The following answer was failed by Professor Terman. ''Somebody was sick; the lawyer wanted his money and the minister came to see how he was.''[2] Professor Terman's high-quality genes evidently made him better disposed toward the good intentions of lawyers than did the genes of his failing respondent. To Professor Terman, it seemed more logical that a minister at the house next door is there to preach a funeral rather than to inquire after the welfare of an ill parishoner.

To the degree that items in I.Q. tests are not so monstrously arbitrary as those we have just cited, they largely consist of arithmetical and vocabulary materials, together with skills of logical analysis, which are largely learned in school. Those who cannot answer have not learned what in theory the school teachers wished to teach them. They are usually the same people who have failed to learn that lawyers do not want the money of their clients and are primarily useful to help one bequeath one's fortune. From this—and the fact that this failure to learn what one should seems to run in families—we are asked to conclude that a low I.Q. score indicates a genetic defect. The tests in fact seem to measure only whether one has learned, and believed, what Professor Terman and his colleagues have learned and believed. To the degree that one has, one may reasonably look forward to enjoying the kind of success that Professor Terman enjoyed. The assumption that one who has not learned these things was prevented from doing so by his bad blood is both gratuitous and self-serving.

The worst contemporary blood, if one regards the I.Q. as a mirror held up to the genotype, is black blood. The average I.Q. score of blacks is lower than that of whites. That fact, together with a very great score overlap between the black and white populations, has been documented in an enormous research literature. To some scholars, at least, racial differences in I.Q. have constituted a further demonstration of the I.Q.'s genetic basis. The dreary and at times revolting literature on race differences has not been reviewed in this book. There is no need to force oneself through it. There is no adequate evidence for the heritability of I.Q. within the white population. To attribute racial differences to genetic factors, granted the overwhelming cultural-environmental differences between races, is to compound folly with malice. That compounding characterized the mental testers of World War I, and it has not vanished.

The interpretation of I.Q. data seems never to be free both of policy implications and of ideological overtones. Professor Jensen began his survey of the I.Q. literature with the conclusion that ''Compensatory education has been tried and it apparently has failed.''[3] The apparent failure was seen to be the inevitable consequence of demonstrated genetical truths. Professor Herrnstein has described how he was ''submerged for twenty years in the depths of environmentalistic behaviorism.''[4] The ascent to the higher spheres of I.Q. testing was noted by *The New York Times,* which cited him as acknowledging that his ''conclusions, if true, amount to a death sentence for the ideal of egalitarianism, a powerful influence in contemporary Western society.''[5] The psychology of the mental testers, we are told, has doomed compensatory education and has killed egalitarianism. That is unqualifiedly bad news—for the underprivileged, for teachers, for egalitarians, and for behaviorists. Professor Herrnstein has said of American behaviorism, "The promises go back almost fifty years, to behaviorism's founder, John. B. Watson, and are coming still."[6] The promises go back much longer than 50 years, but they have seldom been expressed more forcefully or eloquently than by Watson. There is no psychology student in America who has not been exposed to a part, a small part, of Watson's dictum about the rearing of a dozen babies. To most students, it has been held out as the *reductio ad absurdum* of a mindless environmentalism run rampant. The full passage, however, contains more than promises. There is considerable analysis, and a full and moving recognition that the promises of behaviorism applied to human affairs cannot be realized without social and political reform. The celebrated passage followed a lengthy and sophisticated discussion of the relation between inheritance of structure and inheritance of function. The passage in its full context restores to us a psychological tradition richer and truer for our time and place than the strait-jacketed ideology of the mental testers:

> Our conclusion, then, is that we have no real evidence of the inheritance of traits. I would feel perfectly confident in the ultimate favorable outcome of careful upbringing of a *healthy well-formed baby* born of a long line of crooks, murderers and thieves, and prostitutes. Who has any evidence to the contrary? . . . One cannot use statistics gained from observations in charitable institutions and orphan asylums. All one needs to do to discount such statistics is to go there and work for a while, and I say this without trying to belittle the work of such organizations.
>
> I should like to go one step further now and say, "Give me a dozen healthy infants, well-formed, and my own specified world to bring them up in and I'll guarantee to take anyone at random and train him to become any type of specialist I might select — doctor, lawyer, artist, merchant-chief and, yes, even beggar-man and thief, regardless of his talents, penchants, tendencies, abilities, vocations, and race of his ancestors." I am going beyond my facts and I admit it, but so have the advocates of the contrary and they have been doing it for many thousands of years. Please note that when this experiment is made I am to be allowed to specify the way the children are to be brought up and the type of world they have to live in.
>
> . . . Where there are structural defects . . . there is social inferiority — competition on equal grounds is denied. The same is true when "inferior" races are brought up along with "superior" races. We have no sure evidence of inferiority in the negro race. Yet, educate a white child and a negro child in the same school — bring them up in the same family (theoretically without difference) and when society begins to exert its crushing might, the negro cannot compete.
>
> The truth is society does not like to face facts. Pride of race has been strong, hence our Mayflower ancestry — our Daughters of the Revolution. We like to boast of our ancestry. It sets us apart . . . . Again, on the other hand, the belief in the inheritance of tendencies and traits saves us from blame in the training of our young . . .[7]

NOTES TO CONCLUSION

1. C. C. Brigham, *A Study of American Intelligence,* (Princeton, Princeton University Press, 1923), p. 29.
2. L. M. Terman, *The Measurement of Intelligence,* (Boston, Houghton Mifflin, 1916), pp. 316–317.
3. A. R. Jensen, "How Much Can We Boost IQ and Scholastic Achievement?", *Harvard Educational Review,* 39, (1969), 2.
4. R. J. Herrnstein, *I.Q. in the Meritocracy,* (Boston, Atlantic Monthly Press, 1973), p. 6.
5. *New York Times,* August 29, 1971, p. 34.
6. Herrnstein, *I.Q.,* p. 7.
7. J. B. Watson, *Behaviorism,* rev. ed. (Chicago, University of Chicago Press, 1930), pp. 103–105.

AUTHOR INDEX

Numbers in *italics* refer to the pages on which the complete references are listed.

B

Babbott, F. L., 29
Babson, S. G., 63, *71*, 162, *173*
Banfield, E. C., 7, *13*
Binet, A., 5, 7, 10, *13*
Blewett, D. B., 82, 103, *107*, *109*
Bramhall, J. L., 63, *71*, 162, *173*
Brigham, C. C., 20, 21, 22, 25, *31*, 176(1), *179*
Bruun, K., 84, *107*
Bulmer, M. G., 163(2), 168(10), *173*
Burks, B. S., 114, 115, 124, *133*
Buros, O. K., 49, *70*
Burt, C., 1, *4*, 35, 36, 37, 38, 39, 40, 41, 42, 43, 45, 46, *68*, *69*, 75, 77, 78, 81, 82, 85, 87, 88, 89, 95, 105, *106*, *107*, *108*, *110*, 150, 153, 154, 156, *158*
Byrns, R., 82, *107*

C

Carlisle, C. L., 2, *4*
Carter, H. D., 79, *106*

B

Churchill, J. A., 63, *71*, 103, *110*, 163, 164, 167, 169, *173*
Clark, P. J., 96, 97(61), 98(67), 99, 103(77), 104(81), *108*, *109*, *110*
Conway, J., 37, 38, 42(27, 30), 45, 46, *68*, *69*

D

Dexter, E., 86, *107*

E

Elderton, E. M., 86, *107*
Ellis, N. R., *157*
Erlenmeyer-Kimling, L., 74, 75, 76, *105*, *106*
Estabrook, A. H., 73, 111, *105*, *133*

F

Fisher, R. A., 90, *108*
Flood, E., 10, *13*
Folano, G., 79, *106*
Foster, J. C., *13*
Freedman, H., 79, *106*

Freeman, F. N., 52, 53, 54, 55, 70, 71, 77, 83, 102, 106, 107, 113, 114(9), 124, 133
Fulker, D. W., 48, 69, 149, 151, 158

G

Gaw, F., 41, 42, 69
Goddard, H. H., 7, 8(12), 13, 16, 31
Gottesman, I., 155, 158
Grant, M., 7, 13, 19, 31
Gray, J. L., 86, 107
Gregor, A. J., 101, 109

H

Halperin, S. L., 147, 148, 158
Healy, J., 82, 107
Herrman, L., 81, 107
Herrnstein, R. J., 1, 2, 3, 4, 5, 7, 12, 43, 69, 75, 82, 87, 89, 94, 106, 107, 108, 112, 123, 125, 126, 130, 131, 133, 134, 135, 146, 150(24), 155, 157, 158, 159, 166, 171, 173, 174, 177, 178, 179
Hildreth, G. H., 77, 106
Hirsch, N. D., 27, 28, 31, 33, 67
Hogben, L., 81, 107
Holzinger, K. J., 52, 53, 54, 55, 70, 71, 77, 83, 102, 106, 107, 113, 114(9), 124, 133
Honzik, M. P., 77, 106, 112, 133
Howard, M., 36, 37, 38, 39, 40(17), 43, 68, 88, 95(57), 108, 156, 159
Huntley, R., 84, 107
Husen, T., 83, 107, 156, 159

J

Jarvik, L. F., 74, 75, 76, 105, 106
Jencks, C., 78, 79, 106
Jensen, A. R., 3, 4, 30, 32, 42, 43, 48, 53, 55, 58, 66, 69, 70, 71, 75, 78, 82, 85, 89, 101, 104(80), 106, 107, 108, 109, 110, 117, 131, 133, 134, 135, 136, 139, 141, 142, 155, 156, 157, 158, 159, 165, 173, 177, 179
Jinks, J. L., 48, 69, 149, 151, 158
Juel-Nielsen, N., 61, 62, 71, 143, 146, 158

K

Kaelber, C. T., 168, 173
Kangas, J., 63, 71, 162, 173

Kaplan, B. J., 165, 173
Karn, M. N., 84, 98, 107, 109
King, R. A., 156(35), 159
Kinnicutt, F., 23, 32
Kushlick, A., 139

L

Laughlin, H. H., 10(18), 11(19, 20, 21, 22, 23, 24, 25), 13, 16, 25, 29, 31
Leahy, A. M., 115, 124, 133

M

McNemar, Q., 57, 71
Markkanen, T., 84, 107
Matarazzo, J. D., 149(22), 158
Matthews, M. V., 81, 107
Maxwell, J., 83, 107
Mehrota, S. N., 83, 107
Mellone, M. A., 138, 157
Merrill, M. A., 125(20), 133
Merriman, C., 64, 71
Mitchell, B. C., 77, 106, 113, 114(9), 124, 133
Morgan, C. T., 156(35), 159
Morse, A. D., 29(23), 32
Moshinsky, P., 86, 107

N

Neel, J. V., 171, 173
Newlyn, D. A., 81, 107
Newman, H. H., 52, 53, 54, 55, 70, 71, 83, 102, 107
Nichols, R. C., 83, 98, 109

O

Osborne, R. T., 101, 109

P

Partanen, J., 84, 107
Pearson, K., 1, 4
Penrose, L. S., 81, 107
Pintner, R., 30, 32, 79, 106
Proctor, C., 99, 103(77), 109
Pugh, T. F., 168, 173

R

Reed, E., 12, *13*
Reed, S., 12, *13*
Roberts, J. A. F., 136, 137, 139, *157*

S

Scarr, S., 165, *173*
Schoenfeldt, L. F., 98, *109*
Schull, W. J., 171, *173*
Shields, J., 47, 49, 50, 52, *69*, *70*, 83, *107*, 142, 143, 146, *157*, *158*, 168, *173*
Shockley, W., 46, *69*
Simon, T., 5(2), *13*
Sims, V. M., 79, *106*
Skeels, H. M., 64, *71*, 112, 124, 125, 128, 130, *133*, *134*
Skodak, M., 64, *71*, 112, 124, 125, 130, *133*, *134*
Smith, R. T., 97, *109*
Snider, B., 84, 98, *107*, *109*
Snygg, D., 112, *133*
Stein, Z., 140, *157*
Stocks, P., 84, 98, *107*, *109*
Stott, D., 156
Susser, M. W., 140, *157*
Sutter, J., 81, *107*
Sutton, H. E., 96, 97(61), 98(67), 104(81), *108*, *109*, *110*
Sweeney, A., 23, 24(13), *32*

T

Tabah, L., 81, *107*
Terman, L. M., 6, 7, 11, *13*, 55, 58(67), *71*, 122, 125(20), *134*, 150, 151, *158*, 177, *179*
Thorndike, E. L., 76, *106*

V

Vandenberg, S. G., 75, 82, 96, 97, 98, 99, 101, 103, 104(81), *107*, *108*, *109*, *110*, *133*, 138, 146, 147, *157*, 171, *173*

W

Wallis, W. D., 120, *133*
Wictorin, M., 83, *107*
Wight, A., 9, 13
Willerman, L., 63, *71*, 164, *173*
Wilson, P. T., 97, *109*

Y

Yerkes, R. M., 8, *13*, 17, 18, 19(6), *31*
Young, K., 15, 26, *30*
Young, N., 63, *71*, 162, *173*